'*Understanding Humanitarian Protection* is an expertly written, systematic intro-
duction to the history, institutions and practi
protection and intervention. Filled with illustrat
studies, and written in a clear and highly acces
resource for teachers and students to grasp the
debates in one concise volume.'

Cecilia Jacob, *The Australian National University*

'Crossley provides a fantastic introduction to the humanitarian protection regime. From R2P to UN reform, humanitarian relief to targeted sanctions, *Understanding Humanitarian Protection* offers a sharp, highly informative, and accessible account of the development of the regime, its key issues, and major controversies.'

James Pattison, *University of Manchester, UK*

'How to protect civilians from war and other man-made crises is one of the key practical and intellectual challenges of our time. Noele Crossley's book provides a useful survey of how different traditions of thought and a wide range of external governments, international organisations, and civil society have tried to meet this challenge. Her conclusion suggests better informed citizens, governments and organisations should build a global regime that eliminates protection "black holes" – territories where third parties cannot alleviate terrible suffering.'

Paul D. Williams, *George Washington University, USA*

Understanding Humanitarian Protection

This new textbook provides an introduction to humanitarian protection, a field of study concerned with international responses to armed conflict, political violence, and humanitarian crisis.

The book engages with a wide range of empirical and normative questions, providing an overview of the academic literature whilst simultaneously discussing the policies and practices associated with protective responses to conflict and humanitarian emergencies that put the lives and livelihoods of vulnerable populations, including civilians, refugees, and minority groups, at risk. Divided into three parts, covering the origins of the humanitarian protection regime, the range of actors involved, and the responsibilities of these actors, the book offers an accessible entry point into the major contemporary debates, providing readers with the conceptual tools for understanding core issues. Key points are reinforced and illustrated through the deployment of selected case studies, and a comprehensive glossary is provided for key terms. Each chapter ends with a summary of key points, questions for further reflection, and a list of recommended reading.

This book will be of much interest to students of human protection, humanitarianism, the Responsibility to Protect, human security, peacekeeping, and International Relations in general.

Noele Crossley is Lecturer (Teaching) in International Organisations & International Security at University College London. She received her PhD from the London School of Economics and Political Science. She is the author of *Evaluating the Responsibility to Protect* (Routledge).

Understanding Humanitarian Protection

Noele Crossley

Routledge
Taylor & Francis Group
LONDON AND NEW YORK

Cover credit: © Getty Images

First published 2022
by Routledge
2 Park Square, Milton Park, Abingdon, Oxon OX14 4RN

and by Routledge
605 Third Avenue, New York, NY 10158

Routledge is an imprint of the Taylor & Francis Group, an informa business

British Library Cataloguing-in-Publication Data
A catalogue record for this book is available from the British Library

Library of Congress Cataloging-in-Publication Data
A catalog record for this title has been requested

ISBN: 978-0-367-43951-4 (hbk)
ISBN: 978-0-367-43950-7 (pbk)
ISBN: 978-1-003-00667-1 (ebk)

DOI: 10.4324/9781003006671

Typeset in Times New Roman
by MPS Limited, Dehradun

For those in need of protection

Contents

Acknowledgements

This book is the result of two years of writing and many more of research and teaching on the subject of humanitarian protection. I would like to thank very generally all those colleagues who have supported my research and teaching over the past decade or so. This book really would not exist without the encouragement and support I have received from you. Needless to say, your influence will be felt between the lines and pages of this book. I am particularly grateful to Eamon Aloyo, Alex Bellamy, Chris Brown, Outi Donovan, Adrian Gallagher, John Gledhill, Mark Hoffman, Cecilia Jacob, Jonathan Monten, James Pattison, Cristina Stefan, and Paul D. Williams. Finally, the team at Routledge has once again been a true pleasure to work with and special thanks are due to Andrew Humphrys and Bethany Lund-Yates.

Glossary of Terms

Accountability Legally, the ability to prosecute a party for violations of rights, negligence, or misconduct. Politically, the ability to seek compensation and redress.

Actor A political entity, such as a state, an individual, or an organisation. There are state-actors (governments, states) and non-state actors (individuals, organisations).

Advocacy Collective efforts by individuals and groups to advance a particular cause, such as human rights. Individuals and groups can form advocacy coalitions, through which they work together to promote an idea or issue.

Agency The ability of an actor to make a choice. Some International Relations theories assume that actors have limited agency. According to structural realism, for example, factors outside of the control of a state limit the options available to it and predispose it to a particular course of action.

Agenda for Peace The title of a 1992 report of the UN Secretary-General. The report outlined preventive diplomacy instruments including fact-finding missions, early warning, and preventive deployment, and called for reforms towards more robust forms of peacekeeping.

Asylum A state's granting of protection to a refugee. The 1951 Refugee Convention and Protocol of 1967 serve as key legal documents. The Universal Declaration of Human Rights of 1948 recognises the fundamental right of individuals to seek asylum from persecution in other states.

Bilateral Relating to two states. 'Bilateral negotiations', for example, are negotiations between two states.

Brahimi Report A report published in 2000. The report summarised the recommendations of a panel appointed by the UN Secretary-General, chaired by Lakhdar Brahimi. The report recommended clearer and more realistic peacekeeping mandates.

Civil society Individuals and groups that are not associated with formal state structures or businesses. Civil society is comprised of non-governmental organisations, charities, and faith-based organisations.

Civil war Armed conflict between two or more groups within a state. A civil war may, or may not, involve a state's government. In some civil wars, belligerent groups are supported by external actors.

Cold War The conflictual relationship among states politically aligned either with the United States or with the Soviet Union in the period after the Second World War. States fought each other in so-called 'proxy wars'.

Collective security A system in which states agree to defend each other from an act of aggression by a third party, or a member state. The United Nations and the North

Atlantic Treaty Organisation are examples of international and regional collective security arrangements, respectively.

Conditionality (aid) The provision of aid to recipient states by a donor state contingent upon the recipient state meeting criteria specified by the donor state. The term can also be used to refer to criteria that a recipient state must meet in order to retain access to funds.

Conflict (armed) Fighting between two or more political groups. The Uppsala Conflict Data Program (UCDP), a leading resource for conflict data, defines a conflict as the use of armed force between the government and at least one other group resulting in at least 25 battle-related deaths annually.

Conflict resolution The actions and processes associated with the ending of armed violence between two or more politically organised groups. This may be narrowly defined, connoting formal negotiations and mediation to end armed fighting. A broader conceptualisation is premised on a longer time frame, wider goals such as positive peace, and considers the role of informal processes (see also *peacebuilding*).

Consequentialism A perspective in international ethics that assumes the morality of an action should be judged by its outcomes. This perspective can be contrasted with the deontological perspective, which assumes that the morality of an action should be judged by the extent to which it conforms to agreed rules.

Constructivism A theory of International Relations which assumes that ideas, values, and identities matter, and that norms of social practice influence the behaviour of actors including states. The theory can be contrasted with realist approaches, which assume that interests are fixed and that norms of social practice have no independent influence on the behaviour of states and other actors.

Contestation (norm) The act of questioning the validity or applicability of a law or social rule. Contestation may be strategic or principled. Contestation can take the form of denial, excuse, or direct challenge.

Cosmopolitanism A perspective in international ethics that assumes that principles of ethics and human rights apply universally to everyone, irrespective of social context. This perspective can be contrasted with communitarian approaches, which assume that rights derive their meaning and validity from group membership and are tied to a particular social context.

De facto Referring to being owing to circumstance, rather than formal constitution. A de facto government is one with control over a given territory although it may not have been formally appointed.

De jure Referring to rights and duties as conferred by law. A de jure government derives this status from its claim to state sovereignty conferred to it by collective recognition of statehood bestowed through UN membership.

Department for Political and Peacebuilding Affairs (DPPA) An office of the UN Secretariat. The department engages in early warning, conflict prevention and mediation, conflict management, and sustaining peace.

Diplomacy (humanitarian, preventive) Deliberation seeking to achieve (mutually beneficial) terms of agreement, typically without recourse to the threat of coercion. 'Humanitarian diplomacy' is a form of diplomacy intending to advance humanitarian goals. 'Preventive diplomacy' is a form of diplomacy intending to prevent armed fighting or atrocities.

Direct prevention Halting or averting mass atrocities, an escalation of violence, armed conflict, and humanitarian suffering. The term refers to immediate measures including early warning mechanisms, preventive diplomacy, and mediation, as well as coercive measures including the threat or imposition of sanctions and the deployment of peacekeepers.

Discourse The language that is used in the context of public exchanges with regard to particular issues. Discourse is particularly important for constructivists, who assume that it is an expression of meaning that is constructed intersubjectively (between individuals and groups).

Donor state A state providing funds to other states. Funds may be used for development projects or humanitarian aid.

Ethnic cleansing The use of violence or intimidation to remove people with a certain ethnicity from a specific area. The term was first used in the context of the conflict in the former Yugoslavia. Ethnic cleansing has not been recognised as an independent crime in international law, but the term has been referred to in UN resolutions.

Foreign policy A states' posture and actions towards other states. The term may refer to broad ideas and principles guiding a state's actions, or to a state's particular preferences and behaviours with regard to a specific issue.

General Assembly The main legislative body of the United Nations. The General Assembly and the Security Council are the two central decision-making bodies of the United Nations.

Geneva Conventions The principal documents of international humanitarian law, which applies during armed conflict. The Conventions describe legal provisions to protect civilians and other non-combatants including aid workers, wounded soldiers, and prisoners of war.

Genocide Acts committed with the intent to destroy a national, ethnic, racial, or religious group, including killing or harming members of the group, inflicting conditions designed to bring about the group's destruction, the prevention of births within the group, and the forcible transfer of children. Genocide was first recognised as a crime by the General Assembly in 1946 and codified as an independent crime in the Genocide Convention of 1948.

Genocide Convention A treaty adopted in 1948 defining the crime of genocide. It was the first human rights treaty adopted by the UN General Assembly (see also *genocide*).

Geo-strategic interests State preferences as they relate to political power and economic wealth relative to other states. The term is associated with realist theory and states' quest for survival and power maximisation.

Global governance Global forms of regulation relying on international institutions, international networks, international civil society, and transnational capitalism. Given the absence of a world government, many forms of global governance are driven bottom-up rather than top-down.

Globalisation The political, economic, and institutional changes resulting from improved international communication and transportation. The term is typically used in the context of discussion of issues that are global in nature, such as climate change or transnational crime.

Good governance A form of political control that is grounded in liberal principles including representativeness, transparency, and accountability. The term is often used in the context of post-conflict statebuilding.

Humanitarian intervention The use of force within another sovereign state on grounds of alleviating human suffering. A wider conceptualisation may refer to any coercive or non-coercive measures to that end within another jurisdiction.

Humanitarian organisation A non-governmental body with the purpose of providing charitable aid to populations in need. Organisations vary with regard to thematic and geographic specialisation.

Humanitarianism Ideas and practices associated with the charitable provision of aid to alleviate human suffering. Humanitarianism is associated with the concepts of humanity, neutrality, and impartiality.

Human protection A practice aimed to prevent and respond to mass atrocities and conflict-induced harm to civilians. The term was used in the 2001 report of the International Commission on Intervention and State Sovereignty that is credited with having articulated in full the Responsibility to Protect (R2P) principle.

Human rights A group of rights belonging to each individual. They precede rights bestowed on individuals by states. These rights were first set out in the Universal Declaration on Human Rights adopted by the UN General Assembly in 1948.

Human security A concept focusing on the security of individuals and groups. The concept recognises the role of a range of political and economic factors in contributing to security.

Humanity A disposition of kindness and empathy towards the plight of those suffering as a consequence of adverse conditions (brought on by war). A term associated with humanitarianism.

Immunity Freedom from prosecution for alleged crimes. In the context of international criminal justice, the term refers to guarantees provided to alleged perpetrators of violations of human rights law or international humanitarian law.

Impartiality A disposition for adjudication based on specified principles. Impartiality as a humanitarian principle describes provision and allocation of relief based on need, rather than any other factors.

Institutionalisation Forming new state and non-state bodies designed to promote norms or principles. The term can also refer to the mainstreaming of principles within existing organisations or procedures.

International Commission on Intervention and State Sovereignty (ICISS) The Commission that articulated the Responsibility to Protect (R2P) principle. Upon concluding its work, the Commission published an influential report, 'The Responsibility to Protect'.

Internally displaced person (IDP) An internally displaced person is an individual who is unable to return to their home due to ongoing conflict or the destruction of property as a consequence of armed conflict. Unlike refugees, IDPs are displaced individuals that have not crossed international borders.

International Criminal Justice The study and practice of human rights law and international humanitarian law. International criminal justice is centred on individual accountability.

International humanitarian law A body of law applicable to situations of armed conflict. The laws provide protections to civilians and other groups affected by armed conflict.

International society A concept associated with English School International Relations theory. International society is made up of states whose behaviour is influenced, but not solely determined by, international law and international institutions.

Intervention In its narrower meaning, intervention refers to the use of military force by states or a group of states within the borders of another state. This can refer to military operations that are authorised by the UN and/or conducted with the state of the host government; or it may refer to intervention conducted without the consent of the host government and/or UN authorisation. In its broader meaning, intervention may refer to any form of interference in the domestic affairs of another state and, in this context, any actions by third parties designed to protect civilians, mitigate humanitarian consequences, and conflict management (see also *humanitarian intervention*).

League of Nations The predecessor organisation to the United Nations. The organisation was established in 1920 at the end of the First World War.

Leverage (political) The ability to achieve a preferred outcome by harnessing one's strengths. In diplomacy, it refers to the ability to influence, to entice or to persuade.

Liberalism A political school of thought underpinned by several foundational principles, including democracy, the rule of law, and free trade. In this context, liberalism is a theory that assumes that international institutions and cooperation can facilitate peaceful conflict resolution and coordinated responses to humanitarian crisis.

Local ownership A principle encouraging participation of national authorities and grassroots civil society organisations. The term is typically used in the context of peacebuilding.

Mandate The authorisation granted by the UN Security Council for the conduct of a peacekeeping operation. A mandate may or may not refer to Chapter VII of the UN Charter, granting intervening parties the right to use 'all means necessary', including the use of force, in implementing a mission.

Mass atrocities Large-scale, systematic violence against civilians and other non-combatants. The term typically refers to genocide, ethnic cleansing, war crimes, and crimes against humanity (see also *ethnic cleansing*, *genocide*).

Mediation The provision by a third party of impartial guidance of negotiations between two or more parties to a dispute. Mediation is used during ceasefire negotiations and negotiations over the terms of a peace agreement.

Moral hazard A concept taken from insurance theory, suggesting that contingency planning can affect behaviour by lowering the costs of negligence or recklessness. In political science, the concept refers to the idea that consistent military intervention by third parties in support of rebel groups may spur rebellion across cases by lowering the cost to rebels and increasing the likelihood of rebel success.

Multilateralism A principle according to which states ought to conduct their foreign policy in coordination with other states. In this context, multilateralism means internationally coordinated responses to immediate crises and, structurally and over longer periods of time, international cooperation on the development of global policies for structural conflict prevention and the coordination of responses to violent conflict, atrocity crimes, and humanitarian emergency.

Multi-stakeholder partnership (MSP) Cooperation between a diverse group of actors including governments, international organisations, and civil society. MSPs are frequently used to foster collaboration on global development and environmental sustainability.

Naming and shaming The action of publicly calling out and condemning norms violations. Naming and shaming is typically, but not exclusively, performed by human rights organisations.

Neutrality Politically not affiliated with either party to a dispute. Neutrality is a traditional principle of humanitarianism.

New humanitarianism An approach to humanitarianism that is, like traditional humanitarianism, premised on three key tenets – neutrality, impartiality, and humanity – but willing to view neutrality as conditional. Where a neutral approach interferes with the protection of human rights, organisations associated with principles of new humanitarianism will be prepared to forego the principle of neutrality.

No-fly zone A no-fly zone is an area that has been designated by the UN, a state, or a coalition of states as territory where no military aircraft is permitted to conduct operations, unless authorised. The patrolling of such designated areas is intended to prevent harm to civilians and the destruction of infrastructure through aerial bombing campaigns by parties to a conflict.

Norm A standard of behaviour that is perceived by individuals to be appropriate in a given social context. Norms emerge through customary practice. The degree to which a norm compels actors to behave in a particular way is determined by a range of factors, including the contextual salience of other norms.

Normative Relating to *ought*, rather than *is*. Relating to ethics and norms.

Outcomes (humanitarian) The results of intervention. In this context, the results of protective measures.

Paternalism An agent's actions and behaviours inhibiting the autonomy and free will of another, justified on grounds of protection. The term is often used in connection with critical discussion of international protection practice and restrictions imposed on national authorities, local actors, and citizens.

Patronage A relationship between a more powerful state and a less powerful state that is mutually beneficial. The weaker state receives support and protection from the more powerful state in exchange for political allegiance.

Peace The absence of fighting or war. 'Positive peace' refers to the absence of structural violence, or to a state of general societal harmony (see also *structural violence*).

Peace enforcement The use of coercive measures in fulfilment of peacekeeping operations mandated by the UN Security Council. This may include, but is not limited to, the use of force (see also peacekeeping).

Peacebuilding (liberal) The processes associated with reconciliation and the rebuilding of institutions and infrastructure after a conflict has ended. 'Liberal peacebuilding' is a term used by critical scholars to refer to the imposition of certain reforms on post-conflict states.

Peacekeeping (multidimensional) The practice of deploying troops to oversee a ceasefire or peace agreement. More recently, a comprehensive set of tasks by military and civilian personnel for the purpose of civilian protection, the prevention of conflict recurrence, stabilisation, and disarmament.

Policy An approach by a state or other actor in a given issue area. Civil society actors such as human rights groups and humanitarian organisations advocate for and promote policies that are more favourable for protecting human rights and providing humanitarian assistance.

Politicisation Actions or processes linking a topic to power dynamics or processes of resource allocation. In this context, looking beyond technical explanations for protection practices or outcomes.

Practice A regularised pattern of collective behaviour in a given social context. For example, peacekeeping as a form of social practice is a type of collective behaviour by states observed in the context of intra-state conflict.

Presidential statement (UN) A public statement by the president of the UN Security Council. Presidential statements do not require a vote.

Preventive diplomacy Negotiation among state representatives to avoid the escalation of hostilities among parties to a conflict. In this context, preventive diplomacy refers to activities by states and international organisations whose objective is to avert harm to civilians and identify avenues for peaceful conflict resolution.

Proportionality A rule of customary international humanitarian law prohibiting use of force causing harm to civilians that is excessive in relation to the anticipated military advantage. It is codified in an additional protocol to the Geneva Conventions.

Proxy war A direct confrontation between a state acting as an agent of another state – the so-called principal – and an adversary of the principal. Proxy wars were common during the Cold War.

Public diplomacy Communicating with the public with the aim of influencing opinion. Public diplomacy can be performed by states or non-state actors.

Rationalism A theoretical approach to the study of International Relations, which assumes that individuals and social entities (such as states) are utility-maximising rational actors. The approach is premised on the assumption that actors have a priori preferences, are able to rank these preferences, and have complete information about costs and benefits of the choices they make.

Realism A school of thought in International Relations that assumes that International Relations are anarchic. States are self-interested and security concerns dictate their foreign policy interests. States face a so-called 'security dilemma' – by increasing their own capacities in pursuit of security, they threaten the security of other states, who in turn must increase their own security by raising their own capacities, or balancing against a more powerful state through alliance with other states.

Rebel group An armed organisation within a state using violent means in pursuit of political objectives. Political objectives typically include secession, a change in government, or a government's change of policies.

Recipient state A state receiving funds from a state or an organisation. Funds may be used for development projects or humanitarian aid, for example.

Refugee An individual who has crossed an international border seeking safety. Refugee flows are typically caused by armed conflict.

Regional organisation An intergovernmental organisation where qualification for membership is determined by geographical proximity. Examples include ASEAN, the AU, or the EU.

Regime A system of rules, norms, and institutions that governs a certain issue area. Regime theorists suppose that regimes influence the behaviour of states and other actors.

Responsibility not to veto (RN2V) A principle suggesting that the permanent members of the Security Council ought to refrain from using their power to block the adoption of Security Council resolutions addressing R2P crisis situations. The principle was included in the ICISS report of 2001.

Responsibility to Protect (R2P or RtoP) A principle suggesting that a state's sovereignty flows from its ability and willingness to protect populations within its jurisdiction and that all states have a collective responsibility to step in if a state is unable to meet its protection responsibilities. The principle was first fully articulated in a 2001 report of the International Commission on Intervention and State Sovereignty (ICISS), although ideas about state sovereignty upon which the principle is based can be traced back much further.

Responsibility While Protecting (RWP) A principle relating to the conduct of actors intervening in conflict for protection purposes. The principle was first articulated in a concept paper by Brazil.

Rhetoric A particular kind of vocabulary, language, and arguments that are being used in public discourse. The analysis of rhetoric features heavily in constructivist work.

Safe areas Places within or near to combat zones providing security to non-combatants. Safe areas have been criticised for failing to provide security, most notably in the case of Srebrenica.

Sanctions (targeted) The imposition of costs, often economic, with the purpose of compelling governmental policy change. Targeted sanctions apply to specified individuals and entities rather than the target state as a whole.

Security Council The main decision-making body of the United Nations. The Council can authorise the use of force through Chapter VII of the UN Charter. Five states on the Council, the 'permanent five' (the United States, Russia, China, the United Kingdom, and France) have the power to veto Security Council resolutions, giving them more power than the other states on the Council.

Sovereignty A constitutive principle of international society, which stipulates that no external party is authorised to interfere in the domestic affairs of other jurisdictions. In the Westphalian understanding, sovereignty is an essential characteristic of statehood.

Special envoy A person representing a government or the UN for a specific purpose. UN envoys are appointed by the Secretary-General.

Structural prevention Long-term efforts by international actors to prevent mass atrocities, violent conflict, and humanitarian suffering. These measures are typically designed to address the root causes of conflict and mass violence.

Structural violence A pattern of observed social behaviour that systematically disadvantages particular groups and individuals. Structural violence is present where political circumstances, rather than practical constraints, explain inequality of opportunity among actors for the realisation of their full potential.

Sustainable Development Goals This is a list of 17 goals for international peace and prosperity. Goal 16 promotes peace, justice, and strong institutions.

Track two diplomacy Negotiation and peacebuilding efforts that are not part of regular, 'track one' diplomacy. This can refer to informal deliberations by officials, or to meetings of unofficial representatives.

World Summit Outcome Document (WSOD) A document summarising the deliberations of the 2005 gathering of world leaders. The document has the status of a UN General Assembly resolution. Paragraphs 138–140 referred to the Responsibility to Protect, signalling broad international support for the principle.

List of Acronyms and Abbreviations

A4P	Action for Peacekeeping
ACHR	American Convention on Human Rights
ACJHR	African Court of Justice and Human Rights
ACT	Accountability, Coherence, and Transparency Group
ADDR	Authority for Demobilization Disarmament and Reintegration
ADMM	ASEAN Defence Ministers' Meeting
AHRD	ASEAN Human Rights Declaration
AI	Amnesty International
AICHR	ASEAN Intergovernmental Commission on Human Rights
APSA	African Peace and Security Architecture
ARF	ASEAN Regional Forum
ASEAN	Association of Southeast Asian Nations
AU	African Union
BRICS	Brazil, Russia, India, China, and South Africa
CDVR	Truth and Reconciliation Commission
CIVCOM	Committee for Civilian Aspects of Crisis Management
CPC	Conflict Prevention Centre
CPCC	Civilian Planning and Conduct Capability
CSCE	Conference on Security and Co-operation in Europe
CSDP	Common Security and Defence Policy
DDR	Disarmament, Demobilisation, and Reintegration
DPO	Department for Peacekeeping Operations
DPPA	UN Department of Political Affairs
EAC	East African Community
ECHR	European Convention for the Protection of Human Rights and Fundamental Freedoms
ECOSOC	Economic and Social Council
ECOWAS	Economic Community of West African States
EEC	European Economic Community
EPNK	European Partnership for the Peaceful Settlement of the Conflict Over Nagorno-Karabakh
EU	European Union
EUCAP	EU Capacity Building Mission in Mali
EUMC	European Union Military Committee
EUMS	European Union Military Staff
EUTM	EU Training Mission

FARC	Revolutionary Armed Forces of Colombia
G4	Group of 4
G20	Group of 20
GDP	Gross Domestic Product
GMA	Global Magnitsky Act
HRW	Human Rights Watch
ICC	International Criminal Court
ICCPR	International Covenant on Civil and Political Rights
ICESCR	International Covenant on Economic, Social and Cultural Rights
ICISS	International Commission on Intervention and State Sovereignty
ICJ	International Court of Justice
ICRC	International Committee of the Red Cross
IDP	Internally Displaced Person
IFHR	International Federation for Human Rights
IFRC	International Federation of the Red Cross and Red Crescent Societies
IGAD	Intergovernmental Authority on Development
IHL	International humanitarian law
INGO	International Non-Governmental Organisation
IRO	International Refugee Organization
KLA	Kosovo Liberation Army
LAS	League of Arab States
LTTE	Liberation Tigers of Tamil Eelam
MICIVIH	International Civilian Mission in Haiti
MINUSMA	UN Multidimensional Integrated Stabilization Mission in Mali
MINUSTAH	UN Stabilisation Mission in Haiti
MONUC	United Nations Organization Mission in Democratic Republic of the Congo
MPCC	Military Planning and Conduct Capability
MSF	Médecins Sans Frontières
MSP	Multi-Stakeholder Partnership
NATO	North Atlantic Treaty Organisation
NGO	Non-governmental Organisation
NHRI	National Human Rights Institutions
OAS	Organization of American States
OCHA	UN Office for the Coordination of Humanitarian Affairs
ODIHR	Office for Democratic Institutions and Human Rights
ODM	Orange Democratic Movement
ODSG	OCHA Donor Support Group
ONUC	United Nations Operation in the Congo
OSCE	Organization for Security and Co-operation in Europe
PanWise	Pan-African Network of the Wise
PBC	UN Peacebuilding Commission
PBSO	Peacebuilding Support Office
PMG	Politico-Military Group
PNU	Party of National Unity
PoW	Panel of the Wise
PSC	Political and Security Committee

R2P	Responsibility to Protect
RECs	Regional Economic Communities
RN2V	Responsibility Not to Veto
RPA	Rwandan Patriotic Army
RWP	Responsibility While Protecting
S5	Small Five
SDG	Sustainable Development Goals
SECDEFPOL	Security and Defence Directorate
SSR	Security Sector Reform
UforP	Uniting for Peace
UN	United Nations
UNAMID	United Nations-African Union Mission in Darfur
UNAMIR	United Nations Assistance Mission for Rwanda
UNAMSIL	United Nations Mission in Sierra Leone
UNDP	United Nations Development Programme
UNEF	United Nations Emergency Force
UNHCR	United Nations High Commissioner for Refugees
UNHRC	United Nations Human Rights Council
UNITAF	Unified Task Force
UNMIK	United Nations Mission in Kosovo
UNOSOM	United Nations Operation in Somalia
UNTSO	United Nations Truce Supervision Organisation
WFP	World Food Programme
WLB	Women's League of Burma
WSOD	World Summit Outcome Document

1 Introduction

The words 'response' and 'responsibility' are related, and for good reason. What *responsibility* do we as individuals, citizens, and members of civil society have towards people affected by armed conflict and political violence? The idea that individuals and states should protect people in other states is not new, but the language of *responsibility* in this context is a fairly recent development. Historically, even minimal and elemental responses to egregious violations of human rights and dignity were perceived as a discretionary right, rather than a duty. This meant that while states *could* act if they wanted to, they were under no obligation to do so. The 'international community' existed as an idea about a society of states with a shared interest in preventing war, but states did not perceive a collective duty for responding to internal crises threatening human rights. Throughout the Cold War years, the protection of state sovereignty was a chief concern for post-colonial states, and the politics of the Cold War prevented strong multilateralism. And, in the absence of an international humanitarian response infrastructure the likes of which we have witnessed in recent decades, a true norm of humanitarian protection was, quite simply, regarded as unattainable idealism.

Determined and persistent campaigning by a coalition of dedicated advocates, the end of the Cold War, and an increasingly developed humanitarian response network has, however, been successful in bringing about significant change. Ideas about humanitarianism and protective intervention and public perceptions about appropriate international responses to conflict and humanitarian emergency have developed very substantially over time, particularly since the turn of the millennium. Several policy milestones, as we shall see, have been significant in this regard, and while there continues to be disagreement about the distribution of responsibilities and the best means of protection, undoubtedly the idea that there ought to be *a response*, and that there is a collective Responsibility to Protect, now shapes the way most people think about conflict and the role of international actors.

This chapter prepares the conceptual groundwork for this book, describing the development of the field of humanitarian protection, in substantive and theoretical terms. We will cover some key concepts and terms that will be useful in subsequent chapters and describe a range of methodological approaches used in the field. The field, as we shall see, draws on a range of traditions, and a wide range of questions can be addressed, including empirical questions that seek to use observation for explanation (e.g. 'Why does conflict happen?' or 'Why are some responses more successful than others?') and normative questions that seek to distinguish between *good*, and *bad* (such as, 'Is a system of sovereign states a good thing?' and 'Is it better if

DOI: 10.4324/9781003006671-1

states share protection responsibilities?'). Throughout the course of this book, you will become familiar with a wide range of such questions, in many cases, addressing very specific problems, in a very detailed, systematic kind of way. In what follows below, we will explore the academic traditions out of which these questions have emerged, and some key terminology.

Humanitarian Protection as a Field of Study

How do international actors respond to conflict and political crises that put the lives of innocents at risk? Humanitarian protection as a field of study describes protective responses by third parties and engages with both empirical and normative questions about the policies and practices associated with protective responses to conflict and humanitarian emergencies that put the lives and livelihoods of vulnerable populations, including civilians in armed conflict, refugees and displaced people, and minority groups, at risk. 'Humanitarian protection' as a field of study encompasses several academic sub-fields, surveying the origins of ideas, the roles and responsibilities of protection agents (including states but also humanitarian organisation and other non-state actors), and the efficacy and legitimacy of protection practices. To begin with, it makes sense to survey a range of definitions of terms that are related, but that do have distinct meanings that are also politically salient. Humanitarian protection as a field of study thus is the product of thinking originating from several issue areas.

One of the strands out thinking that informs humanitarian protection as a field of study is the scholarly literature on 'humanitarian intervention', itself originating from the policy and practitioner debates on the legitimacy of multilateral and unilateral interventions of the 1990s (see Box 1.1). 'Humanitarian intervention' emerged during the Cold War, when interventions into internal armed conflicts increased. After the end of the Cold War, intervention became a common practice. The end of the Cold War allowed for greater international cooperation on humanitarian crises.

'Human security' which was first mentioned in the 1992 report of the UN Secretary-General, 'An Agenda for Peace', and referred to again in the UNDP reports of 1993 and 1994. 'Human security' promoted an approach to security that focused on the security of the individual and communities, rather than states. The push represented the interests of states of the Global South, for whom the traditional emphasis on civil and political rights did not go far enough in providing the conceptual requisites for policy-making geared at addressing the causes of insecurity in their entirety – causes spanning not just the insecurity deriving from civil conflict and state repression, but also from the structural violence and deprivation caused by global inequality and fewer opportunities for developing states to enjoy the benefits of global trade. In the world of academe, a whole new research agenda on the causes and consequences of human insecurity subsequently emerged. This new research agenda changed the field dramatically in that it promoted a departure from state-centric accounts of security, and a more comprehensive understanding of the meaning of security not limited merely to survival but also expanded to include access to opportunity, and all of those factors required for individual and communal flourishing. 'Human security' can thus be defined as the study of tcoordinated through the UN. In he causes and consequences of insecurity of individuals and the communities upon which individuals' livelihoods depend, in the context of political and economic volatility.

Box 1.1 Humanitarian Intervention

Humanitarian intervention emerged as a concept throughout the Cold War, where, despite the patronage of either the United States, or the Soviet Union, humanitarian justifications for third-party interventions in civil war became more frequent, until they became commonplace after the end of the Cold War. The end of the Cold War brought an end to Security Council deadlock and with it the opportunity for genuinely multilateral responses to conflict and humanitarian crisis. However, the fact that the UN Security Council could now act did not mean that states agreed on coordinated policies in every crisis situation. For example, in the case of Kosovo, although there were compelling reasons for decisive action on humanitarian grounds, international responses were not coordinated through the UN. Instead, the North Atlantic Treaty Organisation (NATO) intervened unilaterally – still, however, invoking humanitarian justifications and in this context, Tony Blair articulated a 'doctrine of the international community', which suggested that unilateral intervention, in the face of conscience-shocking crimes could be legitimate. In sum, therefore, humanitarian intervention can be defined as the use of force by a state, or by a coalition of states, with the intention of preventing, or responding to, humanitarian crisis.

The protection of civilians, in contrast, is a term associated with UN peacekeeping. It is a staple of common vocabulary in UN resolutions, reports, and national foreign policy documents. Civilians are the object of protection, which therefore presupposes a distinction between combatants on the one hand, and non-combatants on the other. This is because the term is used to denote the actions that states and peacekeepers authorised by the UN take to protect non-combatants – civilians – affected by political violence. As such, the concept is embedded in a broader regime of which international humanitarian law forms an integral part. International humanitarian law distinguishes between combatants and non-combatants – the protection of civilians builds on this distinction, permitting the UN, through peacekeeping missions, to intervene to protect individuals not engaged in armed hostilities.

Several big debates characterise the field of humanitarian protection. First, questions that are drawn from International Relations theory. Realist thinkers argue that states as key actors will only act where it is in their interest to do so, while liberal thinkers argue that institutions – the UN, and other collective security arrangements – can and do make a difference. Second, the field of humanitarian protection is characterised by questions that are drawn from political theory. What role should military intervention play in protecting vulnerable populations? While some thinkers are sceptical about the use of force in pursuit of humanitarian objectives, others argue that military intervention may be justified if other measures are unlikely to succeed. Third, a set of questions about the extent to which ideas and values and emerging norms of protection can compel and constrain states and other actors to respond reliably, and in ways that are in line with some key principles and rules underpinning the protection regime. Finally, a range of critical perspectives have discussed the extent to which the regime, like regimes in other fields, reflects unequal power relations, reproducing, and potentially reinforcing, the structures and practices that weaken developing states, empower protectors at the expense of the protectee, and marginalise the role of women. While these debates have been dynamic and have served to move thinking about these questions forward in productive ways, many of these questions are perennial and characterise the field. While the idea that sovereignty entails specific non-negotiable responsibilities and that the international community has a responsibility, at the very least, to assist states in meeting their primary protection responsibility has grown in influence, the precise conditions under which the principle of sovereignty cedes to an international responsibility to protect (see Box 1.2) are still unclear.[1]

Given its diverse origins, humanitarian protection as a field of study thus draws on empirical case study research as well as normative argumentation. However, the two are also related in significant ways. Empirical research is grounded in basic premises and core assumptions about good outcomes, such as fatalities and conflicts prevented. Political theorists, by contrast, may focus on what makes a war just, such as having good reasons for waging a war. Although on many occasions, basic premises of empirical scholarship map well onto core assumptions about the common good, this is by no means a given and great attention therefore needs to be paid to concepts and their meanings. For example, is a war sufficiently good if it protects innocents, or is a war only then a good war if it also ends tyranny? In modern language, we might ask whether a peacekeeping intervention that prevents civilian fatalities is good enough, or whether we expect more, in terms of good governance, say, or the advancement of gender equality? Conversely, can an intervention be good if it causes harm but ends tyranny? What are the thresholds for what is acceptable, and where does one draw the

Box 1.2 The Responsibility to Protect

The 'Responsibility to Protect' is a term coined in a report of the International Commission on Intervention and State Sovereignty (ICISS), published in 2001. The express objective of the Commission had been to forge an international consensus about how harm to vulnerable populations in conflict could be prevented or mitigated without, however, promoting interventionist norms threatening to undermine state sovereignty – a norm highly valued by many peoples subjected to colonial repression. The Commission developed a formula, 'sovereignty as responsibility' that sought to overcome the dilemma. 'Sovereignty as responsibility' imposed certain conditions on governments in the exercise of their duties as sovereigns. Where a state was unable or unwilling, the Commission suggested, to protect its populations from harm, the Responsibility to Protect would fall to the international community. 'Sovereignty as responsibility' has had a strong impact on the international discourse since then. International consensus about the central premises of the report was reflected in the endorsement of the principle at the UN World Summit in 2005, where states committed to the principle that states have a responsibility to protect populations from genocide, ethnic cleansing, war crimes, and crimes against humanity.

line? Who gives protection, who receives it, and when? How is the act of protecting justified? These questions are steeped in politics and may lie beneath the jargon. Consequently, understanding the meanings of concepts and the arguments with which they are historically associated is of paramount importance.

Theory and Definitions

Humanitarianism and Humanitarian Protection

Humanitarianism has a long tradition rooted in the First World War, the efforts of Henri Dunant and the creation of the International Federation of the Red Cross and Red Crescent Societies (IFRC) in 1919.[2] The organisation superseded the Red Cross, founded in 1863 by Dunant, several years after first efforts to organise relief aid for those wounded in the Battle of Solferino. Dunant spearheaded an initiative for relief societies with the task of caring for injured combatants. Shortly following the establishment of the Red Cross, the first Geneva Convention was adopted by several governments. Humanitarianism, the relief of human suffering as a consequence of war, through the provision of provisional shelter, food, medical treatment and supplies, has since been transformed into a professionalised industry, with a number of state-funded organisations and charities, both secular and faith-based, providing relief during conflict-induced humanitarian crises. Many of these organisations also provide aid during crises that do not result from conflict, and many also run long-term projects that are not exclusively focused on providing rapid relief. While some organisations are truly universal in scope, other organisations focus on particular regions, or specialise in a particular area of providing relief. Some organisations belong to the wider UN system, while others are independent.

Humanitarian protection (see Box 1.3) encompasses the provision of humanitarian relief to populations in need during conflict and other complex humanitarian emergencies, but is not limited to the provision of relief. A related concept, 'human protection' was articulated in former UN Secretary-General's Cyril Foster Lecture at Oxford in 2008, where Ban Ki-Moon summarised it as 'a subset of the more encompassing concept of human security'.[3] The practice of humanitarian protection thus can be described as encompassing measures designed to prevent, and respond to, harm and suffering of populations as a result of complex humanitarian emergency. The 'complexity' of the humanitarian emergency is a result of the political factors that inhibit a resolution of the conflict or the effective provision of humanitarian aid. Consequently – although Ban Ki-Moon had actually referred to humanitarian emergency in the broadest sense – 'human protection' or 'humanitarian protection' are frequently understood to entail international responses to humanitarian crises that result from armed conflict (such as in Rwanda or Darfur), or to responses to humanitarian crisis that is exacerbated by latent political conflict, for example when a government is unwilling to allow access to populations in need of humanitarian relief, thereby unnecessarily increasing civilian suffering (such as in the case of Myanmar in the aftermath of Cyclone Nargis, or the politicisation of humanitarian relief efforts in Yemen, where conflict has produced the world's worst recent humanitarian crisis).

The practices associated with humanitarian protection arose against the backdrop of a long history of ideas about intervention.[4] These ideas have found expression in academic works, they have led to the establishment of dedicated organisations, they

Box 1.3 Humanitarian Protection

'Humanitarian protection' is a broad term. Conceptually, it is similar to 'human protection', a term coined by former Secretary-General Ban Ki-Moon at the 2008 annual Cyril Foster Lecture at the University of Oxford. 'Human protection' encompasses responses to situations in which populations are threatened by harm from direct violence, or from the indirect consequences of conflict. It has since entered the academic discourse as a term standing for a comprehensive approach to aiding affected populations during conflict. 'Humanitarian protection' engages with the role of international actors in providing assistance and relief in complex humanitarian emergencies, where access to affected populations is difficult given political volatility and insecurity on the ground. Humanitarian protection thus draws on related concepts, including the protection of civilians, and the Responsibility to Protect. As opposed to 'humanitarian intervention', which has traditionally been associated primarily with military intervention, protective action associated with humanitarian protection refers to tailored responses by international actors, also including non-state actors, to individual crises. These responses may include the use of force as a last resort if this is deemed an effective protective measure, but in many cases will be limited to other measures, including preventive diplomacy and threats of economic or other sanctions. The term differs from 'human security' in that it focuses on the role of specific actors within the protection paradigm and the measures available to them.

have shaped the formulation of national security strategies, and they have influenced the policy-making of states. These ideas have promoted the expansion of peacekeeping practice; and they have led to the campaign for the recognition of the plight of people displaced within state borders – internally displaced people (IDP), who are not afforded the same legal protections as people who cross international borders. These ideas also led to renewed debate on just war ethics. The concept of 'intervention' first emerged as military intervention throughout the Cold War, but it was not until the end of the Cold War that references to its 'humanitarian' variant became commonplace.

However, the term 'humanitarian intervention' remains contentious, given the military nature of the responses and the inability of interveners to avoid civilian casualties. Humanitarian and faith-based civil society organisations continued to express reservations, and the principle, articulated succinctly in the Blair Doctrine, devised as a response to the crisis in Kosovo, and used to justify NATO's intervention there, has been the subject of debate. Developing states in particular have expressed reservations.[5] To address concerns around the potential misuse of humanitarian justifications for self-interested intervention, an international Commission, comprising an international panel of experts, funded by the Canadian government, elaborated a framework that aimed to reconcile non-aggression and sovereignty norms as enshrined in the UN Charter. The principle drew on the 'sovereignty as responsibility' formula articulated in the context of IDP protection and employed a framework resting on three pillars: prevention, reaction, and rebuilding.[6] The report attempted to reframe the way international actors, including states, perceived conflicts and their role in responding to them. The principle was endorsed at the UN World Summit in 2005 though in a slightly narrower form. While the initial report referred to 'man-made crises putting populations at risk', the World Summit Outcome Document focused more narrowly on situations in which 'national authorities manifestly fail to protect their populations from genocide, war crimes, ethnic cleansing and crimes against humanity'.[7]

Nevertheless, the endorsement of the principle constituted a major milestone. The 'Responsibility to Protect' became a central concept in subsequent years, with continued campaigning for more robust and effective human rights-based international responses to conflict and complex humanitarian emergencies.[8] The campaign can be said to have been successful in that it became a frame of reference that even critics wary of the formalisation of interventionist and, potentially, paternalistic practices began to adopt. It also provided the impetus for the creation of new institutions at the international, regional, and domestic levels, all tasked with protecting populations from mass atrocity crimes, and in laid the groundwork for a new academic field of study on the protection of populations at risk during conflict.

From 'International Security' to 'Human Security'

International Security as an academic field of study emerged in the Cold War era, influenced by realist thought in the context of Cold War rivalry and, in particular, the development of nuclear weapons. Following the end of the Cold War, throughout the 1990s, a thawing of relations between the Western bloc and Russia and post-Soviet countries signalled the beginning of a new era of multilateral policy-making and it was in this era that liberal thinking about foreign policy, cooperation, and the role of institutions once again became influential. Theories of collective security, such as that articulated by Kupchan and Kupchan, suggested those systems of collective security, shaped by ideas and underpinned by domestic support, could provide security in a state of anarchy.[9] The authors suggested that if states formed a community within which a state that violated the principle of non-aggression was punished collectively, they could prevent armed conflict among states.

The impetus for this theorising came from the collective response during the Gulf War of 1990–1991. In 1990, the UN Security Council voted to authorise 'all necessary means' to expel Iraq from Kuwait, marking the beginnings of a post-Cold War, unipolar order in which the UN was better able to implement a range of goals pertaining to human rights, international peace and security, and development. It was in this particular context of thawing relations and the expansion of multilateral initiatives, reflected in a growing number of international organisations with ever broader and more complex tasks, that wider notions of 'international security' emerged.[10]

Also throughout the 1990s, in the immediate aftermath of the collapse of the Soviet Union and with it, the end of the Cold War, a separate strand of scholarship began to advocate for a new approach to understanding security that focused on the security of individuals and groups, rather than merely the security of states. This approach to the study of security emerged from the realisation that new forms of conflict called for new conceptual tools to address the issues that threatened vulnerable populations. Civil war, not war among sovereign states, was now the prevailing form of political conflict. In addition to focusing on individuals and groups, this approach also advocated for a more comprehensive understanding of the nature of threats to individuals and groups, to include not just threats to lives and immediate sources of bodily harm but also to livelihoods and the long-term well-being of groups and communities. This approach became known as 'human security', promoted by Mary Kaldor, who outlined its utility for scholars,[11] and Roland Paris, who questioned the concept's analytical utility, given the vagueness of the term, yet suggested it was helpful in that it reframed the study of security in a productive way.[12]

From 'Direct Violence' to 'Structural Violence'

Peace research has a long history but in its contemporary form – understanding the causes and consequences of conflict through scientific inquiry – it is the product of pioneering work of a number of scholars, including, most prominently, Johan Galtung in the 1950s.[13] The origins of the recent field of study of the causes of conflict, and conditions of peace, must therefore be viewed in the context of renewed efforts to bring academic rigour to a field of study inspired by anti-war campaigning during the Cold War. The Vietnam War and the anti-war campaigning associated with it provided the impetus for research in this field, resulting in the publication of some foundational research. The early work in the fieldrigour to a field of study inspired by was dominated by debates over definitions of war, peace, conflict, and violence – as might be expected from a young discipline. Pathbreaking essays included Johan Galtung's reflections on the distinction between direct violence – a situation in which one actor, in Galtung's words, 'commits the violence as *personal* or *direct'*, – as opposed to structural violence, where the conditions are such that 'violence is built into the structure and shows up as unequal power and consequently as unequal life chances', establishing the distinction between negative peace as the absence of violence, versus positive peace as both the absence of direct, as well as of structural violence. Structural violence, Galtung argued, caused deprivation – opportunities forgone due to externally imposed systemic conditions. For example, where people die as a result of starvation or malaria, this is the result of systemic inequality, given sufficient resources, worldwide, to provide food to everyone, and the knowledge about the effective prevention and treatment of malaria. 'Violence', Galtung suggests, is 'the cause of the difference between the potential and the actual, between what could have been and what is'.

The field today has become vastly more complex with a range of methodological traditions actively engaged in the study of conflict, its causes, and its consequences. It is characteristically pluralist methodologically, with quantitative, qualitative, and critical approaches all represented in vibrant research agendas. Critical approaches have, recently, focused on the role of international actors in intervention and post conflict rebuilding, such as Séverine Autesserre's work on the everyday politics of intervention,[14] or Roland Paris' work on human security.[15] Furthermore, a rich literature on causes and consequences of civil war has generated new theories about the causes of conflict, including grievance-based explanations (suggesting that perceived injustices explain the resort to violence), as well as greed-based arguments, articulated, for example, by Paul Collier and Anke Hoeffler, where the main driver of conflict is hypothesised to be an interest in the acquisition of resources among actors mobilising groups during conflict.[16]

International Relations, Constructivism, and the Study of Norms

International Relations as a discipline is defined by a debate between idealists on the one hand and realists on the other. Idealism led to the creation of the League of Nations, the precursor organisation to the United Nations,[17] and, more broadly, argued that collective systems of security could provide the assurances states required to be able to forfeit defensive alliance systems that inevitably constituted a threat to others. The disintegration of the collective security structures as a consequence of the Second World War gave rise to realist thought. These realists suggested that human nature – 'a world' according to Hans Morgenthau, 'of opposing interests and of conflict among them'[18] – foreclosed the possibility of cooperation; that, in an anarchic system, or, as Kenneth Waltz suggested, a 'self-help' system,[19] any measures designed to increase one's own security were perceived as a threat by others.[20] This constituted the 'first great debate' in international politics.

Subsequent debates revolved around the extent to which cooperation among states was possible, in an anarchic, self-help system, and the role that international organisations (specifically, now, in the security domain, the UN) played in helping to achieve cooperation in managing conflict and preventing war. The debate now played out within the rationalist paradigm based on an assumption that actors (still, primarily, states) acted in their own best interests, according to defined preferences (still relating solely to maximising security), to maximise utility (and avoid costs). Either side, again, differed in their perceptions of the role and independent influence of international organisations. While neo-realists argued that where forms of international cooperate emerge, they merely reflect converging interests in a given issue area, and institutions are tools of powerful states, liberal institutionalists suggested that institutions could foster cooperation by reducing transactions costs, providing mechanisms for monitoring and verification, and by providing a venue for repeated interactions among actors, that result in reputational costs where actors renege on commitments made, thus reducing prospects for future cooperation.[21]

Finally, the most recent debate has played out among rationalists and reflectivists – an umbrella term for all of those approaches that are not based on rationalist assumptions. These include constructivist and critical approaches. While constructivists argued that 'anarchy was what states make of it'[22] – in other words, that social constructions of identities and roles, such as, for example, perceptions of enmity and friendship among states – mattered, critical theorists – including feminist and post-colonial thinkers – argued that specific kinds of discourses (meaning the way in which language was used to describe phenomena) elevated particular issues and perspectives, while marginalising others. 'Theory is always *for* someone and *for* some purpose',[23] Robert W. Cox suggested in 1981. This scholarship flagged that the theoretical prism for understanding the production of knowledge was an overtly political process, and that rationalist accounts – both in their neo-realist and liberal institutionalist variants – failed to consider questions related to global inequality among states, and the role of gender in international relations. Both constructivist and critical approaches are relatively newer additions to the field, and as such have been developing substantially in recent years – a well-established body of work now exists in both areas, that often also overlap; and these have provided many new and useful ways of thinking about protection practice, as we shall see further on.

From 'International Society' to 'Global Society'

The field of Global Governance provides a theoretical prism for understanding the role of a wide range of international actors. Scholars such as Michael Barnett and Kathryn Sikkink have surveyed the role of norms and changing perceptions about actors and their responsibilities.[24] Some positivist work has begun to survey the institutional structure of global governance, focusing on the determinants of successful cooperation. While some of these approaches focus on governance through an institutionalist lens, other approaches have been more sociologically oriented, also bringing in the role of identities, values, perceptions, and norms.

The central difference between Global Governance and International Relations is that where the latter is premised on a state-centric understanding and questions typically revolve around politics among states, particularly the politics of security and insecurity, and the auxiliary role that other actors play in this regard, Global Governance takes a more holistic approach, surveying the role of a range of actors, including international civil society, business, and regional actors. This approach can be described as 'polycentric', outlined by thinkers such as Mathias Koenig-Archibugi, as opposed to traditional state-centric approaches.[25] Its origins in globalisation theory – essentially descriptive in nature – explains the orientation towards understanding the nature of international affairs, and the role that discrete units of actors play in the international realm, as well as the factors that allow for successful cooperation in a range of governance domains. Consequently, the field differs significantly to other approaches both in terms of the key units that form the basis of theorising in the field, as well as with regard to the questions to which it seeks answers.

While much of the field today is dominated by questions around the efficacy of institutions, some work in the field has also engaged with ethical questions related to the politics of governance structures. In a range of issue areas, normative positions align along a spectrum of positions flanked by cosmopolitan thought – the idea that rights, values, and norms apply universally and that a duty is owed to all individuals, irrespective of context – at one end, and communitarian philosophy – the assumption that rights, duties, and obligations are grounded in particular communities – on the other.[26] Central themes include the distribution of power among international actors and the extent to which international institutions reflect global inequalities and reinforce them; the history of colonialism and how it has produced global structures within which inequalities are amplified; and the role and duties of international actors tasked with specific roles in the international realm – how far do their responsibilities extend, and how can obligations be identified; what are the appropriate mechanisms for assigning responsibilities, and, in the absence of competent judicial authorities, whether there are any mechanisms for arbitration and accountability.

The Epistemic Community: Drawing on the Work of Policymakers and Practitioners

International public policy, also referred to as global public policy, is a fairly recent field of study. Traditionally, it focuses on the process of policy-making, for example in the areas of health, education, or trade, and the role of state actors as well as civil society in making policy. It focuses on policy recommendations and assessing effects of policy. As such, public policy uses methods of decision theory – what accounts for preferences of policymakers – and counterfactuals – what are the results of these decisions, and what the outcomes have been, had other decisions been made by these actors. The field draws on International Relations as a field of study in that it uses neo-realism, liberal institutionalism, as well as constructivist approaches to explain and understand policy-making in the international realm, but is better understood as a sub-field of Global Governance, given the consideration given to non-state actors in accounting for the process of policy formation.[27] As opposed to the more traditional approaches, including International Relations and peace and conflict studies, international public policy is explicitly policy-oriented. Whereas most other approaches eschew policy recommendations, international public policy scholarship seeks to inform and guide the work of policymakers. The field is determinedly positivist in outlook, and characteristically employs quantitative approaches. The express aim of this type of scholarship is to cater to national and international policymakers – officials in charge of portfolios in the domains of international trade, the environment, and international security, as well as practitioners with roles in international organisations, think tanks, or advocacy groups – who require hard facts to justify their policy choices.

The Structure of the Book

The book is structured in three parts: *Origins*, *Actors*, and *Responsibilities*. In each of these three parts, the central literature and questions defining the field are outlined. Each chapter surveys a range of empirical questions, but each chapter also engages with normative questions about the duties of international actors in enacting their responsibilities, such as the choice of appropriate measures for responding to individual humanitarian protection crises.

Part I – *origins* – discusses the development of institutions and norms that underpin the humanitarian protection regime. Chapter 2 outlines the establishment of the United Nations as a successor organisation to the League of Nations in the aftermath of the Second World War. It describes the drafting of the UN Charter, and the subsequent gradual building of the constituent parts of the international human rights regime, comprising also, in the legal sphere, international humanitarian law and associated international, regional, and national institutions and courts. It describes practices of intervention throughout the Cold War, and the way in which humanitarian justifications for intervention gradually became more frequent as outlined in Nicholas Wheeler's study of Cold War state practice describing significant changes in the international discourse.[28] The chapter describes, further, changes in humanitarian practice and a shift away of practitioner support for strict interpretations of principles of impartiality and neutrality, and the emergence of human rights-based approaches. Chapter 3 then describes the way in which international actors begin to rethink humanitarian intervention after the end of the Cold War, in the context of the peacekeeping failures of the 1990s, the Rwandan Genocide, and Security Council deadlock and subsequent NATO intervention in the case of Kosovo.

Part II – *actors* – comprises three chapters. Chapters 4–6 discuss the role of states and regional organisations, the role of regional actors, as well as civil society actors. A range of protection practice is associated with each type of actor: states and regional organisations (Chapter 4), the United Nations (Chapter 5), and humanitarian organisations and civil society (Chapter 6). Different types of actors respond differently to conflict and humanitarian emergency – each chapter outlines typical practice and the extent to which practice is changing in the context of the development of the protection regime. Chapter 4 discusses states as norm proponents and sceptics. While some states have contested some of the principles associated with the regime (for different reasons, as will be outlined), the key principles associated with the humanitarian protection regime now enjoy widespread support among most states. The politics of norm advocacy and contestation have also played out at the UN and at the regional level. Chapter 5 discusses the role of the UN. Chapter 6 outlines campaigning for the Responsibility to Protect by the Global Centre for the Responsibility to Protect and the International Coalition for the Responsibility to Protect, among other organisations spearheading efforts in support of the establishment of international principles and associated institutions for the co-ordination of robust response mechanisms.

Part III – *responsibilities* – is divided into three subsections, *prevention*, *reaction*, and *rebuilding*, respectively, each engaging with different tasks associated with the protection regime: mediation and preventive diplomacy, peacekeeping and humanitarian relief, and peacebuilding and criminal accountability. While each of these tasks relates to different points in the conflict cycle, the boundaries are fluid in that numerous international responses associated with each of these pillars can occur before, during, or after conflict. For example, mediation efforts can seek to prevent conflict or help end an already ongoing conflict. Similarly, peacekeepers can be deployed during conflict or during post-conflict stabilisation. Chapter 7 outlines mediation and preventive diplomacy. Chapter 8 discusses humanitarian relief and peacekeeping, and Chapter 9 discusses peacebuilding and international criminal justice. Each chapter outlines the nature of international responses to conflict and humanitarian emergency and discusses the extent to which recent practice suggests protection norms have taken root; and each chapter also discusses the continued contestation of humanitarian protection principles and norm advocates' policy efforts to address these concerns.

Summary

- The practice of humanitarian protection is intrinsically political in nature, and close attention needs to be paid to definitions, their meanings, and their use. Although some research and policy-relevant material uses technical jargon, analytical choices may reflect normative assumptions and policy preferences.
- Humanitarian protection as a field of study has diverse origins, ranging from the history of ideas on humanitarian justifications for the use of force; the provision of humanitarian relief to populations affected by the ravages of war; and the protection of refugees and IDPs. It is also a field for which both empirical and normative questions are important.
- The terms 'humanitarian intervention' and 'humanitarian protection' have distinct meanings. While 'humanitarian intervention' is about the use of force,

'humanitarian protection' is about preventing and mitigating harm to civilians in humanitarian emergencies. The differences is salient because protection norms proponents seek to dissociate the practice of protection from the use of force.

- International norms of protection, according to constructivists, inform the decision-making of relevant actors including states. Sustained advocacy for the Responsibility to Protect, in this view, has changed perceptions about appropriate international responses to conflict and humanitarian crises that put the lives and livelihoods of people at risk.
- International public policy seeks to take a bird's eye view of international humanitarian protection. Its role is to guide international policy-making following consideration of reliable empirical research. It is up to policymakers to draw on these recommendations when formulating policy for international protection responses.

Questions for Reflection

- *Do concepts such as 'sovereignty', 'responsibility', and protection have fixed meanings?*
- *Which ideas had the greatest bearing on the conceptualisation of humanitarian protection as a field of study?*
- *What is the difference between 'humanitarian intervention' and 'humanitarian protection', and when should these terms be used?*
- *Can protection norms compel states to respond decisively and robustly to humanitarian protection crises?*
- *Can international public policy articulate best practice for responding to protection crises?*

Further reading

- Barnett, Michael, (2011): *Empire of Humanity: A History of Humanitarianism* (Ithaca, New York: Cornell University Press).
- Bellamy, Alex J. and Edward Luck (2018): *The Responsibility to Protect: From Promise to Practice* (Cambridge: Polity Press).
- Finnemore, Martha (2003): *The Purpose of Intervention: Changing Beliefs about the Use of Force* (Ithaca, New York: Cornell University Press).
- Keck, Margaret E. and Kathryn Sikkink (1998): *Activists beyond Borders: Advocacy Networks in International Politics* (Ithaca, New York: Cornell University Press).
- Wheeler, Nicholas (2002): *Saving Strangers: Humanitarian Intervention in International Society* (Oxford: Oxford University Press).

Notes

1 Jennifer Welsh, 'Norm Contestation and the Responsibility to Protect', *Global Responsibility to Protect* 5, no. 4 (2013): 365–96.

2 David P. Forsythe and Barbara Ann Rieffer-Flanagan, *The International Committee of the Red Cross: A Neutral Humanitarian Actor*, 2nd ed. (Abingdon, Oxon: Routledge, 2016).
3 United Nations Secretary-General, 'Cyril Foster Lecture at Oxford University: "Human Protection and the 21st Century United Nations"', *United Nations*, 2 February 2011, https://www.un.org.
4 Alex J. Bellamy, *Global Politics and the Responsibility to Protect: From Words to Deeds (Paperback) – Routledge*
5 Ramesh Thakur, 'Developing Countries and the Intervention-Sovereignty Debate', in *The United Nations and Global Security*, ed. Richard M. Price and Mark W. Zacher (New York, N.Y.: Palgrave Macmillan, 2004).
6 ICISS, 'The Responsibility to Protect: Report of the International Commission on Intervention and State Sovereignty', 2001.
7 United Nations, '2005 World Summit Outcome', *United Nations*, 16 September 2005.
8 Ramesh Thakur, 'The Responsibility to Protect at 15', *International Affairs* 92, no. 2 (1 March 2016): 415–34, https://doi.org/10.1111/1468-2346.12557.
9 Charles A. Kupchan and Clifford A. Kupchan, 'The Promise of Collective Security', *International Security* 20, no. 1 (1995): 52–61.
10 Union of International Associations, 'Yearbook of International Organizations', 2019.
11 Mary Kaldor, *Human Security: Reflections on Globalization and Intervention*, 1st ed. (Cambridge: Polity, 2013).
12 Roland Paris, 'Human Security: Paradigm Shift or Hot Air?', *International Security* 26, no. 2 (1 October 2001): 87–102.
13 Johan Galtung, 'Violence, Peace, and Peace Research', *Journal of Peace Research* 6, no. 3 (1 September 1969): 167–91.
14 Séverine Autesserre, 'Peaceland, Cambridge Core, May 2014, https://doi.org/10.1017/CBO9781107280366.
15 Roland Paris, 'Saving Liberal Peacebuilding', *Review of International Studies* 36, no. 2 (April 2010): 337–65.
16 Paul Collier and Anke Hoeffler, 'Greed and Grievance in Civil War', *Oxford Economic Papers* 56, no. 4 (1 October 2004): 563–95.
17 Jill Steans et al., *An Introduction to International Relations Theory: Perspectives and Themes*, 3rd ed. (Harlow: Routledge, 2010).
18 Hans Morgenthau, *Politics among Nations*, 7th ed. (Boston: McGraw-Hill Education, 2005), 3.
19 Kenneth N. Waltz, *Theory of International Politics*, Reissue edition (Long Grove, Ill: Waveland Pr Inc, 2010), 104.
20 John Mearsheimer, *The Tragedy of Great Power Politics*, Updated edition (New York: W. W. Norton & Company, 2014).
21 Robert O. Keohane, *After Hegemony: Cooperation and Discord in the World Political Economy*, with a new preface by the author edition (Princeton, NJ: Princeton University Press, 2005), 244–5.
22 Alexander Wendt, 'Anarchy Is What States Make of It: The Social Construction of Power Politics', *International Organization* 46, no. 2 (1992): 391–425.
23 Robert W. Cox, 'Social Forces, States and World Orders: Beyond International Relations Theory', *Millennium* 10, no. 2 (1 June 1981): 126–55, emphasis in the original.
24 Michael N. Barnett and Kathryn Sikkink, 'From International Relations to Global Society', in *The Oxford Handbook of Political Science* (Oxford: Oxford University Press, 7 July 2011).
25 Mathias Koenig-Archibugi, 'Understanding the Global Dimensions of Policy', *Global Policy* 1, no. 1 (2010): 16–28
26 Michael Zürn and Pieter de Wilde, 'Debating Globalization: Cosmopolitanism and Communitarianism as Political Ideologies', *Journal of Political Ideologies* 21, no. 3 (1 September 2016): 280–301.
27 Diane Stone, 'Global Public Policy, Transnational Policy Communities, and Their Networks', *Policy Studies Journal* 36, no. 1 (2008): 19–38.
28 Nicholas Wheeler, *Saving Strangers: Humanitarian Intervention in International Society* (Oxford: Oxford University Press, 2003).

Part I

Origins

2 Human Rights and the Cold War

Following a survey of key definitions and the main theoretical approaches in Chapter 1, this chapter now turns to the origins of the protection regime and ideas about human protection practice. The origins of the terms that characterise the language that is used to describe and justify, or critique or contest, protection practice say much about how these terms are understood today. Their interpretation is politically salient. For example, who is a protectee? What is the role of interveners? Under what circumstances are decisive interventions justified, and what tools are available? Chapters 2 and 3 outline a history of ideas that have shaped the thinking of scholars and practitioners and influenced the present protection regime and the norms and principles associated with this regime. Of particular interest are the creation of the United Nations and the articulation of fundamental and inalienable rights; the emergence of humanitarian practice; the invention of UN peacekeeping; and, towards the end of the Cold War, ideas challenging prevailing conceptions about neutrality as a default principle shaping the responses of third parties such as UN peacekeepers and humanitarian organisations.

The United Nations and Human Rights

The United Nations was established at the end of the Second World War, succeeding the League of Nations as a collective security organisation. It was a second attempt at achieving what the League had failed at: preventing a relapse into a world of war. At the same time, the creators of the organisation sought to draw on lessons learned, above all the need for a grounding in realism. The creators of the organisation understood that a universal security organisation required the support of the great powers. For this reason, five influential states received a permanent seat on the organisation's central executive body, the Security Council: the United States, the United Kingdom, France, Russia, and China. However, the organisation was more than simply a collective security organisation, as it was also tasked with promoting the independence of colonial territories.[1]

Human rights were firmly ingrained in the Charter as a foundational purpose of the organisation. These origins define the structure of its organs, and the ethos underlying its work, to this day – although critics note that the articulation of the principles underpinning the organisation could be viewed as much as the product of a conflagration of interests, as of shared idealism.[2] The Charter is idealist and defines a range of principles, but these principles are ambiguous in and of themselves and have often conflicted with each other. The Charter spelled out rights for collectively

DOI: 10.4324/9781003006671-3

enforcing principles of international peace and security for states with the will and power to realise these, without however creating enforceable duties and obligations.

The future shape of the organisation was established at Dumbarton Oaks, in the United States. The structure of the organisation as it emerged at the 'Washington Conversations on International Peace and Security Organization', reflected interests of the leaders of the United States, Russia, and the United Kingdom: Roosevelt, Stalin, and Churchill. The future structure of the organisation ceded as much influence to other states (including France and China, who would become permanent members of the Security Council) as was needed, but not more than was necessary,[3] creating an organisation 'based fundamentally on the great power structure than one built on international law and due process'.[4] The Charter was signed on 26 June 1945 in San Francisco in the United States, at the United Nations Conference on International Organization. It outlawed the use of force – save for the use of force in self-defence – and explicitly outlawed any form of aggression. The only circumstances in which the use of force is permitted, otherwise, is when authorised by the Security Council. Article 7(42) establishes the right of the Security Council to authorise enforcement measures.

The prohibition on interference in the internal affairs of states has, however, been difficult to reconcile with the provisions for the promotion and protection of human rights in the UN Charter and other documents of international law. The UN Charter made ample reference to human rights, and its first article explicitly stated the promotion of human rights was one of the organisation's central purposes. Yet, the drafters of the Charter did not stipulate the conditions under which principles of human rights protection trumped state sovereignty, in case these were being violated domestically. The Charter made no mention of thresholds or triggering circumstances – such as the anticipation of imminent state collapse. The drafters of the Charter were driven by a desire to prevent inter-state war, not civil war and internal armed conflict, which mostly characterises present-day conflict.

In the immediate aftermath of the war, two events were momentous in laying the groundwork for much of the thinking about political violence and responses to it, including its punishment: the Nuremberg Trials, and the drafting of the Genocide Convention. The trials, held in Nuremberg, Germany, in the immediate aftermath of the war during 1945 and 1946, were conducted by an International Military Tribunal that had been created by the United States, the United Kingdom, the Soviet Union, and France in London in August 1945. Individuals – leaders of the Nazi regime – and groups – such as the Nazi secret police, the Gestapo, were charged. The trials constituted the beginnings of international criminal law, a mechanism for enforcing the rights associated with the international human rights regime, identifying four major categories of crimes (crimes against peace, war crimes, crimes against humanity, and genocide), and making sure that individuals could be held accountable.[5] The trials were the first time states collectively prosecuted suspects for crimes against humanity in a special tribunal. Consequently, the trials marked the beginning of an emerging regime comprised of institutions and norms underpinning international criminal law.[6]

The Genocide Convention was adopted in December 1948, and entered into force in January 1951. It defined the crime of genocide. The term 'genocide' had been coined by Raphael Lemkin in *Axis Rule in Occupied Europe*.[7] 'Genocide' refers to crimes committed against groups, 'the criminal intent to destroy or cripple permanently a human group'.[8] Given that the Nuremberg trials had been limited to crimes committed during wartime, a small number of states – India, Cuba, and Panama – advocated for a UN resolution addressing atrocities committed prior to the war.[9] The resolution subsequently adopted by the General Assembly defined genocide as 'a denial of the right of existence of entire human groups', recognising it as crime under international law.[10] Two years later, in 1948, states adopted the Convention for the Prevention and Punishment of the Crime of Genocide (the Genocide Convention) in Paris. Article II defines the crime of genocide: 'acts committed with intent to destroy, in whole or in part, a national, ethnical, racial or religious group'.[11]

Since then, criminal tribunals, such as the International Criminal Tribunal for Rwanda, or Yugoslavia, have been used to prosecute and punish the crime of genocide. Genocide remains the only crime, in both international humanitarian law and human rights law, that relates to the violation of the rights of a group. Other atrocity crimes – war crimes and crimes against humanity – relate to the targeting of individuals, although these crimes describe actions that target individuals based on group identity. Such mass atrocity crimes may be committed by state actors, governments, armies, and policing forces, or non-state actors such as militias. It is worth noting that different international documents refer to different sets of crimes. For example, the Rome Statute, providing the legal basis for the International Criminal Court (ICC), outlines the court's jurisdiction to prosecute the crimes of genocide, crimes against humanity, war crimes, and the crime of aggression. The Responsibility to Protect principle, on the other hand, refers to genocide, ethnic cleansing, war crimes, and crimes against humanity. Taken together, these documents suggest the emergence of a protection regime.

'Ethnic cleansing', not referred to in the Rome Statute, but included in the Responsibility to Protect paragraphs of the World Summit Outcome Document, is the wholesale deportation or murder of ethnic groups.[12] The term describes patterns of violence that are aimed at removing an ethnic group from a territory, through mass killing, removal, or transfer. While such acts have been carried out since antiquity, it was not until the horrors of the wars in the Balkans, discussed in more detail in Chapter 3, that the term entered the international discourse as a separate category of political violence.[13] The term has also been used to describe patterns of violence observed in conflicts in East Timor, and, more recently, violence against the Rohingya minority in Burma. The recognition of such types of violence as a separate category of crime – despite its omission from the Rome Statute – constituted a major milestone in the development of the protection regime. In this way, the particular patterns of political violence observed after the end of the Cold War influenced the international discourse and with it shaped the work of policymakers, scholars, and practitioners.

The documents above pertain to the deterrence and punishment of crimes committed against individuals and groups during conflict as well as during times of peace. The second body of law relevant in understanding the human protection regime are the sources of law pertaining to humanitarian practice and conduct during times of war. Therefore, while the Genocide Convention and the Universal Declaration of Human Rights laid the foundation for the human rights regime and international criminal justice mechanisms, the Geneva Protocols constituted the cornerstone documents of international humanitarianism. The Geneva Protocols of 1949 were devised to regulate the conduct of armed groups in order to mitigate harm to noncombatants and alleviate human suffering. The Geneva Conventions of 12 August 1949 comprise provisions pertaining to the treatment of wounded and sick members of the armed forces in time of war, in the field and at sea; the treatment of prisoners of war; and the protection of civilians in time of war. The Fourth Convention outlines provisions for the treatment of civilians and humanitarian relief. These provisions 'cover the whole of the populations of the countries in conflict without any adverse distinction based, in particular, on race, nationality, religion or political opinion, and are intended to alleviate the sufferings caused by war' (Article 13), the right of parties to a conflict and parties to the treaty to establish safety zones for the provision of relief (Article 14) and neutralised zones to shelter the wounded and the sick, including combatants, and civilians (Article 15).[14]

However, as was the case for the laws pertaining to human rights, international humanitarian law has been criticised for failing to compel responsible actors – states and humanitarian aid organisations – to provide humanitarian relief in a principled and even way. Throughout the Cold War years, relief responses were highly variable, given that ideology played a role in the way in which warring parties interpreted and applied these norms.[15] During the Cold War, conflicts in Korea and Vietnam showed the importance of the role of non-state parties to a conflict – a gap in international humanitarian law, which referred only to state parties. The Red Cross proposed to address putting forward a set of draft rules in 1957. Unsuccessful, the issue was re-visited in Vienna 1965, but only at the Istanbul conference of 1969 was a resolution finally passed that brought about the diplomatic impetus for the articulation of additional protocols also covering obligations of non-state parties. However, selective application remained a problem, and once again, the norm of state sovereignty served to obstruct the even application of protection norms. The Soviet Union exploited this gap in 1979, during its invasion of Afghanistan, claiming that, as a purely internal matter (the Soviet Union claimed it was interfering upon the invitation of the government), international humanitarian law pertaining to the treatment of prisoners of war, did not apply. To this day, selective application and the ambiguity of conflict, which makes it difficult to distinguish between situations in which humanitarian law applies from those in which human rights law applies, continue to hamper the efficacy of the protection regime.

The Cold War and Principles of Neutrality, Impartiality, and Humanity

In the years that followed, the Cold War defined international politics. The world was divided into the Western bloc, the Soviet bloc, and the so-called 'Third World' – unaligned states, or states whose allegiance may have been subject to change. Each of these blocs, headed by the US and close allies on the one hand, and Russia and its satellite states on the other, presided within their respective spheres of influence. Within their respective blocs, these states were hegemonic, in that they controlled not only relations among states within these spheres but also exerted significant influence over domestic affairs. The conflict between the West and the Soviet Union was one of ideas as much as one of control over territory and access to resources. While the Soviet Union was premised on socialism and a planned economy, the Western bloc was constituted by states that subscribed to liberalism, a free market economy, and parliamentary democracy.

The Soviet era proxy wars generated human rights violations and war crimes on a large scale, but the human rights discourse did not become a dominant feature of international politics until the end of the Cold War and the transition following the collapse of the Soviet Union. During the Cold War, the norm of state sovereignty continued to serve to shield the authority of either party within their spheres of influence. Millions perished under Communism as a consequence of forced labour and collectivisation programmes, or in direct targeting of political dissidents, yet intervention was neither feasible, given the military power of the Soviet Union, nor normatively permissible, given states' interpretation of Charter obligations. The US pursued a policy of 'containment' and pursued regime destabilisation through covert operations but did not seek to alter the normative status quo protecting the absolute sovereignty of states. Towards the end of the Cold War, however, human rights justifications gradually became more salient in that they were employed as a tool of voicing dissent. The diffusion of human rights norms allowed Soviet dissidents to critique Soviet policies, particularly in Eastern Europe.[16] The language of human rights helped activists hold leaders accountable, and, towards the end of the Cold War, Soviet leaders seeking change themselves began adopting human rights language, reflecting a significant change in the international discourse.

The same was not true, however, for early Cold War proxy wars foughtactors to abide by international out in the 'Third World'. Here, both sides projected their military power in an effort to expand their political influence and gain strategic advantage. While human rights violations characterised many of these conflicts, intervention was rarely justified on humanitarian grounds. Self-defence was the justification provided for pursing strategic interests in the 'Third World'. Nicholas Wheeler's influential study, *Saving Strangers*, describes three cases – the Bangladesh War of 1971, Vietnam's intervention in Cambodia, and Tanzania's intervention in Uganda.[17] The UN Security Council interpreted India's use of force against Pakistan as a breach of the prohibition on the use of force, rather than as a rescue of the Bengali people that had been subjected to repression by the Pakistani government (and India had justified the use of force on the grounds of self-defence, rather than in response to the atrocities that had been committed), and states sanctioned Vietnam for its intervention in Cambodia in the same year, against the Pol Pot regime, although an estimated two million people had died in massacres and as a result of forced labour. However, once again, the discourse gradually began shifting towards the end of the Cold War. In 1979, Tanzania intervened to overthrow Idi Amin's murderous regime in Uganda – although the intervention lacked the full endorsement of international actors, it received tacit approval, indicating that a change in the public perception of appropriate grounds for intervention was occurring. Nevertheless, intervention was still regarded as an exception from the rule, as an exceptional measure in exceptional circumstances, and the norm of non-intervention still served as a powerful deterrent to the invocation of the use of force on humanitarian grounds. These perceptions would gradually change after the end of the Cold War, during the 1990s and beyond.

Another feature of international responses to atrocities and humanitarian suffering during the Cold War was the absence of non-violent, habitual practices in responding to these situations. During the Cold War, the use of force was perceived as the only effective means of compelling states and other actors to abide by international norms. International actors still lacked an effective mechanism of coordinating international responses through diplomatic measures, sanctions, and criminal justice. A protection 'toolkit' was not yet available to states and other relevant actors. Consequently, although the use of military force on humanitarian grounds was contentious, it appeared the only means of responding, effectively, to large-scale, systematic human rights violations. This would gradually change after the end of the Cold War, as would the ad hoc nature of these responses, with the emergence of a range of institutions specialised in providing coordinated response to conflict and complex humanitarian emergencies.

Among organisations engaged in delivering humanitarian assistance, both features – the absence of a permissive normative framework, as well as of effective coordinating mechanisms – similarly characterised Cold War responses. Traditional principles of neutrality and impartiality underpinned the ethos of humanitarian relief work during this era. For practical reasons, as well as a matter of principle, humanitarian organisations such as the ICRC (the Red Cross) would not access an affected area and provide relief without the consent of the host government. Throughout the Cold War years, however, this too, began to change. Arguments in favour of a rights-based approach to delivering humanitarian relief – an approach that was prepared to depart from strict principles of neutrality – were first aired. In the context of the war, French doctors, volunteering for the Red Cross in Nigeria, providing medical relief in Biafra, led by Bernard Kouchner, appalled by the ICRC's approach, established Médecins Sans Frontières (MSF),[18] to deliver aid where others would not. Within the humanitarian relief sector and among policymakers and academics alike, these changes were accompanied by controversy – on the one hand, such an approach allowed humanitarian organisation to voice criticism, defending human rights, on the other hand, it ran the risk of alienating governments or groups in de facto control of disputed territories, preventing access to populations in need, and, potentially, preventing access to affect populations in future conflicts.

Despite the intricate relationship between protection and humanitarianism, the latter and armed intervention continued to be understood as distinct issues, and accordingly were addressed by different actors during the Cold War years. A shift in the international discourse to recognise the ways in which protective intervention and humanitarianism were related did not appear until after the end of the Cold War. However, thinking about intervention, and humanitarian justifications for intervention, nevertheless underwent profound changes during the Cold War.

One conflict, in particular, influenced international thinking about armed intervention during the Cold War. The conflict in Congo elicited the first large-scale, internationally coordinated UN peacekeeping response, the United Nations Operation in the Congo (ONUC), established by Security Council resolution 143 of 14 July 1960. The authorisation of the mission was remarkable in that states agreed on a peacekeeping mission, despite the fact that Cold War politics determined strategic interests and, in many other cases, inhibited a coordinated international response. Resolution 161 of 1960 authorised ONUC to employ 'all means necessary' in implementing its mandate, in other words authorising peacekeepers to use force, if necessary, to prevent military clashes and help maintain a ceasefire. For the most part, interventions during the Cold War, where they involved the use of force, were undertaken outside of the UN framework and did not involve humanitarian justifications, but even where states acted in unison through the UN, they did so not on the grounds of the need to protect civilians, but on the grounds of a need to end hostilities, and bring about regional stability. In fact, the goal in the case of the Congo had been to prevent the Cold War standoff destabilising the region following Belgium's withdrawal from the region after independence.[19] Consequently, a multilateral response was possible in this case not in spite of the fact that Cold War dynamics determined Security Council responses, but precisely because of Cold War dynamics. However, even though this explained the rationale for the peacekeeping mission, it did not attain this goal; further escalation of the crisis led to a deterioration of the situation on the ground. After three years of fighting, the government regained control, and the UN's withdrawal from Congo began to be planned in 1963, and was completed in 1964.

The academic literature of the time regarded the international response to the crisis in Congo as a 'test' of the concept of preventive diplomacy, as a demonstration of the flexibility of the Charter and the executive capacity of the UN Secretary-General, and, most importantly perhaps in terms of its legacy for UN peacekeeping, as a prototype of what would later be referred to as 'state-building'.[20] However, the norm of state sovereignty continued to define the way international actors considered international responses to conflict, atrocities, and humanitarianism – the violation of state sovereignty continued, for many decades, to be seen as an exceptional measure in exceptional circumstances, and where intervention was authorised, the explicit justification provided was to assist governments in regaining or maintaining control, or observing ceasefires between belligerent parties.

The Cold War and the Development of Peacekeeping

Although the maintenance of international peace and security is a core function of the UN, it was not until the end of the Cold War that UN peacekeeping as we know it today became an established international practice.[21] The Charter of the UN had initially foreseen a military committee consisting of senior military personnel from the P5, an inactive body that, according to the UN Charter, was to be used to provide assistance with regard to military operations authorised by the UN.[22] During the Cold War years, robust action by the Security Council was inhibited by the Cold War and divisions among the great powers on the Security Council. Today, international peacekeeping is associated with the deployment of blue helmets to active conflicts, but the earlier peacekeeping operations were different in nature from the operations that are typically deployed today. The UN's first peacekeeping operation was the United Nations Truce Supervision Organisation (UNTSO), consisting of military observers dispatched to Palestine in 1948. The mission was established in May 1948. UN Security Council resolution 50 decided that a ceasefire would be supervised by the UN with the support of military observers. Several months later, another observer mission was sent to Kashmir. In January 1949, the UN Security Council authorised the United Nations Military Observer Mission Group in India and Pakistan (UNMOGIP), again to supervise a ceasefire, this time between India and Pakistan. The peacekeeping mission operated in Jammu and Kashmir, a contested state bordering India and Pakistan. In 1950, the UN Security Council authorised the American-led operations to defend South Korea, a mission that was authorised only because of the absence of Russia and China on the Security Council during the voting procedure.

In 1956, in what constituted a major milestone in the development of peacekeeping practice, the UN deployed United Nations Emergency Force (UNEF), following the Suez Crisis of October 1956, upon the initiative of Dag Hammarskjöld, in Egypt. The mission established a new form of peacekeeping. UNEF helped establish three main principles that would subsequently form the heart of the UN's peacekeeping ethos for many decades: consent, neutrality, and minimal use of force.[23] The observer missions that had preceded the UN's first peacekeeping operation had been premised on the assumption that an impartial, third party can provide monitoring of a buffer zone between belligerent parties after hostilities have ended. This peacekeeping mission built on and expanded the neutrality principle, a central pillar of first-generation peacekeeping. UNEF was the UN's first real peacekeeping force.

As neutral third parties, peacekeepers would not be perceived by belligerent groups as parties to a conflict, allowing these forces to keep a peace that might still be fragile. The idea was that peacekeepers would, through their presence, prevent the recurrence of armed hostilities between both parties, allowing a long term, political resolution of the conflict and post-conflict stabilisation. However, the dispatch of peacekeepers remained a rare occurrence throughout the early Cold War years, and where the UN authorised peacekeeping missions, these were generally limited in their objectives. The features of the mandate given to these operations ensured that they were not seen as parties to the conflict, and the forces deployed did not take part in any combat operations. The peacekeeping mission in Congo 1960–1964 was the first UN peacekeeping mission that was authorised to use force to enforce peace, and the only mission of this kind until the UN mission in Somalia after the end of the Cold War. The mission was significant also because it was the first to include a significant civilian component. UN peacekeeping would take a much more prominent role after the collapse of the Soviet Union, and the implosion of the bipolar system of global politics that had defined International Relations for many decades until the 1990s. In the post-Cold War context, the UN emerged as the main authority on matters of peace and security – but it was still ill-equipped to take on this responsibility.

Towards the end of the Cold War, a call for a wider application of UN peacekeeping operations emerged.[24] These changes were the result of efforts by the states that had been traditional troop contributing states and Eastern European states and the Soviet Union. These states recognised a need for greater cooperation to jointly tackle newly emerging security challenges in the post-Cold War order. During the 1980s the Nordic states (Denmark, Finland, Iceland, Norway, and Sweden) were the strongest advocates for UN peacekeeping and contributed a third of the UN's peacekeeping troops. In 1983, the Nordic states called for the Security Council to intervene preventively in situations threatening international peace and security. They also recommended the establishment of fact-finding missions and military observers. In a letter in 1991, titled 'Shaping the Peace', the Nordic states proposed the integration of peacemaking and peacekeeping, as well as the deployment of peacekeeping missions before, during, and after conflict, as well as during humanitarian crises, rather than merely as a force to observe a ceasefire and peace agreements. This call was supported by the UN Eastern European Group. While this group had, during the Cold War, regarded peacekeeping as an illegal practice and refused to pay into the UN budget, the position of this group changed towards the end of the Cold War and with the appointment of Mikhail Gorbachev in 1985, Soviet states began supporting the deployment of UN peacekeeping operations and began paying their debts to the UN. These developments signalled a departure from traditional forms of UN peacekeeping; many of the ideas tabled during this time would be explored further and implemented after the end of the Cold War, during the 1990s and beyond.

The Cold War and Humanitarian Relief

Humanitarianism, during the Cold War years, was practiced, and perceived, as an activity distinct from peacekeeping. Both of these domains operated, largely, as distinct spheres, one directed by states, mandated through the UN, the other operated by the UN through the Department of Peacekeeping Operations. Humanitarian aid was provided by non-governmental organisations. Gradually, coordinated humanitarian relief became institutionalised. The Department of Humanitarian Affairs at the UN was established following the adoption of UN General Assembly resolution 46/182, which provided the United Nations with a stronger mandate for coordinating global humanitarian responses to complex humanitarian emergences. The emergence of coordinated response mechanisms also resulted in more scholarship on the processes and procedures of effective humanitarian relief coordination.[25] Peacekeeping forces became a means not only of monitoring peace agreements but also of facilitating the provision of humanitarian aid to affected populations through buffer zones and safe havens that provided protection to civilians and provided access for humanitarian relief. Similarly, during the Cold War years, the notion that humanitarian aid work should always abide by principles of neutrality and impartiality was challenged.

Arguments in favour of a departure from strict principles of neutrality and impartiality were first articulated in the context of the Biafra War. The Biafra War was a secessionist conflict between the Igbo people, who fought for secession, and the Nigerian government that sought to prevent partition. The region of Biafra declared independence in 1967, precipitating three years of fighting, ending in Biafra's surrender. The Nigerian government used a dual strategy of force and blockade in its attempt to regain control over territory lost to the insurgents. The military operation resulted in a famine, widely publicised around the world. The ICRC played a central role in co-ordinating relief efforts to affected populations. However, Nigerian forces denied humanitarian access to affected civilians, prompting a group of French humanitarians working for the ICRC, among them Bernard Kouchner, to urge for a more robust response to the crisis that also challenged notions of absolute sovereignty and the authority of governments that failed to grant access to affected civilian populations.

The crisis resulted in a rift among aid workers – a rift that would later become a central cleavage between traditionalists, and the 'new', rights-based humanitarianism of the post-Cold War era. Consequently, the crisis also had a lasting impact on the major policy debates among humanitarians, and the self-perception of practitioners in the field. The academic literature of the time reflected the debates playing out in the policy domain. Some argued that intervening based on need, without government consent, if necessary, while it provided urgently needed relief to civilians, also served to bolster insurgent groups, and in doing so might contribute to a prolongation of conflict, and with it, humanitarian suffering.[26] The case vividly demonstrated that humanitarians were faced with difficult choices in situations of complex humanitarian emergency – and created a schism among humanitarians. While some humanitarians sought to remain loyal to traditional humanitarian principles, others perceived this position to be untenable in the face of the humanitarian suffering that they witnessed. Among the latter group were several disaffected French doctors that had been sent by the ICRC, one of whom was Bernard Kouchner, who would later become French foreign minister.

Bernard Kouchner played a central role with regard to the establishment of Médecins Sans Frontières (MSF, or Doctors Without Borders). In the context of the crisis as it unfolded, Kouchner developed the idea of a *droit d'ingérence*, the 'right to interfere'.[27] The phrase can be translated into English as either a right, or a duty, to intervene or interfere. The concept of 'le droit d'ingérence' was discussed widely and continues to frame the public discourse on intervention and humanitarianism in the Francophone world, and within the humanitarian domain, the idea that sovereignty should not prevent access to civilian populations and preventive responses were discussed much earlier than in the Anglophone world, where these debates, particularly regarding the idea of 'humanitarian intervention', were not discussed in as much depth until several decades later, in the 1990s, in the context of the Kosovo war. For these reasons, Kouchner's campaign, and the emergence of MSF as an organisation willing to depart from traditional principles of neutrality and impartiality, are regarded as a significant antecedent to the development of the idea of 'sovereignty as responsibility', and its articulation as policy in a report entitled the 'Responsibility to Protect',[28] in the early 2000s. Kouchner stated 'I invented MSF to go where the others were not able to go',[29] and *sans frontiérisme* (without borders) became a guiding principle of the organisation. The formation of MSF thus signalled the beginning of the era of new ways of thinking about humanitarianism in the context of conflict and complex emergencies. The new humanitarianism suggested that the delivery of humanitarian aid ought to be attuned to politics, rather than operate under the assumption that humanitarian aid could ever be apolitical. Critical scholars noted that control over a territory – hence access to affected populations – defined relief workers' everyday lived experience. Without permission to access affected areas, humanitarians were helpless. Consequently, negotiating access necessitated, to a certain degree, taking sides. This more nuanced understanding of the relationship between humanitarianism and conflict issued in the era of the 'new humanitarianism'.[30] While some humanitarians continue to maintain strict principles of neutrality and impartiality, others are more vocal and more prepared to take a political stance.

The 1990s were a time of considerable political upheaval in a range of policy domains. The collapse of the Soviet Union brought with it a thawing of relations among former great powers that meant that states saw the possibility for cooperation in a range of issues areas that had not existed previously. Particularly Security Council politics were seen to have undergone a major structural shift, with the veto power of Russia, China, the US, Britain, and France no longer perceived necessarily as an inhibitor of decisive collective responses. This, in combination with the conflicts that emerged as a result of the power vacuum that resulted from the withdrawal of great power patronage of states in both spheres of influence, provided a structural context amenable to coordinated multilateral, global responses to intra-state conflict. Humanitarianism changed profoundly during this decade, also as a result of experiences in conflicts including crises in Kurdish areas in Iraq in 1991, the Rwandan genocide, and Kosovo in 1998, the growing integration of practices of peacekeeping and humanitarian relief, and the wider broadcasting of humanitarian crises through improved communications technology.[31]

In the humanitarian domain, the discourse associated with the new humanitarianism became more influential. While 'humanity' remained the principal tenet of all humanitarians, many organisations recognised that in some instances, adherence to these principles risked undermining other protection norms. The new humanitarians promoted rights-based approaches to humanitarian relief. These approaches suggested reframing humanitarianism, to replace a narrow understanding of humanitarianism as simply addressing the symptoms – a band-aid approach – to an approach to humanitarianism that entailed the promotion of justice, and human dignity. Gradually, the new humanitarianism began to influence the policy of a range of organisations but neutrality remains a central tenet for some relief organisations, including the ICRC.[32] To mediate between these two approaches, Mary Anderson developed the idea of a 'marketplace' of aid providers. This approach suggested that organisations, collectively, fulfil the dual role of voicing criticism and taking a political stance, while other organisations decline to comment and retain access to vulnerable populations, providing much-needed relief.[33] Recent scholarship continues to grapple with these issues.[34] However, the schism between the new humanitarians on the one hand, and the traditionalists on the other, continues to persist. Recent scholarship has also voiced concern about the 'new humanitarianism', suggesting that the more robust policies associated with it, including closely coordinated responses with peace enforcement measures, constitute a militarisation of humanitarianism.[35]

Summary

- The United Nations was established at the end of the Second World War. The UN Charter and the Genocide Convention provide the legal groundwork for human rights protection and mass atrocity prevention.
- The Geneva Conventions and the Additional Protocols are the basic documents of international humanitarian law. International humanitarian law regulates conduct during armed conflict. It serves to protect non-combatants, such as civilians and former soldiers.
- The Charter of the UN refers to universal human rights. At the same time, it also unequivocally enshrines states sovereignty as a constitutive principle of international society.
- Peacekeeping as a multilateral practice in response to conflict emerged during the Cold War years. Initially, however, the objectives of peacekeeping missions were limited and narrowly circumscribed.
- Neutrality, impartiality, and humanity are three traditional core tenets associated with humanitarianism. However, humanitarians have questioned the unconditional application of the principle of neutrality, as illustrated in the Biafra case study.

Questions for Reflection

- *What were the first human rights treaties, and what did they stipulate?*
- *What are the Geneva Conventions, and what is their role?*
- *Is there a contradiction in the UN Charter with regard to the norm of state sovereignty and the protection of human rights?*
- *What is the 'new peacekeeping' and what explains its emergence?*
- *How relevant, in your view, has neutrality been as a principle guiding the actions of humanitarian agencies?*

Further reading

- Donnelly, Jack (2013): *Human Rights in Theory and Practice*, 3rd ed. (Ithaca and London: Cornell University Press).
- Fox, Renée (2014): *Doctors without Borders* (Baltimore: Johns Hopkins University Press).
- Howard, Lise Morje (2008): *UN Peacekeeping in Civil Wars* (Cambridge: Cambridge University Press).
- Moorhead, Caroline (1999): *Dunant's Dream: War, Switzerland and the History of the Red Cross* (London: Harper Collins).
- Rieff, David (2002): *A Bed for the Night: Humanitarianism in Crisis* (London: Random House).

Notes

1 Thomas G. Weiss and Sam Daws, eds., *The Oxford Handbook on the United Nations* (Oxford: Oxford University Press, 2018), https://doi.org/10.1093/oxfordhb/9780198803164.001.0001.

2 Mark Mazower, *No Enchanted Palace: The End of Empire and the Ideological Origins of the United Nations*, Reprint edition (Princeton Oxford: Princeton University Press, 2013).

3 Robert C. Hilderbrand, *Dumbarton Oaks: The Origins of the United Nations and the Search for Postwar Security* (Chapel Hill: University of North Carolina Press, 1990).

4 Warren Kimball, 'Reviews of Books – Dumbarton Oaks: The Origins of the United Nations and the Search for Postwar Security by Robert C. Hilderbrand', *The American Historical Review* 96, no. 5 (1991): 1511.

5 Bruce Broomhall, 'Scope', in *International Justice and the International Criminal Court: Between Sovereignty and the Rule of Law* (Oxford: Oxford University Press, 2004).

6 Patricia M. Wald, 'Genocide and Crimes against Humanity', *Washington University Global Studies Law Review* 6, no. 3 (2007).

7 Raphael Lemkin, William A. Schabas, and Samantha Power, *Axis Rule in Occupied Europe: Laws of Occupation, Analysis of Government, Proposals for Redress*, 2nd ed. (Clark, NJ: The Lawbook Exchange, Ltd., 2008).

8 Raphael Lemkin, 'Genocide as a Crime under International Law', *American Journal of International Law* 41, no. 1 (n.d.): 147.

9 William A. Schabas, 'Origins of the Genocide Convention: From Nuremberg to Paris', *Case Western Reserve Journal of International Law* 40 (2009, 2007): 35.

10 General Assembly resolution 96(1), adopted on 11 December 1946.

11 United Nations General Assembly, 'Convention on the Prevention and Punishment of the Crime of Genocide', 1948.

12 H. Zeynep Bulutgil, 'Social Cleavages, Wartime Experience, and Ethnic Cleansing in Europe – H Zeynep Bulutgil, 2015', *Journal of Peace Research* 52, no. 5, (2015): 577–90

13 Andrew Bell-Fialkoff, 'A Brief History of Ethnic Cleansing', *Foreign Affairs* 72, no. 3 (1993): 110–21, https://doi.org/10.2307/20045626.

14 International Committee of the Red Cross, 'Geneva Convention Relative to the Protection of Civilian Persons in Time of War (Fourth Geneva Convention)', 12 August 1949.

15 Stephanie Carvin, 'Caught in the Cold: International Humanitarian Law and Prisoners of War during the Cold War', *Journal of Conflict and Security Law* 11, no. 1 (2006): 67–92.

16 Daniel C. Thomas, 'Human Rights Ideas, the Demise of Communism, and the End of the Cold War', *Journal of Cold War Studies* 7, no. 2 (1 April 2005): 110–41, https://doi.org/10.1162/1520397053630600.

17 Nicholas Wheeler, *Saving Strangers: Humanitarian Intervention in International Society* (Oxford: Oxford University Press, 2003).
18 Tim Allen and David Styan, 'A Right to Interfere? Bernard Kouchner and the New Humanitarianism', *Journal of International Development* 12, no. 6 (2000): 825–42.
19 Jane Boulden, 'United Nations Operation in the Congo (ONUC)', *The Oxford Handbook of United Nations Peacekeeping Operations*, 9 July 2015, https://doi.org/10.1093/oxfordhb/9780199686049.013.21.
20 Harold Karan Jacobson, 'ONUC's Civilian Operations: State-Preserving and State-Building', *World Politics* 17, no. 1 (1964): 75–107, https://doi.org/10.2307/2009388.
21 For a history of UN peacekeeping see Marrack Goulding, 'The Evolution of United Nations Peacekeeping', *International Affairs* 69, no. 3 (1993): 451–64; James Dobbins, 'A History of UN Peacekeeping', in *Charter of the United Nations*, ed. Ian Shapiro and Joseph Lampert (New Haven: Yale University Press, 2014), 195–209.
22 Alexandra Novosseloff, *The UN Military Staff Committee: Recreating a Missing Capacity* (Abingdon, Oxon: Routledge, 2018).
23 Paul F. Diehl, 'First United Nations Emergency Force (UNEF I)', in *The Oxford Handbook of United Nations Peacekeeping Operations* (Oxford, Oxford University Press, 2015).
24 Chen Kertcher, 'From Cold War to a System of Peacekeeping Operations: The Discussions on Peacekeeping Operations in the UN During the 1980s up to 1992', *Journal of Contemporary History* 47, no. 3 (2012): 611–37.
25 Burcu Balcik et al., 'Coordination in Humanitarian Relief Chains: Practices, Challenges and Opportunities', *International Journal of Production Economics* 126, no. 1 (1 July 2010): 22–34, https://doi.org/10.1016/j.ijpe.2009.09.008.
26 M.-A. Pérouse de Montclos, 'Humanitarian Aid and the Biafra War: Lessons Not Learned', *Africa Development* 34, no. 1 (1 January 2009), https://doi.org/10.4314/ad.v34i1.57357.
27 Noele Crossley, *Evaluating the Responsibility to Protect: Mass Atrocity Prevention as a Consolidating Norm in International Society*, 1st ed. (Milton Park, Abingdon, Oxon; New York, NY: Routledge, 2016).
28 ICISS, 'The Responsibility to Protect: Report of the International Commission on Intervention and State Sovereignty', 2001.
29 T. Allen and D. Styan, 'A right to interfere? Bernard Kouchner and the new humanitarianism', *Journal of International Development*, 12, no. 6 (2000): 825–42.
30 Fiona Fox, 'New Humanitarianism: Does It Provide a Moral Banner for the 21st Century?', *Disasters* 25, no. 4 (2001): 275–89, https://doi.org/10.1111/1467-7717.00178.
31 Adam Roberts, 'The Role of Humanitarian Issues in International Politics in the 1990s', *International Review of the Red Cross* 81, no. 833 (March 1999): 19–43, https://doi.org/10.1017/S1560775500092324.
32 Barbara Ann Rieffer-Flanagan, 'Is Neutral Humanitarianism Dead – Red Cross Neutrality: Walking the Tightrope of Neutral Humanitarianism', *Human Rights Quarterly* 31 (2009): 888.
33 Mary B. Anderson, 'To Work, or Not to Work, in "Tainted" Circumstances: Difficult Choices for Humanitarians', *Social Research* 74, no. 1 (2007): 201–22.
34 Monica Adami, 'Disorder within the Humanitarian Sector: The Old versus New Humanitarianism Debate', *Disasters* 45, no. 2 (2019), https://doi.org/10.1111/disa.12426.
35 David Chandler, 'The Road to Military Humanitarianism: How the Human Rights NGOs Shaped a New Humanitarian Agenda', *Human Rights Quarterly* 23 (2001): 678.

3 Rethinking Protection after the Cold War

After the end of the Cold War, the traditional principles of protection practice that had informed international responses to humanitarian crises were no longer taken for granted. International actors questioned, in particular, the value of neutrality as an unconditional principle of humanitarian action. Several crises prompted international actors to rethink a principle that had shaped humanitarian policy for decades. This chapter describes these developments. It is important to note that these debates have not been settled – the schism between the principled defenders of neutrality and those in favour of human rights-based approaches that argue that any response should be guided, above all, by an immediate concern for the rights and dignity of affected individuals and groups continues to persist and is reflected in many of the debates that characteristically appear in the context of international responses to humanitarian crisis. In the post-Cold War era, two cases in particular contributed significantly to the development of human protection ideas: the case of Rwanda in 1994, where international actors failed to intervene decisively to prevent genocide, and the case of Kosovo in 1999, where military intervention was justified on humanitarian grounds but lacked Security Council authorisation. Both of these cases significantly shaped ideas, principles, and protection practice.

An Agenda for Peace and the New Peacekeeping

'An Agenda for Peace: Preventive diplomacy, peacemaking and peace-keeping' was a 1992 report of the UN Secretary-General, Boutros Boutros-Ghali. The report aimed to improve the UN's capacity for preventive diplomacy and peacekeeping. The report emerged out of the immediate post-Cold War context and must be seen in this light. The report took a comprehensive view of conflict management, engaging with issues of direct and structural prevention (in other words, both preventing an escalation of crises that are already ongoing, as well as addressing long-term, structural issues that may cause conflict, including inequality), as well as responses in ongoing conflicts (the use of force to halt armed conflict – *peacekeeping* – as well as the use of force to monitor ceasefires and peace agreements – *peacebuilding*). The report used the language of responsibility, suggesting that the 'primary responsibility for the maintenance of international peace and security' lies with the Security Council, and that 'this responsibility must be shared by the General Assembly and by all the functional elements of the world Organization' and also requires the 'concerted attention and effort of individual States, of regional and non-governmental organizations' (para 16), although the 'foundation-stone of this work is and must remain the State' (para 17).[1]

DOI: 10.4324/9781003006671-4

The report was significant for a number of reasons. First, owing to the context out of which it emerged. The end of the Cold War, and with it the end of a bipolar order, allowed international actors to conceive of truly multilateral responses to conflict management. These actors now found themselves in an environment that was no longer unfavourable to collective action, but that was conducive to it. At the same time, the power vacuum left by the end of the Cold War, felt in many parts of the world, precipitated the need for the provision of protection and security where power transitions and the collapse of former mechanisms of governance created insecurity.

Second, the report was significant because it defined a number of key terms that have become points of reference in the protection discourse and the practice of protection: *preventive diplomacy*, 'action to prevent disputes from arising between parties, to prevent existing disputes from escalating into conflicts and to limit the spread of the latter when they occur', *peacemaking*, 'action to bring hostile parties to agreement, essentially through such peaceful means as those foreseen in Chapter VI of the Charter of the United Nations', and peacekeeping, 'the deployment of a United Nations presence in the field'.[2] The report also introduced the term 'peace enforcement'. 'Peace enforcement' capabilities, the report envisioned, were to be developed by the UN in coordination with member states, in order to 'respond to outright aggression, imminent or actual'.[3] The wording was thus both visionary and prescriptive.

The report was significant also because it thematised protection and responsibility, and was progressive in that sense, while remaining loyal to the principle of state sovereignty. 'The foundation-stone of this work is and must remain the State', the report suggested, while also suggesting – a bold statement at the time – that the time of 'absolute and exclusive sovereignty … has passed; its theory was never matched by reality'.[4] In this sense, the report foretold the development of a new language of responsibility, and set the tone for a path of advocacy leading to the articulation of the Responsibility to Protect principle about a decade later.

Finally, the report also discussed the relationship between conflict management and the provision of humanitarian aid, and in doing so, projected a particular vision of appropriate practice, based firmly on traditional principles of humanity, impartiality, and neutrality. In discussing both practices, the report also reflected a beginning trend towards deeper integration of protection practice and better coordination among international protection actors. Suggesting that peacekeeping increasingly 'requires that civilian political officers, human rights monitors, electoral officials, refugee and humanitarian aid specialists and police play as central a role as the military',[5] the report was reflective of a beginning trends towards a more comprehensive, integrated approach to peacekeeping practice.

Consequently, the report reflected a changed international environment, while also moving the discourse forward in a way that provided more scope for international actors to respond to protection crises. Importantly, it showed a greater preparedness by international actors to move away from a traditional interpretation of state sovereignty. In the decade to come, developing peacekeeping practice would be put to some important tests, but would meet with failures throughout the course of the 1990s. One of these was the UN's response to the genocide in Rwanda in 1994.

The United Nations and the Rwandan Genocide

The Rwandan genocide was the worst episode of mass killing since the Second World War, a genocide in which an estimated 800,000 people perished during no more than 100 days, in the spring and summer of 1994. Rwanda had been under colonial rule by Germany, Britain, and Belgium until Belgian control ended in 1962. Colonial rule had produced a society in which ethnicity was politicised, and ethnicity remained politicised after independence.[6] Ethnic delineations defined, to a large extent, who was targeted by the genocidaires. The genocide began following the shooting down of a plane carrying the Rwandan president, Juvenal Habyarimana, on 6 April 1994. Hutu militia, the Interahamwe, carried out most of the killings, systematically targeting Tutsi and moderate Hutu.[7] UN forces, led by Roméo Dallaire, were present on the ground but were not, however, equipped with a mandate to intervene to protect civilians – resolution 893 of January 1994, which established UNAMIR (United Nations Assistance Mission for Rwanda), to promote the implementation of the Arusha Peace Agreement, provided a mandate only to contribute to the security of the state's capital, Kigali, and to monitor compliance with the ceasefire and the Arusha Peace Agreement, the resettlement of displaced persons, and assistance with the coordination of humanitarian relief efforts.[8] As a consequence, the UN mission was ill-equipped to respond to the impending catastrophe.

On 21 April 1994, two weeks after the onset of the genocide, the UN took a decision that, in retrospect, was one of the gravest mistakes in its history. A report by the Secretary-General, published a day earlier, outlined three options for the UN's response to the crisis: first a massive reinforcement of UNAMIR, and change in the mandate, allowing it to coerce both parties to observe a ceasefire, restore law and order, and end the killing of civilians; second, a significant reduction in the size of the mission, whereby the force commander and a small number of peacekeepers would act as intermediaries between the parties, in an effort to bring about a ceasefire, and for the co-ordination of humanitarian relief. The third alternative was a complete withdrawal of UNAMIR.[9] However, following the killing of ten Belgian peacekeepers, the Security Council, concerned for the security of UN personnel and failing to anticipate the magnitude of the impending crisis, opted for the second alternative, a reduction in force size – effectively amounting to a withdrawal of UNAMIR as a military force.[10] Kofi Annan, head of UN peacekeeping at the time, suggested in his memoirs that 'We believed it to be the best – indeed, the only – option that we could take'.[11]

Consequently, despite the UN's presence on the ground, there was no meaningful international protection intervention during the crisis. It was not until mid-May that the Security Council increased its force level up to 5,500 troops, imposed an arms embargo, and authorised UNAMIR to 'take action in self-defence against persons or groups who threaten protected sites and populations'.[12] On 22 June 1994, the Security Council authorised, under Chapter VII of the UN Charter, to use 'all necessary measures' to achieve humanitarian objectives through a temporary humanitarian mission, under national command and control. The aim of the mission was to contribute, 'in an impartial way, to the security and protection of displaced persons, refugees and civilians at risk in Rwanda'.[13]

At the end of June 1994 – by which time the killing was already subsiding, with few Tutsi still alive in Rwanda – the UN authorised a temporary peacekeeping operation that was to be replaced with a more expansive UN mission.[14] The resolution finally authorised states to use 'all necessary means' under Chapter VII of the UN Charter to protect displaced people, refugees, and civilians, secure humanitarian areas, and provide security to humanitarian relief workers. France, which had proposed the mission, sent forces through Opération Turquoise. However, critical scholars questioned France's involvement in Rwandan politics before, during, and after the genocide.[15] France had provided supplies to the Rwandan national army and Hutu militia, in line with Security Council resolution 929, but inconsistent with the objectives of an arms embargo imposed by the Security Council.

Collective soul-searching and a deep sense of regret and shame defined the international mood in the years following the genocide, and the trauma lingers to this day, a daunting reminder of the consequences of inaction. Scholars searched for explanations for collective apathy, identifying the experience of intervention failure in Somalia, as well as incomplete information about the true scale of the horror unfolding in Rwanda, as possible explanations. Others identified bureaucratic obstacles, and geopolitical interests, as explanations for inaction.

Among international actors involved in the crisis, throughout the 1990s and into the 2000s, the experience of Rwanda and efforts to promote better early warning and preventive action mechanisms came to define careers and legacies. Kofi Annan, in his memoirs, concluded that 'in 1994, there was simply no culture or precedent in the international system of UN intervention in an internal conflict to use military force decisively to protect civilians'.[16] Annan would spend the rest of his diplomatic career and his tenure as UN Security-General promoting a new understanding of state sovereignty, and the idea that states had a responsibility to intervene, using robust measures where necessary, to prevent genocide and mass atrocities. Similarly, Roméo Dallaire, force commander of UNAMIR, recounted his experiences in his memoirs, a scathing critique of collective inaction.[17] Together with the Kosovo crisis, discussed in further detail further on, the crisis in Rwanda constituted the single most significant case in accounting for the collective desire to revisit principal questions pertaining to the law, ethics, and practices of protective intervention, the prerequisites of legitimate sovereignty over a given territory, and the meaning of international peace and security itself.

Francis Deng and 'Sovereignty as Responsibility'

The changes throughout the Cold War heralded the beginning of a protection regime that also provided protection and assistance to refugees and internally displaced persons. Both the regulative and institutional backbone of refugee protection emerged throughout the Cold War years. Institutionally, the regime came into being with the establishment of offices dedicated to refugee protection at the League of Nations and, later, following the end of the Second World War, the International Refugee Organization (IRO), the precursor organisation to the United Nations High Commissioner for Refugees (UNHCR).[18] Importantly, efforts to protect people fleeing violence, or forced to leave places of habitual residence, were framed as refugee protection throughout the Cold War years, because the protection of civilians within state boundaries was perceived as a responsibility of the sovereign state, which external actors had no right to interfere with. This interpretation of international law changed after the end of the Cold War.

Leading efforts to reconceptualise the protection of displaced people was Francis Deng.[19] Francis Deng suggested that state sovereignty ought to be interpreted as entailing a duty for the protection of all people within a jurisdiction from harm, and a duty of assistance. Deng prepared the Guiding Principles on Internal Displacement of 1998 in his capacity as Special Representative of the UN Secretary-General for Internally Displaced Persons. The Guiding Principles did not create new legal obligations but instead restated and compiled human rights and humanitarian law as it pertains to displaced people. The Guiding Principles were drawn up based on two studies prepared by Francis Deng for the Commission on Human Rights, which illustrated that internally displaced people enjoyed fewer protections than did refugees who crossed state borders. The document comprised 30 guiding principles: general principles, principles pertaining to protection from displacement, principles on protection during displacement, principles relating to humanitarian assistance, and principles relating to return, resettlement, and reintegration. They stated that 'national authorities have the primary duty and responsibility to provide protection and humanitarian assistance to internally displaced persons' (3.1) and that an offer of assistance from 'international humanitarian organizations and other appropriate actors ... shall not be regarded as an unfriendly act or an interference in a State's internal affairs and shall be considered in good faith' (25.2). The push for the recognition of rights of displaced persons (IDPs) was particularly salient in a context where more crises were intra-state – civil wars – than traditional inter-state wars.

These efforts to expand the protection afforded to internally displaced persons were of particular salience in the emergence of the protection regime because it suggested that the role of international actors, and their perceived legitimacy in pursuing these protection objectives, was expanding, despite member states' continued commitment to the norm of state sovereignty. However, critical scholars also noted that framing IDP protection as a legitimate task of bodies with technical expertise allowed states, non-governmental organisations, and bureaucracies to take on roles and responsibilities that perhaps belonged to local actors,[20] and a rich body of critical literature on liberal interventionism – which we will revisit in later chapters, emerged in response to these and other developments.

NATO's Intervention in Kosovo

The intervention of the North Atlantic Treaty Organisation (NATO) in Kosovo in 1999 was significant because, despite the end of the Cold War, the inability of the Security Council to authorise robust measures in response to the persecution and threat of forced displacement of ethnic Albanians provided a vivid illustration of the structural issues that afflicted the decision-making procedure of the UN Security Council. This in turn indicated that politics and strategic interests would continue to trump humanitarian and human rights considerations in situations where parochial – geo-strategic or economic – interests mattered greatly to the permanent members of the Security Council.

Throughout the early 1990s Kosovo had witnessed local unrest, but it was not until March 1998 that the conflict escalated, with direct confrontations between state security forces and Kosovo Liberation Army (KLA) militia. Analysts feared imminent humanitarian disaster, a view shared among Security Council members, who disagreed, however, on the most appropriate means for addressing the crisis.[21] In May and June of 1999, the Security Council passed a series of resolutions, demanding Yugoslavia's co-operation with an OSCE verification mission and access for humanitarian relief operations. In June, the council authorised the enforcement of the withdrawal of Yugoslav forces from Kosovo and the establishment of United Nations Mission in Kosovo (UNMIK).[22] However, given Russia's objections, the UN did not authorise military peace enforcement measures. In the face of impending humanitarian crisis, NATO decided to act without the explicit authorisation of the Council, launching an air campaign. Russia strongly criticised the intervention, despite the humanitarian justification provided by the Western allies.

It is difficult to assess the true impact of the intervention in terms of harm averted, as well as the human and political costs.[23] The intervention protected innocent civilians, but it also imposed its own human costs – the air strikes alone killed an estimated 500 civilians. Furthermore, the intervention, analysts suggested, may have hardened the Serbian position, resulting in increased persecution of Kosovar Albanians. Some also suggested that the KLA may have increased its attacks on Serb forces in anticipation of protective third-party intervention, resulting in further state repression and a greater number of civilian deaths. Finally, the tally also included political costs – the fallout over Kosovo continues to persist and may have weakened trust in the ability of international actors to resolve conflict through the UN and in accordance with international law. Moreover, the inability to agree on a common course of action also hampered the post-conflict peacebuilding efforts. Kosovo declared independence from Serbia in 2008, and has been recognised by the United States and several EU member states, but a majority of UN member states, including Serbia and Russia, have not recognised Kosovo as a sovereign state, and Kosovo's ambiguous status will likely remain unresolved for the foreseeable future.

The crisis again resulted in widespread discussion, in the years that followed, of criteria for legitimate and legal protective intervention. A report by the Independent International Commission on Kosovo concluded that the intervention had been illegal according to international law, but nevertheless legitimate.[24] Throughout the course of the crisis, the UK developed a doctrine of humanitarian intervention, first aired in a speech by Tony Blair before the Chicago Economic Club, in which he suggested that humanitarian intervention was justified when certain criteria were met, and when it was also in the national interest.[25] The debate in the aftermath of Kosovo, therefore, provided the impetus for a resurgence in reflection, among scholars and policymakers, of the conditions under which – in a changed international environment – intervention on humanitarian grounds was justifiable and appropriate, given existing legal provisions. In doing so, it promoted renewed debate on legitimacy criteria for the use of force. However, the language of 'humanitarian intervention' was viewed critically, as too narrowly concerned with military measures. The articulation of the Responsibility to Protect principle shortly after the crisis sought to address these problems.

The Articulation of the 'Responsibility to Protect'

Kofi Annan and Two Concepts of Sovereignty

In September 1999, UN Secretary-General Kofi Annan published an article in the *Economist*, entitled 'Two Concepts of Sovereignty'.[26] In it, Annan suggested that state sovereignty was being redefined, and argued for a transformation of international practice to take into account 'new actors, new responsibilities, and new possibilities for peace and progress'. The article was significant because it indicated that the Secretary-General actively supported efforts to reconceptualise 'sovereignty as responsibility', in agreement with the basic assumptions inherent in the formula that Francis Deng had drawn up in the context of the protection of internally displaced people. In effect, Kofi Annan was acting not simply as impartial arbiter and mediator of states' interests, in his capacity as Secretary-General, but also as a norm entrepreneur seeking to promote a greater sense of responsibility for preventing harm to individuals, and actively intervening to stop behaviour causing harm to civilian populations in crisis situations. Annan's efforts must be seen in the light of his personal experience as well as the immediate context of political debates playing out at the time.

The immediate impetus for the article, however, were crises in Kosovo and East Timor, both referred to in the article. The crisis in East Timor emerged shortly after the crisis in Kosovo, another reminder of the need for swift humanitarian responses, and the difficulty of doing so effectively without government consent. These crises, and the debates they gave rise to, showed that there was a tenuous consensus that the international system of response to humanitarian crises and systematic, large-scale human rights violations needed reform – although there remained much disagreement about the trajectory of this reform, the rules and institutions that ought to underpin a new regulative framework, and the agents that were key to driving the change.

Undoubtedly, however, change had been set in motion: the preceding years had resulted in a broad consensus that institutionalised apathy was no longer condonable. Disagreement about the shape and form the changes were meant to take were apparent also within the inner circle of the first generation of advocates for the responsibility protect, as evidenced by disagreement over the permissibility of unilateral humanitarian intervention. While Michael Ignatieff, one of the commissioners for the report, for example, argued at the time that the Responsibility to Protect justified unilateral intervention in Iraq, Gareth Evans argued that the use of protection language in the context of the Iraq War threatened to undermine support for the principle.[27]

In the years following the publication of the article, Annan would continue to advocate for the principle – support for the principle was to become one of the central pillars of his legacy as UN Secretary-General.[28] For example, the Secretary-General's report on the Prevention of Armed Conflict, of June 2001, used the language of responsibility, highlighting both a need for prevention – a theme engaged with in depth in the report of the International Commission on Intervention and State Sovereignty, as will be discussed in the next section, as well as referring to a 'responsibility to ensure that vulnerable people are protected' and 'to ensure that genocides such as that perpetrated in Rwanda are prevented from ever happening again'.[29]

Several years later, Annan created the High-Level Panel on Threats Challenges, and Change. Its report of 2004, *A More Secure World: Our Shared Responsibility*, again included criteria for intervention.[30] The Secretary-General's report of 2005, *In Larger Freedom*, endorsed the report of the High-Level Panel, and the criteria contained in the report. All this goes to show that the Secretary-General had been in favour of less ambiguity, and more clarity, on the principles that ought to guide international decision-making in response to emerging humanitarian crises of utmost concern. Annan's effort in this regard did not come to fruition, at least not in the short term – the criteria were not included in the 2005 report, discussed later – but his advocacy for the principles underpinning the emerging protection regime was to be of lasting significance.

The ICISS Report: The Responsibility to Protect

With support from the Canadian government, the International Commission on Intervention and State Sovereignty (ICISS) conducted a series of roundtables and consultations internationally and, in December 2001, published a report entitled 'The Responsibility to Protect'.[31] The report also drew on scholarly and policy research organised to support the work of the Commission, led by Thomas G. Weiss and Stanlake J.T.M. Samkange. The Commission set itself the task of reframing the terms of the debate in order to find a way of overcoming the limitations to protective intervention that a strict interpretation of state sovereignty as non-interference in the domestic affairs of states posed. The report of the Brundtland Commission, published in 1987, served as an example. The Brundtland Commission sought to reconcile the economic imperative of economic growth, poverty alleviation, and development (and the effects on the environment this necessarily entailed) with the aims and objectives of environmental protection. In adopting 'sovereignty as responsibility' as a formula for overcoming the tensions between the imperative of human rights protection on the one hand, and non-interference in the domestic affairs of sovereign states on the other, the Commission sought to chart a path forward that would allow the UN and other international actors to act in line with both imperatives.

The final report was the product of intense deliberations at a series of roundtables and consultations in major cities around the world. Gareth Evans and Mohamed Sahnoun co-chaired the commission. The other commissioners were Gisele Côte-Harper, Michael Ignatieff, Klaus Neumann, Eduardo Stein Barillas, Ramesh Thakur, Fidel Ramos, Vladimir Lukin, Cyril Ramaphosa, Cornelio Sommaruga, and Lee Hamilton. The commission set an agenda for each of the roundtables, steering the discussion towards four core issues: the language associated with intervention and protection; criteria for the use of force; the source of legitimate authority and due process; and the role of prevention. The final report outlined three dimensions of the Responsibility to Protect: the responsibility to prevent; the responsibility to react; and the responsibility to rebuild.[32] The responsibility to prevent outlined early warning and analysis, root cause prevention, and direct prevention efforts, the responsibility to react outlined measures short of military action, including political and economic sanctions, such as arms embargoes. The report also included six criteria for military intervention: right authority, just cause, right intention, last resort, proportional means, and reasonable prospects.

Soon after the publication of the report, the Iraq War interfered with advocacy efforts for the Responsibility to Protect. Advocates for the principle feared the use of the language of protection in the context of the Iraq War might undermine support for the principle. Nevertheless, supportive states and individuals continued to advocate for the principle throughout the 2000s. Some states objected to the principle fearing it might weaken the norm of state sovereignty. Critics suggested the principle could be utilised to justify intervention by powerful states with interests that were not exclusively humanitarian. The central idea of 'sovereignty as responsibility' was progressive, and given the nature of the changes it entailed, still controversial. The notion that under some circumstances the principle of state sovereignty should yield to norms associated with the human rights regime, including international humanitarian law, was new and a clear departure from traditional thinking. States with a colonial history were sceptical, particularly in view of the fact that ICISS' proposal had been spear-headed by actors associated with the Global North and that the final report gave a disproportionate amount of attention to coercive responses to crises, including military intervention. Advocacy for the Responsibility to Protect principle, in the decade that followed, would continue to encounter concern and apprehension about the possible misuse of the principle.

The World Summit and the Responsibility to Protect

The endorsement of the Responsibility to Protect principle at the World Summit of 2005 was a significant milestone in the development of the principle and the broader development of global norms of human protection. In the run-up to the summit, several states were at the forefront of advocacy for the principle, lobbying other states to endorse the principle through mention in the outcome document.[33] The most supportive states were Argentina, Australia, Canada, Colombia, Croatia, Germany, Ireland, New Zealand, Norway, Peru, Rwanda, South Korea, Sweden, and Tanzania. The permanent five members of the Security Council were sceptical about the principle, although the reasons for their scepticism varied. While the US was reluctant to commit to a principle that might create an obligation to intervene where this was not in its national interest, China and Russia were concerned the principle might weaken the norm of state sovereignty, and the UK and France expressed reservations on the grounds that the inclusion of criteria did not necessarily help to create the necessary political will for robust collective responses. As in other issue areas, both procedural matters (whether to include criteria), as well as substance (the scope of protection, and the identification of protection agents) were matters of political concern. The fact that states disagreed so profoundly on these fundamental questions reflected the political salience of the proposed changes. The inclusion of the Responsibility to Protect principle was therefore of great symbolic significance, despite the fact that as a General Assembly resolution, the recommendations were not binding on states. A painful caveat for norm proponents was the absence of criteria in the final version of the paragraphs as included in the outcome document. Still, the inclusion of the Responsibility to Protect paragraphs outlined the substance and scope of an emerging, though as yet tenuous, consensus on changing norms of human protection, and the roles and responsibilities of states.

The formulation of the Responsibility to Protect principle in the outcome document also constituted a narrowing of the scope of the principle, as well as a raising of the threshold for action. According to the outcome document, the Responsibility to Protect fell to other actors when a state was 'manifestly failing' to protect its populations from the four atrocity crimes: genocide, ethnic cleansing, war crimes, and crimes against humanity. Not included were other human rights violations during peace time, humanitarian disaster, and the indirect consequences of conflict – including the protection of displaced people – for civilian populations, where governments were unable or unwilling to protect effectively. The reference to the 'manifestly failing' threshold meant that the Responsibility to Protect would shift from states as those primarily responsible for the protection of populations within their respective jurisdictions, to international actors only when it was deemed that national authorities were manifestly failing to discharge their protection duties. Not only did this mean a limitation in terms of the ability of international actors, including civil society, to invoke protection responsibilities for other human rights violations – it also introduced a further ambiguous threshold that could be invoked for action, but also be used to justify inaction – predisposing the principle to politicisation; a structural impediment likely to result in inconsistent implementation of the principle.[34]

In the years that followed the summit, annual deliberations on the principle revealed state positions and reflected continued resistance to the principles.[35] The most outspoken critics of the principle included Cuba, Venezuela, and Sudan. States that rejected the Responsibility to Protect in statements during Security Council meetings and annual General Assembly deliberations did so on the grounds that the principle might be abused by powerful actors to intervene in the affairs of other states, including where this was not fully justified on humanitarian grounds. Some states also feared that an intervention authorised with reference to the principle might gradually expand in scope – a slippery slope towards neo-colonial occupation. Consequently, states that were sceptical of the principle also opposed the creation of a joint office of the Special Advisor for the Responsibility to Protect and the Special Advisor for Genocide Prevention.

The 2009 report of the Secretary-General, *Implementing the Responsibility to Protect*, was an attempt to address the ambiguity of the Responsibility to Protect principle as endorsed in the outcome document of the world summit.[36] The report outlined a three-pillar framework for international responses to mass atrocities: first, the primary responsibility of each state to protect domestic populations. Second, the responsibility of international actors to assist states in meeting their primary protection responsibilities. And, third, the responsibility of the UN and member states to protect vulnerable populations if states were unable or unwilling to do so. These pillars were not intended to outline a sequence; rather, each existed simultaneously and the measures outlined in each of the pillars were to be applied based on need, and tailored to each case.

Ban Ki-Moon's Cyril Foster Lecture on Human Protection

While the world summit outcome document and the 2009 report on implementing the Responsibility to Protect served to narrow, delimit, and define the principle, Ban-Ki-Moon's Cyril Foster lecture at the University of Oxford in 2011 set the principle in a broader context of human protection. By relating the concept to a broader protection agenda, arguably it promoted a more expansive understanding of protection needs, as well as corollary protection responsibilities.[37] The lecture had been drafted by the then UN Special Adviser for the Responsibility to Protect, Edward Luck. In the lecture, the Secretary-General suggested that human protection was 'a subset of the more encompassing concept of human security' designed to protect vulnerable populations during crises, irrespective of whether these crises occur as a result of violent conflict or have other, or non-anthropogenic (man-made) causes. Human protection, as conceived by Luck for the Secretary-General, therefore included duties and responsibilities associated with preventing harm to vulnerable populations resulting from complex humanitarian emergencies. This included response to conflict (including peacekeeping, peacebuilding, and humanitarian relief), the prevention of conflict (preventive diplomacy and mediation), and the development of international institutions promoting legal accountability. Ultimately, human protection was about saving lives – effectively, grounded in cosmopolitan, utilitarian, and consequentialist values. In tying the Responsibility to Protect principle to this broader agenda, the Secretary-General promoted a more expansive understanding of the scope of protection, implicitly suggesting, perhaps, that state sovereignty was contingent upon an ability and willingness to meet all protection responsibilities, and that no exception would be made for emergencies that did not meet the manifestly failing threshold, or arose out of crisis situations that were not necessarily rooted in politics.

The tension between those who favoured a narrower approach to interpreting the principle, and those who supported a more expansive reading, played out in several fields. It was reflected also in the debate about the extent to which humanitarian relief aid should be prepared to depart from principles of neutrality and impartiality – in other words, focusing on relieving the symptoms of the conflict and the adverse effects on affected populations – rather than addressing structural and root causes (embodied in a human rights-based approach). In focusing on the protection of vulnerable populations above all else, 'human protection' aligned, ideationally, well with the human rights-based approach that, while not neglecting the need for addressing the immediate needs of individuals caught in the crossfire of conflict, also recognised the need to consider the structural conditions out of which the plight of affected populations arose in the first place.

The Responsibility to Protect and the Protection of Refugees and IDPs

In recent years, several scholarly works have engaged with the relationship between the Responsibility to Protect principle and the protection of refugees and IDPs. The Responsibility to Protect and the displacement of civilians in conflict are related concepts but have distinct meanings and a discussion of the relationship between the two concepts has received more scholarly attention in recent years. Both concepts originate in collective efforts to prevent, and respond to, harm to people affected by conflict, and are closely related to each other, given that displacement is often the result of human rights violations.[38] However, the narrowing down of the 'Responsibility to Protect' principle in the World Summit Outcome document to focusing on a narrower range of issues meant that the protection of displaced people was no longer, conceptually, necessarily encompassed by the Responsibility to Protect principle. At the same time, both issues are in practice closely associated with each other, and it is no surprise, therefore, that in the decade or so after the World Summit, with continued and sustained advocacy for the Responsibility to Protect, scholars and policymakers would begin to engage in more depth with the relationship, both empirically and politically, of both concepts.

In recent years, scholars of the Responsibility to Protect have suggested that the Responsibility to Protect also encompasses the Responsibility to Protect IDPs, who are not protected by the Refugee Convention of 1951 as they do not cross borders. Birnie and Welsh, for example, suggest that states may have a remedial responsibility to provide safe areas to civilians affected by conflict.[39] However, conditions in safe areas are often dire, as they are designed to provide temporary shelter and humanitarian relief. For this reason, the protection of displaced people, Birnie and Welsh argue, should also include the provision of asylum, the prevention of displacement in the first place, as well as efforts to facilitate the return of IDPs. Walter Kälin, former Representative of the UN Secretary-General on the Human Rights of Internally

Displaced Persons, interpreted the Guiding Principles on Internal Displacement as a form of soft law whose conversion into hard law should be promoted at all levels, including regional treaties and peace agreements.[40] These examples show that scholars and international policymakers continue to engage with the relationship between the two related concepts of IDP protection and the Responsibility to Protect, and the trend appears to be towards a renewed emphasis on the interconnectedness of IDP protection and R2P.

The Arab Spring: Collective Responses to Libya and Syria

Libya and Syria, both crises which unfolded against the backdrop of the Arab Spring, were viewed as 'test cases' for the new protection principle. While the conditions that had led to the crises in both cases were relatively similar – two states headed by increasingly unpopular autocrats and facing growing domestic dissent – international responses to these crises varied considerably. The Arab Spring, a series of popular uprising sweeping through Arab states, led to revolts in Libya in February 2011 and in March of the same year in Syria. In Libya, the violent uprising began in Benghazi, and then spread to other cities, resulting in increasingly violent clashes between the regime's security forces and rebels. In Syria, direct confrontation between protesters and security forces were precipitated by the shooting of protesters in Deraa. In the case of Libya, international actors responded by authorising a no-fly zone in March, and a NATO-led air campaign, authorised by the UN, to protect civilians. In Syria, the UN endorsed a peace plan drafted by the UN's envoy, Kofi Annan, and rebel groups received military and financial support from Turkey, Gulf states, the US, and several European states. There was no concerted, robust response – military or otherwise – from the United Nations Security Council.

While the Responsibility to Protect principle had been invoked to justify NATO's response in Libya, it did little to compel international actors to act decisively, and in a coordinated manner, in the case of Syria.[41] States, it seemed, continued to prioritise strategic interests over humanitarian concerns. The verdict, in both cases, was that the Responsibility to Protect had failed – at least in part – to compel states to act in unison and with resolve (as in the case of Syria), and in good faith with the principles associated with the doctrine (as in the case of Libya). While states acted in a timely manner, and with resolve, in the case of Libya, through the NATO intervention that was authorised by the UN Security Council, the intervention was criticised for overstepping the terms of the mandate. In the case of Syria, on the other hand, Russia's strategic interests foreclosed the possibility of a unified military response authorised by the UN, as well as coordinated, multilateral protective intervention.

Once again, scholars attempted to assess outcomes. Despite a decisive response by NATO in the case of Libya, analysts concluded the success of the intervention was mixed, at best. Alan Kuperman suggested the intervention might have produced a moral hazard in that it emboldened the rebellion, and in doing so possibly led to more violence than would have been observed in the absence of intervention, especially given that the intervention ultimately developed into a wider effort to bring about regime change.[42] By this reading, not only did NATO's intervention in Libya fail to save lives, but it may have cost additional lives. In the aftermath of the crisis, Ramesh Thakur, who had served as an ICISS commissioner, suggested that 'good intentions do not automatically shape good outcomes'.[43]

The difficulties associated with both crises rekindled scepticism and provided munition to critics of the Responsibility to Protect principle. The crises demonstrated the continued difficulty in implementing norms of protection, despite the fact that norms of humanitarianism, protection, and multilateralism had, two decades after the end of the Cold War, become firmly established standards for measuring legitimate responses to conflict and complex humanitarian emergencies. Still, both cases also showed that the norms advocacy of the 1990s and 2000s had resulted in a comprehensive international regime geared at protecting vulnerable populations. Both crises saw at least some measure of coordinated responses from states, the UN, regional organisations, and the civil society sector. This, in turn, suggests that international practice had changed significantly since the end of the Cold War. Neither the institutions nor habitual protection practice had existed in this shape or form during the Cold War era.

Summary

- 'An Agenda for Peace' was a 1992 report of the UN Secretary-General that aimed to improve the UN's capacity for preventive diplomacy and peacekeeping. The report emerged from the immediate post-Cold War political context.
- The ICISS report of 2001 outlines three protection responsibilities: prevention, reaction, and rebuilding. The principle of 'Responsibility to Protect' as endorsed in the World Summit Outcome Document of 2005 is more narrowly circumscribed. The outcome document states that the Responsibility to Protect applies when a state is 'manifestly failing' to protect its populations from four atrocity crimes: genocide, ethnic cleansing, war crimes, and crimes against humanity. Not included are other human rights violations during peace time, humanitarian disaster, or the protection of displaced people.
- The principle of 'human protection' as outlined by the Secretary-General in a speech in 2011 is premised on a comprehensive understanding of protection responsibilities. Human protection was defined by the Secretary-General as a subset of human security. Human protection is understood as the protection of vulnerable populations during armed conflict or arising from non-anthropogenic causes.
- The case of Rwanda in 1994 and Kosovo in 1999 were significant cases for the development of the protection regime. The aftermath of the Rwandan genocide saw concerted efforts to put in place more robust mass atrocity prevention measures, whereas the crisis in Kosovo led to renewed debate on legitimacy criteria for the use of force in the absence of a Security Council mandate.
- In the early 2010s, the Arab Spring put newly articulated protection principles to the test. Responses to crises in Libya and Syria illustrated persistent obstacles to the implementation of protection principles. NATO's intervention in Libya was criticised for overstepping its mandate, while states were unable to forge a coordinated, multilateral response to the crisis in Syria.

Questions for Reflection

- *Why was 'An Agenda for Peace' a significant document?*
- *What are the key differences between R2P as defined in the ICISS report, and R2P as defined in the World Summit Outcome Document?*

- *What are the advantages and disadvantages, in both scholarly and practical terms, of a wider conceptualisation of protection as embodied in the concept of 'human protection'?*
- *In what ways have the Rwandan genocide and the crisis in Kosovo shaped the development of the protection regime?*
- *In your view, have norms of protection influenced international responses to crises in Libya and Syria?*

Further reading

- Annan, Kofi, with Mousavizadeh (2012): *Interventions: A Life in War and Peace* (London: Penguin).
- Bellamy, Alex (2006): 'Whither the Responsibility to Protect? Humanitarian Intervention and the 2005 World Summit', *Ethics & International Affairs* 20(2): 143–69.
- Deng, Francis M. (1995): 'Frontiers of Sovereignty: A Framework of Protection, Assistance, and Development for the Internally Displaced', *Leiden Journal of International Law* 8(2): 249–86.
- Melvern, Linda (2006): *Conspiracy to Murder: The Rwandan Genocide* (Verso, London).
- Nahlawi, Yasmine (2020): *The Responsibility to Protect in Libya and Syria: Mass Atrocities, Human Protection, and International Law* (Abingdon, Oxon: Routledge).
- Orchard, Phil (2019): *Protecting the Internally Displaced* (Abingdon, Oxon: Routledge).
- Sorpong, Peou (2002): 'The UN, Peacekeeping, and Collective Human Security: From an Agenda for Peace to the Brahimi Report', *International Peacekeeping* 9(2): 51–68.

Notes

1 United Nations Secretary-General, 'An Agenda for Peace: Preventive Diplomacy, Peacemaking and Peace-Keeping: Report of the Secretary-General', 1992.
2 United Nations Secretary-General, 5.
3 United Nations Secretary-General, 12.
4 United Nations Secretary-General, 4.
5 Article 52 of 'An Agenda for Peace'.
6 Mahmood Mamdani, *When Victims Become Killers: Colonialism, Nativism, and the Genocide in Rwanda* (Princeton, NJ: Princeton University Press, 2001).
7 Gerard Prunier, *The Rwanda Crisis: History of a Genocide*, 2nd revised ed. (London: C Hurst & Co Publishers Ltd, 1998).
8 United Nations Security Council, 'Rwanda', 5 October 1993.
9 United Nations Secretary-General, 'Special Report of the Secretary-General on the United Nations Assistance Mission for Rwanda', 20 April 1994.
10 United Nations Security Council, 'Adjustment of the Mandate of the UN Assistance Mission for Rwanda due to the Current Situation in Rwanda and Settlement of the Rwandan Conflict', 21 April 1994.
11 Kofi Annan, *Interventions: A Life in War and Peace* (New York: Penguin, 2013), 48.

12 United Nations Security Council, 'The Expansion of the Mandate of the UN Assistance Mission for Rwanda and Imposition of an Arms Embargo on Rwanda', 17 May 1994.
13 United Nations Security Council, 'Establishment of a Temporary Multinational Operation for Humanitarian Purposes in Rwanda until the Deployment of the Expanded UN Assistance Mission for Rwanda', 22 June 1994.
14 United Nations Security Council.
15 Hazel Cameron, 'The French Connection: Complicity in the 1994 Genocide in Rwanda', *African Security* 8, no. 2 (3 April 2015): 96–119, https://doi.org/10.1080/19392206.2015.1036669.
16 Annan, *Interventions*, 59.
17 Roméo Dallaire, *Shake Hands with the Devil: The Failure of Humanity in Rwanda* (Toronto: Random House Canada, 2003).
18 Erika Feller, 'The Evolution of the International Refugee Protection Regime', *Washington University Journal of Law & Policy* 5 (n.d.): 129–40.
19 Ingvild Bode, 'Francis Deng and the Concern for Internally Displaced Persons: Intellectual Leadership in the United Nations', *Global Governance* 20 (2014): 277.
20 Frederick Laker, *Rethinking Internal Displacement: Geo-Political Games, Fragile States and the Relief Industry* (New York: Oxford: Berghahn, 2021).
21 Independent International Commission on Kosovo, *The Kosovo Report: Conflict, International Response, Lessons Learned* (Oxford University Press, 2000), 142.
22 United Nations Security Council, 'S/RES/1239', 14 May 1999; United Nations Security Council, 'S/RES/1244', 10 June 1999; United Nations Security Council, 'Resolution 1203 (1998)' (UN, 24 October 1998).
23 Benjamin A. Valentino, 'The True Costs of Humanitarian Intervention', *Foreign Affairs*, no. November/December (2011).
24 Kosovo, *The Kosovo Report*.
25 Lawrence Freedman, 'Force and the International Community: Blair's Chicago Speech and the Criteria for Intervention', *International Relations* 31, no. 2 (1 June 2017): 107–24, https://doi.org/10.1177/0047117817707395.
26 Kofi Annan, 'Two Concepts of Sovereignty', *The Economist*, 16 September 1999.
27 Michael Ignatieff, 'Getting Iraq Wrong', *New York Times Magazine*, 5 August 2007; Gareth Evans, 'When Is It Right to Fight?', *Survival* 46, no. 3 (1 September 2004): 59–81, https://doi.org/10.1080/00396330412331343733.
28 Stewart Patrick, 'The U.N. Kofi Annan Left Behind', *Foreign Policy*, https://foreignpolicy.com/2018/08/22/the-u-n-kofi-annan-left-behind/.
29 United Nations Secretary-General, 'Prevention of Armed Conflict', 7 June 2001.
30 United Nations General Assembly, 'A More Secure World: Our Shared Responsibility', 2 December 2004.
31 ICISS, 'The Responsibility to Protect: Report of the International Commission on Intervention and State Sovereignty', 2001.
32 ICISS.
33 Alex J. Bellamy, 'Whither the Responsibility to Protect? Humanitarian Intervention and the 2005 World Summit', *Ethics & International Affairs* 20, no. 2 (June 2006): 143–69, https://doi.org/10.1111/j.1747-7093.2006.00012.x.
34 Roland Paris, 'The "Responsibility to Protect" and the Structural Problems of Preventive Humanitarian Intervention', *International Peacekeeping* 21, no. 5 (2014): 569–603.
35 Jonas Claes, 'Protecting Civilians from Mass Atrocities: Meeting the Challenge of R2P Rejectionism', *Global Responsibility to Protect* 4, no. 1 (1 January 2012): 67–97.
36 United Nations, 'Implementing the Responsibility to Protect', 2009.
37 United Nations Secretary-General, 'Cyril Foster Lecture at Oxford University: "Human Protection and the 21st Century United Nations"', *United Nations*, 2 February 2011, https://www.un.org.
38 Elizabeth Ferris, 'International Responsibility, Protection and Displacement: Exploring the Connections between R2P, Refugees and Internally Displaced Persons', *Global Responsibility to Protect* 8, no. 4 (2016): 390–409.
39 Rutger Birnie and Jennifer Welsh, 'Displacement, Protection and Responsibility: A Case for

Safe Areas', *Global Responsibility to Protect* 10, no. 3 (21 May 2018): 332–61, https://doi.org/10.1163/1875984X-01003005.

40 Walter Kälin, 'Consolidating the Normative Framework for IDPs', *International Journal of Refugee Law* 30, no. 2 (13 October 2018): 314–17, https://doi.org/10.1093/ijrl/eey026.

41 Nathalie Tocci, 'On Power and Norms: Libya, Syria and the Responsibility to Protect', *Global Responsibility to Protect* 8, no. 1 (29 February 2016): 51–75, https://doi.org/10.1163/1875984X-00801004.

42 Alan J. Kuperman, 'A Model Humanitarian Intervention? Reassessing NATO's Libya Campaign', *International Security* 38, no. 1 (1 July 2013): 105–36, https://doi.org/10.1162/ISEC_a_00126.

43 Ramesh Thakur, 'R2P after Libya and Syria: Engaging Emerging Powers', *The Washington Quarterly* 36, no. 2 (1 April 2013): 73, https://doi.org/10.1080/0163660X.2013.791082.

Part II

Actors

4 States and Regional Organisations

While support for protection principles has grown steadily, some scepticism about the Responsibility to Protect principle remains among states, whose role in the advocacy for the principle was outlined briefly in Chapter 3 on the emergence of the Responsibility to Protect. This chapter takes a closer look at the role of states and regional organisations in advocating for protection principles, pushing for a reinterpretation of existing principles, and implementing protection principles domestically and regionally. Advocacy and contestation are central concepts for understanding the politics of protection. Advocacy and contestation are processes that describe efforts to promote or prevent policy change, respectively. The idea that a Responsibility to Protect imposes a certain conditionality on state sovereignty has greater implications for governments of states with weaker state capacities than it does for stronger states with robust defensive capabilities. This chapter looks at the statements and voting behaviour of states, discussing the role of states as advocates for stronger protection responsibility, as well as the role of states with regard to norm contestation. It also discusses the role of regional organisations in promoting and implementing protection norms at the regional level.

Norms Advocacy and States

States can be important drivers of normative change. Although much constructivist scholarship focuses on the role of non-state actors, including regional organisations and civil society actors, the role of states as drivers of normative states is significant: states set the agenda within international institutions; their interpretation of Charter provisions, treaties, and customary practice is indicative of norms; and their practice and conduct in response to ongoing crises communicates, to a wider audience, their support for protection norms. State governments also have control over the legitimate use of armed force, and as such their interpretation of customary practice and international norms is of major significance.

Early efforts to promote the 'protection of civilians' during armed conflict is to be found in the codification of the rules for protection of civilians in the 1907 Hague Regulations. These applied to immediate combat zones and were designed to protect civilians against the effects of hostilities by requiring a warning prior to bombardment or siege, to allow civilians to leave or take shelter.[1] The Fourth Geneva Convention of 1949 expanded on this principle, requiring immunity from attack for civilian hospitals, medical transports, and medical personnel as well as the establishment of safety zones for the wounded, sick, and for civilians.[2] These legal provisions stipulated what states *could not* do in conflict but did not say what they *should* do. The 'protection of

DOI: 10.4324/9781003006671-6

civilians' discourse emerging in the 1990s following the Rwandan genocide, on the other hand, was an active principle of protection. The 'protection of civilians' was referred to explicitly for the first time in Security Council Resolution 1270 on Sierra Leone. In recent years, the vast majority of UN peacekeeping missions have been deployed under a 'protection of civilians' mandate.[3]

Similarly, the concept of 'human security' has played an important role in shaping the way international actors understand protection responsibilities. Initially promoted by Canada and Norway, 'human security' was first discussed by states through the 'Oslo-Ottawa axis', an informal arrangement comprising a small group of foreign ministers as well as the UN High Commissioner for Refugees, for discussion of issues relating to peacekeeping.[4] This informal group saw its role as that of intermediary to assist developing states in renegotiating the terms of their relationship with Bretton Woods institutions, international donors and powerful multinational corporations – a key objective for developing states. This group saw the promotion of a human rights and humanitarian agenda as a means of increasing their international influence by drawing on the power of ideas and norms. Promotion of the humanitarian agenda permitted Norway, a state that was not member of the European Union, to create a thematically focused international coalition, augmenting its status among its international peers in its role as a humanitarian big player.

Similarly, states had an important role in advocating for the Responsibility to Protect, although many states were also sceptical as will be discussed further on.[5] In 2000, Canadian Prime Minister Jean Chretien announced the establishment of the International Commission on Intervention and State Sovereignty (ICISS), which would be responsible for articulating the ideas that were to form the basis of the principle of 'sovereignty as responsibility'. In this way, states were agenda-setters, advancing international law and providing new policy impetus, and they were and remain principal implementers by their contributions to the UN's budget. For example, the UN Office for the Coordination of Humanitarian Affairs (OCHA) receives about five per cent of its funding from the regular UN budget, with more than 90 per cent of the budget contributed by states through the OCHA Donor Support Group (ODSG).[6] States also play a role in multi-stakeholder partnerships (MSPs), where public and private actors work to achieve a common purpose.[7] Through their contribution to UN and other budgets, states exert significant influence with regard to the themes that are prioritised and how programmes are implemented. When states decide to reduce donor funding, this results directly in declining protection standards.[8] The role of states is crucial for implementation, particularly as they control humanitarian funding. Still, as we have seen, state bureaucracies are also themselves important drivers of change with regard to policy and human rights advocacy.

The role of states is salient not only because of their political status and funding ability but also because of the symbolic significance of their support for protection principles and practice. Their position on protection principles says much about the strength of the normative protection regime, and the wording used in Security Council resolutions and other documents in significant as it suggests changing state practice vis-à-vis the UN Charter provisions. For example, the 'protection of civilians' has had a significant impact on military policies of the UN, the UK, and NATO.[9] Although progress has been slow, civilian protection is becoming institutionalised within military doctrines, for example through restrictions relating to the bearing of arms; as well as the push for incorporating civilian agencies in planning. Similarly, the Security

Council has used R2P language more frequently following its invocation in the case of Libya in 2011.[10] Not all efforts at promoting new concepts succeed, however. For example, the language of 'human security' has become less influential in recent years, possibly because it is a wider concept, but perhaps also because of its even greater challenge to state sovereignty.[11]

Finally, states influence international protection practice through their own state conduct as well as through the establishment of domestic protection structures. States have drawn up national implementation mechanisms for atrocity prevention, and similarly, regional organisations have established mechanisms for promoting and implementing protection principles at the regional level.[12]

However, states are, of course, not the only agents of normative change, nor are they always catalysts for normative change. Some governments have opposed the Responsibility to Protect principle, although reasons for doing so have varied. These will be explored in more detail in the next section. Nevertheless, states are central agents for the promotion of international protection standards, both for directing immediate responses to humanitarian protection crises and for structural prevention efforts. States are also principal actors with regard to advocacy for normative change.

Reasons for Norm Contestation by States

Different states have had different reasons for opposing normative change but contestation has changed in recent years to revolve not so much around the substance of protection norms per se, as the means and modalities of implementing these policies. Some states remain cautious about the Responsibility to Protect and human rights-based approaches to humanitarian aid. Sometimes the resistance may be principled, as when a state opposes policies that may threaten to dilute the principle of state sovereignty; sometimes the resistance may be strategic, for example when a government is itself party to a conflict and the implementation of protection policies threaten to weaken its authority. For example, Sri Lanka, which had officially endorsed R2P, rejected international criticism for its military operations during its war against the Liberation Tigers of Tamil Eelam (LTTE), as well as international efforts to support the domestic prosecution of suspected war criminals after the end of the conflict (see Box 4.1).[13] Similarly, the government of Sudan, itself implicated in violence against civilians in Darfur, rejected the R2P in formal and informal UN deliberations, as have numerous other states including Iran, North Korea, and Syria.[14] However, most of the substantive contestation pertains to the use of force – the other practices associated with the protection regime, including the provision of humanitarian assistance are less contentious given that aid and long-term assistance policies generally require the consent of the government and do not threaten to undermine its authority.

Norm contestation can take various forms. Alan Bloomfield refers to actors who contest protection norms as 'norm antipreneurs'.[15] Actors contesting norms of protection or the principles associated with them may use a range of strategies, Bloomfield suggests, in contrast to the strategies employed by 'norm entrepreneurs' (as outlined by Finnemore and Sikkink).[16] An actor may defend an entrenched status quo by preventing new precedents, blocking efforts to reform institutions, or using tactics designed to delay changes, and all three tactics have been used with regard to contestation of R2P.[17] Before 2005, states blocked initiatives to require P5 states to avoid use of their veto, as outlined in the ICISS report. In 2007, the Human Rights Council

Box 4.1 Sri Lanka: Counterinsurgency and the Responsibility to Protect

Following 26 years of conflict in which 100,000 people had perished, and 20,000, mostly Tamil, people had disappeared, the Sri Lankan government re-established control over territory held by the LTTE, in May 2009. The UN condemned human rights violations on both sides, particularly in the final stages of the conflict. While the government was accused of torture, executions, forced disappearance, sexual abuse, and indiscriminate shelling of civilian populations, the LTTE was accused of suicide attacks, assassinations, the recruitment of child soldiers, as well as using civilians as shields against government attacks by preventing them from fleeing rebel-held areas. The Sri Lankan government framed the military operations against the LTTE as a counterinsurgency effort that constituted part of the War on Terror. The case illustrates both the tension between principles that may be used to legitimise international non-interference in the domestic affairs of a state and the Responsibility to Protect principle, as well as the tension between counterinsurgency responses that fail to discriminate between combatants and non-combatants and the responsibility for civilian protection and state duties under international humanitarian law. Following the end of the conflict, the UN called for the establishment of a hybrid war crimes tribunal, but the government refused the proposal on the grounds that the prosecution of war crimes was a domestic issue, and that Sri Lankan courts were capable of investigating suspected crimes. The case demonstrated that invoking the Responsibility to Protect is difficult in postcolonial contexts; especially where a government can utilise an alternative frame – counterterrorism – to justify harsh counterinsurgency tactics, even where these may run counter to international humanitarian law and established norms of civilian protection.

investigated human rights abuses in Darfur, but a discussion of the outcome report was blocked by states politically aligned with the government of Sudan.[18] When Western states pushed for an application of the Responsibility to Protect principle to the conflict in Darfur by the Security Council, China objected on the grounds that there remained different interpretations of the concept.[19] In the same year, the UN Secretary-General sought the establishment of a Special Adviser for the Responsibility to Protect, but the Fifth Committee of the United Nations (that is responsible for budgetary matters) resisted the reform, although the additional resources were made available under Ban Ki-Moon's term in office in 2010.

Norm appropriation, that is, the invocation of a norm in circumstances in which it does not apply, can be another form of norm contestation. As a permanent member of the Security Council, Russia's position towards R2P is significant. However, Russia's intervention in Georgia is referred to as an example of misuse of the R2P norm. Russia's intervention was disproportionate and violated international humanitarian law.[20] However, as Badescu and Weiss note, the subsequent reception among international actors of the intervention, despite the invocation of R2P language, may have helped sharpen the conceptual meaning of R2P by delineating the boundaries of the norm.[21]

As a permanent member of the Security Council, China's position on R2P is ambiguous, although it has been fluid.[22] While China's rhetoric and voting behaviour suggests it was more sceptical of the principle up until 2005, China has subsequently engaged with the concept. Nevertheless, it has continued to resist the idea of using force to implement pillar three. The use of force for protection purposes contradicts two of its key foreign policy principles, non-intervention, and the non-use of force, which are both enshrined in China's 'Five Principles of Peaceful Co-Existence', first promoted by China in the 1950s.[23] China abstained on resolutions on Darfur has vetoed Security Council sanctions on Myanmar and Zimbabwe, respectively. In 2011, however, China supported Security Council resolution 1970 and acquiesced to resolution 1973 on Libya. Since then, in an effort to re-frame the third pillar of R2P, China has promoted its own principle of 'Responsible Protection'.[24]

Lack of agreement on the substance and the procedures associated with the protection regime have given rise to efforts at reframing or refining the protection principle. Brazil's proposal of 'Responsibility While Protecting'[25] is an example of the latter, and should be understood in the context of Brazil's role on the Security Council at the time of NATO's intervention in Libya.[26] As a Brazil, Russia, India, China, and South Africa (BRICS) state with growing international economic and diplomatic influence, Brazil sought to represent the views of other BRICS states and states of the Global South who regarded the military operations in Libya as overreaching the terms of the mandate provided by the UN Security Council under Resolution 1973 of 17 March 2011. The concept note highlighted the need for sequencing of the three pillars as contained in the Secretary-General's report on *Implementing the Responsibility to Protect*, comprising, in the first pillar, a state's primary Responsibility to Protect, second, states' collective responsibility to assist states in meeting their protection responsibility, and third, collective responses by states to protection crises. Furthermore, it urged for a restrictive approach to the use of force based on the 'do no harm' principle: '[t]he use of force must produce as little violence and instability as possible and under no circumstances can it generate more harm than it was authorized to prevent', and proposed the establishment of Security Council mechanisms to monitor and assess the implementation of Security Council mandates.[27] By 2012, however, following Brazil's end of term on the Council, Brazil ceased actively promoting the concept – a result also, partially, of the diplomatic pushback, including from states in the Global South.[28] However, the concept left its mark on subsequent discussions of the Responsibility to Protect, in that it demonstrated that the conduct of the intervention mattered significantly for its perceived legitimacy, as well as with regard to support for the principle more generally – if interventions that received broad support at the outset were conducted in a way that did not meet expectations, this might lower the chances of support for future protection interventions. Ultimately, while Brazil's letter can be read as an effort to remind states of the need to comply with international law,[29] the RWP concept had wider implications by calling for renewed debate.

In summary, the idea that the protection of civilians and other vulnerable groups can be enforced without the consent of the host government and with force if necessary has been resisted by some states. In many cases, national security concerns such as combating violent extremism and sources of terrorist violence constitute alternative frames states may draw on to justify particular kinds of responses to political conflict and their humanitarian consequences. However, the degree of contestation should not be overstated – on the whole, there is agreement among states that situations of humanitarian emergency and large-scale, systematic human rights abuses are exceptional circumstances requiring robust and concerted international responses.

Norms Advocacy and Regional Organisations

Regional organisations are sites of norms advocacy, but they can also be sites of norm contestation. Some regional organisations play more important roles, with regard to humanitarian protection, than others – while the role of some organisations is delimited to economic and trade policy, for example, other organisations are much more relevant with regard to advancing the protection regime. Some regional organisations have made progress with regard to institutionalising the Responsibility to Protect, whereas others have less clearly articulated policies, or lack the capacity for doing so.[30] The European Union, has prioritised its work on the preventative and rebuilding aspects of the Responsibility to Protect, and is cautious about pillar three responses and the use of force. A 2004 report of the European Union, *A Human Security Doctrine for Europe*,[31] urged the European Union to articulate foreign policy objectives in line with a human security agenda, which entailed placing a priority on human rights, multilateralism, and partnership with local and regional actors, and proposed the formation of a 'human security response force', ideas that influenced the European Security Strategy of 2008. Similarly, the League of Arab States (LAS) adopted the Arab Human Rights Charter in 2004 and has established a Peace and Security Council. The Arab League supported UN Security Council resolution 1973, authorising the intervention in Libya. The African Union (AU) not only supported the development of the Responsibility to Protect principle but also greatly influenced its development, and its Constitutive Act is the world's most interventionist in that according to Article 4 (h), it explicitly permits the AU to intervene in a member state in response to war crimes, genocide, and crimes against humanity.

Conflict prevention is now part of the core mandate of not only the AU, the EU, and the LAS but also of the Organisation for Security and Cooperation in Europe (OSCE), ECOWAS, and the East African Community (EAC), a sub-regional organisation, as well as ASEAN.[32] ASEAN has developed fora for conflict resolution, including the ASEAN Regional Forum (ARF) and the South China Sea Security Dialogue. The OSCE, similarly, established a Conflict Prevention Centre (CPC), and, as part of its conflict prevention framework, the OSCE includes the Office for Democratic Institutions and Human Rights, the Representative on Freedom of the Media, as well as good offices provided by the Personal Representatives of the Chairman-in-Office. Comparing each of these organisations along six criteria – Charter endorsement, non-interference in the affairs of a member state, capacity building, preventive diplomacy, institutional arrangements for conflict management, and direct engagement efforts – Carment and Fischer conclude that the OSCE, the AU, and ECOWAS have comparatively more expansive institutional remits, or have been engaged more directly, while ASEAN and OAS states continue to express reservations about interference in the domestic affairs of states.[33]

At the same time, regional institutions are also sites of contestation. For example, Zähringer and Brosig suggest that, despite the AU's strong commitment to R2P principles, there remains a gap between commitment and action – the authors refer to this as 'organised hypocrisy'.[34] While the AU has expressly committed to the R2P principles, it must also consider members states' national interests and the broader international political climate, particularly the role of powerful third parties. This meant that, while the AU expressed support for Security Council Resolution 1970 on Libya, it officially requested a deferral of the ICC case on the Libyan situation. The AU also expressed its support, in principle, for Security Council resolution 1973, but criticised its implementation.

Similar dynamics can be observed with regard to ASEAN and R2P implementation, where a study conducted by Zain Maulana found that among ASEAN states, there is scepticism about the applicability of the R2P principle with regard to individual cases and, in any case, are considered domestic issues.[35] The discrepancy between practices of norm interpretation and application has also been described by Amitav Acharya as a form of 'norm localization', where norms are amended to suit cognitive priors of local actors.[36] In this case, the protection norm collides with the sovereignty norm that forms a cornerstone of East Asian international relations. However, David Capie speaks of a 'localization myth',[37] when the principles associated with the norm are applied using an 'a la carte' approach, picking aspects of the norm perceived as less threatening. The origins of a norm – whether it originated within a region, or whether it was adopted following international advocacy – matters in so far as actors may be more willing to champion norms over which they perceive to hold ownership.

In summary, regions play an important role both for advancing normative change as well as in terms of immediate responses to acute crises. If anything, regions have become more important than they have been in the past. In a globalised world, regional organisations manage relations among their member states but also exert significant influence in the domestic affairs of their member states, and, although to varying degrees, regions represent their member states internationally and can be an important catalyst for normative change. The next section now turns to the relationship between regional organisations and their international counterparts. This relationship can be mutually reinforcing, but sometimes, authority located at different levels can also result in contradictions and competition, with detrimental consequences for the ability of international actors to respond decisively and effectively.

Regional Protection Regimes and International Institutions

Regional institutions underpin the international human protection regime, but their role is not spelt out clearly and there is contestation about the procedures for locating authority for conflict management and humanitarian response. It is not clear whether, in any given crisis, the immediate response ought to be coordinated by regional actors, or whether the primary authority rests with international institutions who, in many cases, have greater budgetary capacities, a longer institutional memory, established expertise and a fully-fledged response apparatus and existing global networks. From a normative perspective, on the other hand, regional organisations may be more appropriate first responders: their legitimacy derives from their constitution as representing regional interests and, particularly for postcolonial states with a history of external interference and political subjugation, a regional response mechanism may be preferable. 'Subsidiarity' is the concept that the right authority, irrespective of capacities, is in the first instance the local, proximate authority.[38] The idea developed out of the domestic context, where the role of the state was perceived as limited, providing a supplement, or *subsidium*, where an issue could not be resolved at the subordinate level, and in this case requiring intervention. The concept has since been applied to international human rights law, originating primarily in the context of discussion of the relationship between international human rights law and human rights law of the European Union, in an effort to conceptualise a relationship that was able to mediate between the cosmopolitan demands of universal human rights, and pluralist approaches.[39] There is now a plethora of scholarship that has begun to extrapolate from the scholarship on rights, and applied the concept to practices and institutional arrangements underpinning norms and their practical application. For example, Amitav Acharya outlines the role of norm subsidiarity with regard to regional orders, suggesting that non-aligned states have used norm subsidiarity to insulate themselves from external interference of external actors.[40] W. Andy Knight applies the concept for understanding the role that regional organisations can play in supporting the UN with regard to peacemaking and preventive diplomacy if Chapter VIII of its Charter were operationalised,[41] and the idea has been extended to understanding the emerging normative architecture between regional organisations and the international human protection regime across the full spectrum of protection responsibilities.[42]

However, there are practical constraints with regard to the extent that the subsidiarity principle can work to regulate global protection practices. Capacities of protection agents are not distributed evenly, and because the institutions of the international protection regime precede those at the regional level, in many cases their organisational and material capacities are greater. This means that international institutions continue to be viewed as responsible for responding, or at least delegating protection responsibility and substantially supporting protective intervention by third parties to whom these responsibilities have been delegated. For example, the African Union – United Nations Hybrid Operation in Darfur (UNAMID) was the first peacekeeping operation jointly conducted by the UN and a regional organisation. However, in addition to obstruction by the host government, the mission's success was also impaired by competing claims to authority by the UN and the AU,[43] and failure to eliminate asymmetries in the relationship between both actors led to what Tieku and Hakak have critically referred to as 'hybrid paternalism'.[44] In theoretical terms, two further objections to the subsidiarity principle may arise.[45] First, it may be seen to undermine the idea that human rights are absolutely 'fundamental' and 'universal', given that it permits, at least to a degree, regional variation in the interpretation of these rights. Second, the absence of normative uniformity across jurisdictions may be seen to challenge the fundamental legal values of certainty and consistency.

However, given the 'soft' nature of international law, these questions remain mostly abstract and in practice, no certain mechanism for adjudicating between competing claims to authority, or protocols for assigning specific duties to particular protection agents across jurisdictions, thematic domains, and levels of authority have yet emerged. For example, in the sphere of mediation, regional actors do, and historically have, played a central role, but there is no systematic means of identifying the most responsible actors and in practice other factors, including political motivation, capacity, and the degree of trust of the parties to the dispute have shaped protection practices. However, there is evidence of institutionalisation. Examples include, at the international level, the UNDP Bureau for Crisis Prevention and Diplomacy and the UNDPPA Mediation Support Unit. At the regional level, the AU's Panel of the Wise and the Pan-African Network of the Wise (PanWise) provide good offices, and tere is a growing role of ASEAN in managing intra-regional disputes.[46] While most mediation efforts therefore remain ad hoc initiatives, the trend towards institutionalisation may be positive as there is empirical research to suggest that, at least for inter-state conflicts, mediation and conflict management are more likely to succeed where they are highly institutionalised and utilise binding procedures.[47] Empirical research on the effects of regional mediation efforts in intra-state wars suggests that although mediated settlements for intra-state disputes are fragile, efforts by regional organisation generally have positive effects.[48]

While in practice political interests and actor capacity explain why states become involved as a third-party mediator, the growing role of regional organisations and the institutionalisation of mediation practices creates normative ambiguity with regard to identifying the most appropriate mediator. The principle that the party with the greatest capacity to do so – in practice powerful states with international leverage – is at odds with the principle of subsidiarity suggesting that regional actors are responsible in the first instance for providing good offices and leading the mediation between parties to a conflict. Identifying a suitable mediator and agreeing on one unified mediation track may therefore be difficult. For example, while the UN was prominent in mediation in Central African Republic (CAR), Cote D'Ivoire, Darfur, and Libya, the sub-regional organisations were key actors in mediation for conflicts concerning Burkina Faso, Guinea-Bissau, Mali, Madagascar, and Zimbabwe.[49] Agreeing on a single mediation track can consume resources and can take time. Delaying the beginning of a mediation process means a slower response to conflicts and mitigation of violence, including violence targeting civilians. The case of Kenya serves as an example.[50] The AU took the lead in the mediation but alternatives had been considered; two regional organisations had been involved to begin with, the East African Community (EAC) and the Intergovernmental Authority on Development (IGAD). The EAC's efforts to lead a mediation were complicated by the fact that the organisation was headed by Ugandan president Museveni, who was perceived as biased towards the incumbent government; and similarly, ODM perceived IGAD as sympathetic towards the incumbent government. At the beginning of the mediation conducted by Kofi Annan, Annan urged all sides that there should be only one consolidated mediation process, to ensure all sides were committed to the process.[51] Still, both sub-regional organisations continued to offer alternative mediation tracks, and it was not until early in February – a month after the elections – that all parties finally agreed to a single mediation process headed by Annan.

With regard to humanitarian relief and peacekeeping, similarly, the role of regional organisations has grown. For example, mirroring bodies at the international level, including the UN Department for Peacekeeping Operations (DPO), the Department of Political and Peacebuilding Affairs (DPPA), the UN Office for the Coordination of Humanitarian Affairs (OCHA), are the AU Department of Political Affairs, the AU Department of Peace and Security, and the AU Department of Humanitarian Affairs.[52] In South East Asia, regional bodies include the ASEAN Secretariat, the ASEAN defence ministers meeting (ADMM), the offices associated with ASEAN's political and security pillar, as well as the ASEAN regional forum (ARF) and the ASEAN plus three, a regional forum including ASEAN and China, Japan, and South Korea.[53] For the EU, the Common Security and Defence Policy (CSDP) comprises a Political and Security Committee (PSC), the European Union Military Committee (EUMC), the Committee for Civilian Aspects of Crisis Management (CIVCOM), the Politico-Military Group (PMG), the Security and Defence Directorate (SECDEFPOL), and the European Union Military Staff (EUMS) as well as the Civilian Planning and Conduct Capability (CPCC) and Military Planning and Conduct

Capability (MPCC). The EU is the principal international peacebuilding actor in Kosovo, with the EU's Special Representative working in close partnership with local authorities, and the EU Commission playing a central role in economic development.[54] However, these organisations need to coordinate their work with institutions associated with pre-existing international structures, particularly those associated with the UN system. For example, the EU works closely with the UN and the OSCE, for coordination purposes as well as to realise synergies, although this also entails a degree of dependency on other institutions and agency loss.[55]

International organisations cooperate with one another formally as well as informally at various levels, including at a macro-level between organisations, a meso-level, among bureaucracies, and a micro-level describing the role of individuals and small organisational units.[56] There are numerous examples of formal or informal inter-organisational cooperation.[57] For example, in the case of Mali following a coup in 2012 in which the elected government was overthrown by a military junta and an insurgency in the northern regions of the country threatened the state's territorial integrity, ECOWAS, supported by France, intervened on the ground. The UN subsequently authorised the UN Multidimensional Integrated Stabilization Mission in Mali (MINUSMA), with a mandate encompassing a range of peacebuilding objectives including the support of reconciliation efforts and security sector reform. Complementing these peacebuilding efforts were the EU Training Mission (EUTM) and EU Capacity Building Mission in Mali (EUCAP), designed to provide support and training to Malian military and security forces, respectively. The case reflects an emerging practice whereby international organisations share tasks at different points in the conflict cycle, specialising on rapid response or longer-term peacebuilding and structural prevention efforts.

While practices have emerged that have given rise to expectations with regard to inter-organisational roles and responsibilities, these have not been formalised or spelt out explicitly, producing ambiguity and inability of swift response where there is an absence of political will. Of the cases of conflict in which the Security Council can agree on a decisive course of action, the UN can field a majority of troops within three months of authorisation, but a significant number of missions are not deployed within this timeframe.[58] The speed by which states deploy forces depends on a range of factors.[59] The UN Security Council continues to be criticised for failing to respond swiftly, and even where it does, coordination problems stymie responses. For these reasons, the UN Secretary-General launched the 'Action for Peacekeeping' (A4P) initiative in March 2018, which among other objectives aimed to 'mobilise greater support for political solutions and for well-structured, well-equipped, well-trained forces'.[60] In many cases, regional organisations need to reconcile different sets of interests by a range of actors.[61] This may be an even greater challenge when coordination among international actors, including those of donor states, is already difficult (see Box 4.2).[62]

The problem also applies in the domain of international criminal justice. There are now mechanisms for prosecution at the international and regional levels, but these mechanisms compete with each other and can allow for 'forum shopping'.[63] At the international level, the United Nations Human Rights Council and the International Criminal Court are central organs. At the regional level in Africa, the African Commission on Human and People's Rights (the Banjul Commission) and the African Court on Human and Peoples' Right are key institutions. Similarly, regional institutions

Box 4.2 Somalia: A History of Peacekeeping Failures

Following the end of the Cold War and the collapse of the military regime in 1991, Somalia disintegrated in a civil war in which warlords took control and Somaliland, a western region of the state, declared independence. Successive peacekeeping operations, UNOSOM, UNITAF, led by the United States, and later UNOSOM II, were established. UNOSOM sought to monitor a ceasefire agreement and facilitate the provision of humanitarian aid. However, the mission was unable to meet humanitarian needs, resulting in widespread starvation. Humanitarian assistance failed to reach those most in need, with the UN and relief units refused access by de facto authorities and coming under attack. In response, the UN Security Council issued a Chapter VII mandate, authorising the use of force to facilitate a secure environment for the provision of humanitarian relief. UNOSOM II, an expanded mission equipped with a Chapter VII mandate, was tasked with peacebuilding and continued provision of humanitarian relief. However, the peacebuilding efforts failed to bring security, and a takeover of the state's capital, Mogadishu, in 2006 prompted a military intervention by Ethiopia. Since then, international actors have been battling al-Shabab, a militant group with suspected ties to Boko Haram and al-Qaeda. The African Union Mission in Somalia (AMISOM) was created in 2007. However, the efforts to stabilise the state have lacked international coordination, particularly among international donors whose security sector reform programmes were poorly coordinated. The case illustrates the obstacles to internationally managing a conflict and coordinating protection responses among international actors and regional organisations. International responses continue to evolve in response to particular crises, and although institutionalised responses are now common, failure to coordinate among institutions and bureaucracies, both vertically and horizontally, may result in poor communication among actors and inefficient distribution of scarce resources. Overall, the record of international actors in this protracted conflict has been poor, characterised by a string of peacekeeping failures and the inability of international actors to bring peace to the state.

structure the human rights system in Europe, Asia, and the Americas.[64] The European human rights system is elaborate and relatively effective, comprising the Council of Europe, established in 1949, that brought about the European Convention for the Protection of Human Rights and Fundamental Freedoms (ECHR) that allows an individual whose human rights have been violated to file a case against a national government. The European Court of Human Rights can be accessed directly by individuals and adjudicates in case of complaints. The Inter-American human rights system is similarly elaborate, but it has been less successful with regard to compliance and enforcement. A cornerstone document is the nonbinding American Declaration of the Rights and Duties of Man of 1948. The Inter-American Commission on Human Rights, established in 1959, monitors cases of alleged violations of the Declaration and reports on the record of human rights compliance of member states. The American Convention on Human Rights (ACHR) of 1969 is a binding regional treaty. In the Asia-Pacific region, the ASEAN Intergovernmental Commission on Human Rights (AICHR) was established in 2009, and human rights are incorporated in ASEAN's Charter, and in 2012, ASEAN states adopted the ASEAN Human Rights Declaration (AHRD), but there is no regional human rights court as is the case for the other regions. The National Human Rights Institutions (NHRIs) play an important role in the promotion of human rights in the region, although they have been deemed insufficiently independent in their funding and their operations.[65] Strengthening the human rights regime in the Asia Pacific is difficult given the high normative value placed on non-interference in domestic affairs and consensus decision-making.[66] Yet, a central shortcoming of the regional system is the absence of a judicial body to hear complaints and issue-binding remedies.[67]

Despite the growing influence of regional bodies, a key problem, as outlined above remains that of a lack of a coordinating system to assign judicial authority, both horizontally, that is, among regional and sub-regional actors, and vertically, among the regional and international levels. This allows for the possibility of 'forum shopping' where a state, in order to avoid prosecution by the International Criminal Court, can refer a situation to a regional court, in anticipation of greater control over the proceedings, where political independence may be weaker and a state may exert more influence.[68] In these ways, a greater number of institutions can create more ambiguity.[69] Yet, a wider range of institutions with jurisdiction over the prosecution of mass atrocity crimes also means that there are more capacities for, and better prospects of, investigation of suspected crimes.

The increasing influence of regional organisations – in a globalising and increasingly multipolar and fragmented world – therefore holds both opportunities and risks. On the one hand, regional organisation provides further opportunities for immediate responses to humanitarian emergency and conflict. Regional responses may also be perceived as more legitimate. On the other hand, however, regional responders may be no less politicised in their responses to crises in neighbouring states – in some cases, their responses may be less impartial than those of more distant responders. Similarly, while regional responses provide additional avenues for the provision of humanitarian relief, peacekeeping, criminal justice and, importantly with regard to the prevention of conflict in the first place, mediation, the absence of a mechanism for assigning responsibilities means that incoherence, and consequently, contestation and inefficacy, remain characteristics of international responses to conflict and humanitarian emergency.

Summary

- States are represented in international organisations. They also hold a domestic monopoly on the use of force. These features arguably give states greater influence than other relevant actors in establishing and maintaining rules in international society.
- The endorsement of the Responsibility to Protect principle in the World Summit outcome document of 2005 represents a milestone in advocacy for the principle. However, some states remained sceptical about the principle.
- Regional organisations, it is argued, play a significant role in terms of norm

localisation. On the other hand, powerful states remain principal actors with regard to policy-making and the implementation of protection principles.

- Powerful states, such as the permanent five members of the Security Council or the BRICs, and large international bureaucracies including the bodies of the UN may have greater capacity than local actors for responding to conflict and humanitarian emergency. On the other hand, absence of local ownership may undermine the perceived legitimacy of international responses to humanitarian crises.

Questions for Reflection

- *Are states the primary promoters of human protection norms?*
- *Is there a consensus among states on the key principles of humanitarian protection?*
- *How significant is the role of regional organisations for the diffusion of protection norms, and their implementation?*
- *How important is the involvement of regional organisations such as the Arab League, the AU, ASEAN, or EU in international responses to conflict and humanitarian emergency?*

Further reading

- Amar, Paul, ed. (2013): *Global South to the Rescue: Emerging Humanitarian Superpowers and Globalizing Rescue Industries* (Abingdon, Oxon: Routledge).
- Cavallaro, James L. et al. (2019): *Doctrine, Practice, and Advocacy in the Inter-American Human Rights System* (Oxford: Oxford University Press).
- Kingsbury, Damien (2013): *Sri Lanka and the Responsibility to Protect* (Abingdon, Oxon: Routledge).
- Nash, Kathryn (2021): *African Peace: Regional Norms from the Organization of African Unity to the African Union* (Manchester: Manchester University Press).
- Schnyder, Melissa and Noha Shawki (2020): *Advocating for Refugees in the European Union: Norm-Based Strategies by Civil Society Organizations* (London: Lexington Books).
- Shelton, Dinah and Paolo G. Carozza (2014): *Regional Protection of Human Rights*, 2nd ed. (Oxford: Oxford University Press).
- Stacey, Jamie (2020): *ASEAN and Power in International Relations: ASEAN, the EU, and the Contestation of Human Rights* (Abingdon, Oxon: Routledge).
- Williams, Paul D. (2018): *Fighting for Peace in Somalia: A History and Analysis of the African Union Mission* (AMISOM) (Oxford: Oxford University Press).

Notes

1 Waldemar A. Solf, 'Protection of Civilians against the Effects of Hostilities under Customary International Law and under Protocol I', *American University Journal of International Law and Policy* 1 (1986): 117.

2 Solf.

3 Anastasia Shesterinina and Brian L. Job, 'Particularized Protection: UNSC Mandates and the Protection of Civilians in Armed Conflict', *International Peacekeeping* 23, no. 2 (14 March 2016): 240–73, https://doi.org/10.1080/13533312.2015.1123628.
4 The role of states in promoting human security is described in Astri Suhrke, 'Human Security and the Interests of States', *Security Dialogue* 30, no. 3 (1 September 1999): 265–76, https://doi.org/10.1177/0967010699030003002.
5 Charles Cater and David M Malone, 'The Origins and Evolution of Responsibility to Protect at the UN', *International Relations* 30, no. 3 (1 September 2016): 278–97, https://doi.org/10.1177/0047117816659586.
6 Andreas Øien Stensland and Ole Jacob Sending, 'Unpacking the "Culture of Protection": A Political Economy Analysis of OCHA and the Protection of Civilians', Security in Practice (NUPI, 2011).
7 Marianne Beisheim and Nils Simon, 'Multistakeholder Partnerships for the SDGs: Actors' Views on UN Metagovernance', *Global Governance: A Review of Multilateralism and International Organizations* 24, no. 4 (10 December 2018): 497–515, https://doi.org/10.1163/19426720-02404003.
8 Beth Elise Whitaker, 'Funding the International Refugee Regime: Implications for Protection', *Global Governance: A Review of Multilateralism and International Organizations* 14, no. 2 (12 August 2008): 241–58, https://doi.org/10.1163/19426720-01402008.
9 Stuart Gordon, 'The Protection of Civilians: An Evolving Paradigm?', *Stability: International Journal of Security and Development* 2, no. 2 (2013): 1–16.
10 Jess Gifkins, 'R2P in the UN Security Council: Darfur, Libya and Beyond', *Cooperation and Conflict* 51, no. 2 (1 June 2016): 148–65, https://doi.org/10.1177/0010836715613365.
11 Kristen Timothy, 'Human Security Discourse at the United Nations', *Peace Review* 16, no. 1 (2004): 19–24.
12 Cecilia Jacob and Martin Mennecke, *Implementing the Responsibility to Protect: A Future Agenda* (Abingdon, Oxon: Routledge, 2020).
13 Kimberly Nackers, 'Framing the Responsibility to Protect', *Global Responsibility to Protect* 7 (2015): 81; Gerrit Kurtz and Madhan Mohan Jaganathan, 'Protection in Peril: Counterterrorism Discourse and International Engagement in Sri Lanka in 2009', *Global Society* 30, no. 1 (2 January 2016): 94–112, https://doi.org/10.1080/13600826.2015.1092421.
14 Patrick Quinton-Brown, 'Mapping Dissent: The Responsibility to Protect and Its State Critics', *Global Responsibility to Protect* 5, no. 3 (1 January 2013): 260–82.
15 Alan Bloomfield, 'Norm Antipreneurs and Theorising Resistance to Normative Change', *Review of International Studies* 42, no. 2 (April 2016): 310–33.
16 Martha Finnemore and Kathryn Sikkink, 'International Norm Dynamics and Political Change', *International Organization* 52, no. 4 (1998): 887–917.
17 Bloomfield, 'Norm Antipreneurs and Theorising Resistance to Normative Change'.
18 Bloomfield, 325.
19 Bloomfield, 325.
20 Cristina G. Badescu and Thomas G. Weiss, 'Misrepresenting R2P and Advancing Norms: An Alternative Spiral?', *International Studies Perspectives* 11, no. 4 (1 November 2010): 354–74, https://doi.org/10.1111/j.1528-3585.2010.00412.x.
21 Badescu and Weiss.
22 Andrew Garwood-Gowers, 'China's "Responsible Protection" Concept: Reinterpreting the Responsibility to Protect (R2P) and Military Intervention for Humanitarian Purposes', *Asian Journal of International Law* 6, no. 1 (January 2016): 89–118, https://doi.org/10.1017/S2044251314000368.
23 Xiaorong Han, 'China, Cambodia, and the Five Principles of Peaceful Coexistence (Review)', *China Review International* 17, no. 3 (2020): 372–76.
24 Andrew Garwood-Gowers, 'R2P Ten Years After the World Summit: Explaining Ongoing Contestation over Pillar Iii', *Global Responsibility to Protect* 7, no. 3–4 (30 October 2015): 300–324, https://doi.org/10.1163/1875984X-00704005.
25 United Nations General Assembly, 'Letter Dated 9 November 2011 from the Permanent Representative of Brazil to the United Nations Addressed to the Secretary-General', 11 November 2011.

26 Kenkel and Stefan outline Brazil's reasons for putting forward the concept note. See Kai Michael Kenkel and Cristina G. Stefan, 'Brazil and the Responsibility While Protecting Initiative: Norms and the Timing of Diplomatic Support', *Global Governance: A Review of Multilateralism and International Organizations* 22, no. 1 (19 August 2016): 41–58, https://doi.org/10.1163/19426720-02201004.
27 United Nations General Assembly, 'A/66/551–S/2011/701'. Articles 6 and 11(e) and 11(h), respectively.
28 Kenkel and Stefan, 'Brazil and the Responsibility While Protecting Initiative', 50.
29 Inger Österdahl, 'The Responsibility to Protect and the Responsibility While Protecting: Why Did Brazil Write a Letter to the UN?', *Nordic Journal of International Law* 82, no. 4 (1 January 2013): 459–86, https://doi.org/10.1163/15718107-08204001.
30 An overview of organisations and roles is provided in Carla Barqueiro, Kate Seaman, and Katherine Teresa Towey, 'Regional Organizations and Responsibility to Protect: Normative Reframing or Normative Change?', *Politics and Governance* 4, no. 3 (11 August 2016): 37–49, https://doi.org/10.17645/pag.v4i3.642.
31 European Union, 'A Human Security Doctrine for Europe', 2004.
32 David Carment and Martin Fischer, 'R2P and the Role of Regional Organisations in Ethnic Conflict Management, Prevention and Resolution: The Unfinished Agenda', *Global Responsibility to Protect* 1, no. 3 (1 January 2009): 261–90, https://doi.org/10.1163/187598409X450776.
33 Carment and Fischer.
34 Natalie Zähringer and Malte Brosig, 'Organised Hypocrisy in the African Union: The Responsibility to Protect as a Contested Norm', *South African Journal of International Affairs* 27, no. 1 (2 January 2020): 1–23.
35 Zain Maulana, 'Norm Implementation and Contestation: The Case of the Responsibility to Protect in Southeast Asia' (PhD, University of Leeds, 2019), http://etheses.whiterose.ac.uk/25915/.
36 Amitav Acharya, 'How Ideas Spread: Whose Norms Matter? Norm Localization and Institutional Change in Asian Regionalism', *International Organization* 58, no. 2 (April 2004): 239–75, https://doi.org/10.1017/S0020818304582024.
37 David Capie, 'The Responsibility to Protect Norm in Southeast Asia: Framing, Resistance and the Localization Myth', *The Pacific Review* 25, no. 1 (1 March 2012): 75–93, https://doi.org/10.1080/09512748.2011.632967.
38 Paolo G. Carozza, 'Subsidiarity as a Structural Principle of International Human Rights Law', *The American Journal of International Law* 97, no. 1 (2003): 38–79, https://doi.org/10.2307/3087103.
39 Carozza.
40 Amitav Acharya, 'Norm Subsidiarity and Regional Orders: Sovereignty, Regionalism, and Rule-Making in the Third World', *International Studies Quarterly* 55, no. 1 (1 March 2011): 95–123, https://doi.org/10.1111/j.1468-2478.2010.00637.x.
41 W. Andy Knight, 'Towards a Subsidiarity Model for Peacemaking and Preventive Diplomacy: Making Chapter VIII of the UN Charter Operational', *Third World Quarterly* 17, no. 1 (1 March 1996): 31–52, https://doi.org/10.1080/01436599650035761.
42 Noele Crossley, 'The African Union and Human Protection: Towards a Regional Protection Regime', *African Security* 13, no. 2 (2 April 2020): 147–70, https://doi.org/10.1080/19392206.2020.1779528.
43 Kilian Spandler, 'UNAMID and the Legitimation of Global-Regional Peacekeeping Cooperation: Partnership and Friction in UN-AU Relations', *Journal of Intervention and Statebuilding* 14, no. 2 (14 March 2020): 187–203, https://doi.org/10.1080/17502977.2020.1725729.
44 Thomas Kwasi Tieku, 'A Curious Case of Hybrid Paternalism: Conceptualizing the Relationship between the UN and AU on Peace and Security', *African Conflict & Peacebuilding Review* 4, no. 2 (2014): 129–56.
45 Carozza, 'Subsidiarity as a Structural Principle of International Human Rights Law'.
46 Jacob Bercovitch, Kwei-Bo Huang, and Chung-Chian Teng, eds., *Conflict Management, Security and Intervention in East Asia: Third-Party Mediation in Regional Conflict*, Asian Security Studies (Abingdon, Oxon: Routledge, 2008).

47 Holley E. Hansen and Stephen C. Nemeth, 'IO Mediation of Interstate Conflicts: Moving beyond the Global versus Regional Dichotomy', *The Journal of Conflict Resolution* 52, no. 2 (2008): 295–325.
48 Scott Sigmund Gartner, 'Signs of Trouble: Regional Organization Mediation and Civil War Agreement Durability', *The Journal of Politics* 73, no. 2 (2011): 380–90, https://doi.org/10.1017/s0022381611000090.
49 Laurie Nathan, 'How to Manage Interorganizational Disputes over Mediation in Africa', *Global Governance: A Review of Multilateralism and International Organizations* 23, no. 2 (19 August 2017): 151–62, https://doi.org/10.1163/19426720-02302002.
50 Gilbert M. Khadiagala, 'Regionalism and Conflict Resolution: Lessons from the Kenyan Crisis', *Journal of Contemporary African Studies* 27, no. 3 (1 July 2009): 431–44, https://doi.org/10.1080/02589000903118862.
51 Elisabeth Lindenmayer and Josie Lianna Kaye, 'A Choice for Peace? The Story of Forty-One Days of Mediation in Kenya', 21 August 2009, https://www.ipinst.org/2009/08/a-choice-for-peace-the-story-of-forty-one-days-of-mediation-in-kenya.
52 Crossley, 'The African Union and Human Protection: Towards a Regional Protection Regime'.
53 Catherine Jones, 'South East Asian Powers and Contributions to Peacekeeping Operations: UN-ASEAN Partnering for Peace?', *Australian Journal of International Affairs* 74, no. 1 (2 January 2020): 89–107, https://doi.org/10.1080/10357718.2019.1693501.
54 Petar Petrov et al., 'All Hands on Deck: Levels of Dependence between the EU and Other International Organizations in Peacebuilding', *Journal of European Integration* 41, no. 8 (17 November 2019): 1027–43, https://doi.org/10.1080/07036337.2019.1622542.
55 Petrov et al.
56 Malte Brosig, 'Whither a Theory of Inter-Organisational Relations: A Burgeon Field of Research between Conceptual Innovation and Fragmentation', *Journal of Intervention and Statebuilding* 14, no. 2 (14 March 2020): 171–86, https://doi.org/10.1080/17502977.2020.1717133.
57 Petrov et al., 'All Hands on Deck'.
58 Magnus Lundgren, Kseniya Oksamytna, and Katharina P Coleman, 'Only as Fast as Its Troop Contributors: Incentives, Capabilities, and Constraints in the UN's Peacekeeping Response', *Journal of Peace Research*, 29 September 2020, 0022343320940763, https://doi.org/10.1177/0022343320940763.
59 Lundgren, Oksamytna, and Coleman.
60 'Secretary-General's Remarks to Security Council High-Level Debate on Collective Action to Improve UN Peacekeeping Operations | United Nations Secretary-General', https://www.un.org/sg/en/content/sg/statement/2018-03-28/secretary-generals-remarks-security-council-high-level-debate.
61 Paul D. Williams, 'Joining AMISOM: Why Six African States Contributed Troops to the African Union Mission in Somalia', *Journal of Eastern African Studies* 12, no. 1 (2 January 2018): 172–92, https://doi.org/10.1080/17531055.2018.1418159.
62 Walter Lotze and Paul Williams, 'The Surge to Stabilize: Lessons for the UN from the AU's Experience in Somalia', SSRN Scholarly Paper (Rochester, NY: Social Science Research Network, 10 May 2016), https://papers.ssrn.com/abstract=2893349; Paul D. Williams, 'Building the Somali National Army: Anatomy of a Failure, 2008–2018', *Journal of Strategic Studies* 43, no. 3 (15 April 2020): 366–91, https://doi.org/10.1080/01402390.2019.1575210.
63 Matiangai Sirleaf, 'Regionalism, Regime Complexes, and the Crisis in International Criminal Justice', *Columbia Journal of Transnational Law* 54, no. 3 (n.d.): 699–778.
64 Carole J. Petersen, 'Bridging the Gap: The Role of Regional and National Human Rights Institutions in the Asia Pacific', *Asian-Pacific Law and Policy Journal* 13, no. 1 (2012, 2011): 174–209.
65 Céline Martin, 'National Human Rights Institutions in Southeast Asian States: The Necessary Foundation for an Efficient ASEAN Intergovernmental Commission on Human Rights', in *National Human Rights Institutions in Southeast Asia: Selected Case Studies*, ed. James Gomez and Robin Ramcharan (Singapore: Springer, 2020), 37–54, https://doi.org/10.1007/978-981-15-1074-8_3.

66 Sriprapha Petcharamesree, 'Asean Human Rights Regime and Mainstreaming the Responsibility to Protect: Challenges and Prospects', *Global Responsibility to Protect* 8, no. 2–3 (24 May 2016): 133–57, https://doi.org/10.1163/1875984X-00803004.

67 Hien Bui, 'The ASEAN Human Rights System: A Critical Analysis', *Asian Journal of Comparative Law* 11, no. 1 (July 2016): 111–40, https://doi.org/10.1017/asjcl.2016.9.

68 Sirleaf, 'Regionalism, Regime Complexes, and the Crisis in International Criminal Justice'.

69 For a discussion, see Harmen van der Wilt, 'Complementary Jurisdiction (Article 46H)', in *The African Criminal Court: A Commentary on the Malabo Protocol*, ed. Gerhard Werle and Moritz Vormbaum, International Criminal Justice Series (The Hague: T.M.C. Asser Press, 2017), 187–202, https://doi.org/10.1007/978-94-6265-150-0_11.

5 The United Nations

Two questions typically underpin the study of the United Nations and its affiliated institutions (the institutions of the 'UN system'). These questions also relate to the UN's role in responding to conflict, providing or coordinating immediate humanitarian relief, and structural prevention efforts. First, the degree to which the UN and the bodies comprising the organisation and its wider network are independent actors. Does the UN have genuine agency? Second, the extent to which the policies and practices of the UN reflect the interests of powerful states, at the expense of interests of weaker or poorer states. Does the UN serve the interests of powerful states? With regard to protection responsibilities, therefore, two questions are at the centre of thinking about the role of the UN. Can the UN act as a truly impartial actor; and can it promote good protection practice independently and in the best interests of those in need of protection? This chapter addresses these questions, surveying the role of the UN in structural and direct prevention of conflict and humanitarian disaster, and its response to ongoing crisis situations. The chapter also discusses UN reform efforts, and efforts to institutionalise structural prevention in the UN system.

The United Nations, Peacekeeping, and Humanitarian Relief

The United Nations can be described as an 'actor' or as an 'arena'. Conceptualising the UN as an 'actor' implies that the organisation possesses 'agency' – the ability to choose from a set of options, at least to a degree, and to pursue policies independently from national interests of member states. The UN as an 'arena' implies that the UN is no more than the sum of its parts and functions to coordinate the interests and policy preferences of its member states, and in so doing its policy and practice reflect the distribution of the balance of power and influence in the international system. In the latter view, states with greater military capacity, more wealth and diplomatic influence are likely to exert a disproportionate influence over the policy agenda and its implementation at the UN. According to the former view, the organisation will, at the very least, have a moderating effect, constraining its more powerful member states in some areas, and compelling them to behave in line with collective interests in other areas. This debate is salient in the context of humanitarian protection as it is in other issue areas, as will be discussed in this chapter; for example, the extent to which states' interests determine the UN's immediate responses to acute humanitarian protection crises, particularly where the use of force is contemplated and states look to the UN for the authorisation of military measures.

DOI: 10.4324/9781003006671-7

There are, therefore, two schools of thought: one according to which the UN is viewed as an arena with no independent agency, and one according to which the UN bodies – such as the Security Council and the Secretariat – possess agency. Empirical research has sought to observe the practice of international actors, in an effort to gauge how independent these actors are, based on the assumption that if these actors were acting independently of national interest (their actions determined solely by humanitarian need), their responses should be driven by the magnitude of rights violations and the scale of the humanitarian crisis. The literature attempting to address these questions suggests there is evidence both for the UN-as-agent thesis as well as for the UN-as-instrument thesis. Unsurprisingly perhaps, both normative factors and national interests appear to play a role.

In a survey of the UN's responses to humanitarian crises, Melissa Labonte observed that the approaches of the Security Council vary significantly.[1] In some crises, the Council takes a *permissive* approach, employing the full range of response options available to states. In some cases, the Council takes a *satisficing* approach, where responses are shaped by what is deemed appropriate and feasible, rather than guided by need and effectiveness. Finally, in a third category of cases, the Council's approach can be described as *conservative*, where a crisis is framed as an internal affair, and national interests of permanent Council members prevent a more robust response.

Nevertheless, quantitative analysis conducted by Martin Binder of 31 humanitarian crises between 1991 and 2004 has shown that the scale of the humanitarian suffering remains a decisive factor for determining Security Council responses.[2] Therefore, although there is variability in Council responses across cases, responses appear not to be determined by states' interests alone, but apparently are guided by norms. This is corroborated by research by Michael Gilligan and Stephen Stedman showing that the UN acts in line with its stated goals, although it is distinctly biased towards conflict in Europe and the Western hemisphere, and other factors – power, cost, and risk – also play a role.[3]

Still, despite the fact that norms appear to influence policy-making to a degree, that is not to say that the levels and distribution of aid are sufficient and effective in meeting need. Recent research by Andrea Everett, for example, has shown that a majority of emergencies receive limited responses at best by international actors, and where they do, the objectives of the mission are too circumscribed, or where objectives are appropriate to meet humanitarian needs, the resources that are allocated are insufficient.[4] While the multilateralisation of international response efforts has helped sharpen the focus of international responders, the absence of strong private motives for intervening, coupled with a greater need for cooperation among multiple actors, can raise transaction costs (the costs associated with a greater need to coordinate responses) and increase collective action problems (where there is agreement on a desirable response, but individual responsibilities are not clearly defined). The UN's peacekeeping mission in Darfur, conducted jointly with the African Union, serves as an example. Case studies by Limpho A. Heywood, Sadiki Maeresera, and Anup Phayal discuss coordination problems, chronic underfunding and impediments for meeting protection responsibilities (see Box 5.1).[5]

The problem of variability is not limited to the authorisation and implementation of UN peacekeeping operations but permeates the entire spectrum of protection practice. For example, with regard to humanitarian relief, research by Neil Narang has shown that there is variation in the allocation of humanitarian assistance across conflicts, and

Box 5.1 The conflict in Darfur, 2003–2020

The conflict in Darfur illustrates the efforts by the UN of working in partnership with a regional organisation – the African Union (AU). The United Nations – African Union Hybrid Peace Support Operation in Darfur (UNAMID) was established in 2007, four years after the escalation of violence in Sudan's westernmost region. At the local level, the conflict manifested as a clash between settled famers and nomadic tribes over grassland for livestock, but these clashes reflected wider governance issues at the state level that also lay at the heart of conflicts in Sudan's other peripheral regions, South Kordofan and Blue Nile, as well as the secession of South Sudan in 2011. In the absence of avenues for fair representation and equal participation at the national level, the Darfur region had witnessed local unrest prior to the escalation of ethnic violence between Arabs and non-Arabs in the mid-2000s. UNAMID's peacekeeping presence was mired by a lack of cooperation with the Government of Sudan, as well as by insufficient funding. While it was equipped with a Chapter VII mandate providing a robust mandate for civilian protection, and the mission's monitoring and reporting capacity helped lower civilian fatalities by raising the prospect of future criminal prosecution for potential perpetrators, to many analysts, the UN's involvement in Darfur had a mixed record, at best. Following the ousting of president Al-Bashir in 2019 by the Sudanese army and the government's signing of peace agreements with five rebel groups in August 2020, there may be prospects for a more durable peace in future. UNAMID's mandate ended in December 2020. But Darfur remains restive, and longer-term consequences of internal displacement are still felt and continue to occupy humanitarian relief programmes continuing to provide aid in the region.

that political interests, rather than humanitarian need, are often important determinants of international humanitarian assistance. The problem is often worse after a conflict has ended than while it is still ongoing, with aid provided to post-conflict states based on donors' interests.[6] Empirical research on the behaviour of human rights and humanitarian relief organisations has shown that responses vary due to hierarchies among organisations and their need to reconcile normative interests with the availability of material resources.[7]

The provision of humanitarian relief may seem less likely to be influenced by great power politics as it is targeted at populations in need. However, the provision of humanitarian relief by third parties may signal to a domestic and international audience that a government is unable to perform its most basic duties, a powerful symbolic gesture that may undermine the authority of a state. In other instances, humanitarian aid may be intentionally withheld by a government or a de facto authority in order to weaken an opponent. The rules of IHL stipulate that starvation of civilian populations constitutes a war crime,[8] and withholding consent for relief operations constitutes a violation of international humanitarian law, as recognised by the Security Council in resolution 2165 pertaining to Syria.[9] Although disregard of international standards regulating the provision of aid are recognised as crimes under international humanitarian law, humanitarian aid remains a highly politicised field of protection practice. Both giving and denying aid are profoundly political acts.

The politics of humanitarian aid is a salient issue and will be revisited in further detail in Chapter 8. The pertinent question with regard to the UN's agency as an impartial actor is whether humanitarian aid coordinated through the UN is more principled than aid sponsored, or provided by, third parties, including intervening powers. Principled relief prioritises relief where it is needed most, irrespective of political considerations. However, even if an organisation would prioritise the delivery of humanitarian assistance based on need rather than other considerations, more recently the application of human rights-based approaches might mean that humanitarian policy is more attune to political context, resulting in variation in humanitarian policy across cases. The key difference is that the variation in humanitarian policy is not explained by parochial interests of individual states, but – at least in theory, and premised on an assumption that international organisations (IOs) *do* have agency – by consideration of case and context, where intervening actors consider the human rights record of de jure and de facto authorities on the ground. For example, humanitarian organisations could retain the principles of humanity and impartiality, while suspending principles of neutrality towards the parties of a conflict if one of these parties was suspected to be responsible for, or complicit in, human rights violations, and demonstrate flexibility with regard to the principle of independence where the support of one or more powerful protective agents is required to facilitate the provision of humanitarian relief.[10] If the UN was at least a partly autonomous actor – if not financially, then at least operationally – one would assume the implementation of its programmes would be determined solely, or at least primarily, by humanitarian need, rather than the partial interests of powerful states. Humanitarian assistance by the UN is coordinated through the UN Office for the Coordination of Humanitarian Affairs (OCHA), which is premised on the principles of 'humanity, neutrality, impartiality, and independence'. It is noteworthy that independence was added as a core principle at a later stage.[11] The field still lacks empirical research on the extent to which humanitarian relief coordinated by OCHA encourages consistent provision of humanitarian relief. In any case, the degree to which humanitarian agencies can instrumentalise humanitarian relief should not be overstated. For states, as for IOs including the UN, reputation matters and the credibility and esteem of their humanitarian aid departments and policies critically depends on the extent to which their responses are perceived to be driven by humanitarian need rather than political interests.

The same questions around politicisation arise with regard to long-term structural conflict prevention efforts and efforts to build state capacity, though with less urgency than with respect to the use of force and military intervention. However, the academic literature has given ample attention to the potential instrumentalisation of structural prevention and response policies by powerful states, with negative implications for the agency of local actors. For example, donor states may choose to engage with projects in states that are more significant for them in terms of other national interests, for example states with which they have strategic alliances, or where they have specific economic interests. Analysis of donor motives for aid by Maizels and Nissanke has revealed that recipient need better explains the donor behaviour of multilateral aid organisations, whereas donor interest better explains bilateral aid.[12] Assuming a similar logic applies with regard to the implementation of structural conflict prevention and human security programmes, multilateral programmes are less likely to be politicised.

In summary, in the domain of human protection and humanitarianism, as in other domains, the UN is indisputably an actor in its own right; the scope and growing density of its institutional architecture attest to this. The influence of the UN has, over time, fluctuated. Following the end of the Cold War, multilateral organisations became more relevant international actors. In the context of processes of global disintegration, reflected in the waning influence of international institutions, multilaterally coordinated conflict prevention and humanitarian action may be more difficult to realise in the years ahead and require relevant actors, including the UN and its member states, to redouble efforts at maintaining and continuing to develop the nascent international human protection regime.

The Role of the United Nations in a Postcolonial World

While the degree of the UN's independent agency in human protection matters is one point of contention, another concerns the extent to which the UN's involvement constitutes a form of paternalism. The critical perspective that underpins the scholarship that engages with this question is distinct from the discussion above, but related in some ways. If the UN is assumed to be an autonomous actor, can it be criticised for constituting a hegemonic agent? Indeed, critical voices criticise the UN's involvement not only on the grounds that it constitutes a form of paternalism, but also on the grounds that it constitutes a form of great power paternalism. Philip Cunliffe, for example, suggests that 'the responsibility to protect represents a paternalistic model of state power and political authority, embodying the most conservative understanding of political responsibility – responsibility for, rather than responsibility to, people'.[13] This argument constitutes the first dimension of the critical argument: the argument that legitimacy is derived from local authority, and external actors ought to have limited influence over local affairs. The second dimension suggests that UN involvement constitutes a form of great power interference. David Chandler suggests that the development of the Responsibility to Protect principle reflected a new balance of power, 'an attempt to codify and win broader international legitimacy for new interventionist norms'.[14]

Separately, but relatedly, there exists a consequentialist argument that suggests humanitarian outcomes are likely to be better if protection practice is anchored locally or, at the very least, is conducted in local partnership; and a utilitarian argument suggesting that all parties – including the intervening parties and other protective agents – are better off if protective responses are driven from the bottom up or at least incorporate local agents in significant ways. These arguments have been explored in a growing body of empirical literature incorporating both quantitative methods and case study research, focusing on arguments around legitimacy, or arguments pertaining to efficacy.[15] These arguments are sometimes conflated in policy-relevant texts and some of the scholarly literature, but they are grounded in different perspectives and, when taken to their logical conclusion, may result in different policy prescriptions and are therefore each worth understanding in their own right.

The first body of work can be termed the emancipatory approach and suggests that intervention by outside actors lacks legitimacy and that local actors should determine protection responses or at least should have a primary role in their coordination. For example, Elisa Randazzo describes the use of the term 'everyday' in what is now known as the 'local turn' in the scholarship on liberal peacebuilding, and its espousal of approaches to peacebuilding that are bottom-up and driven by local actors, rather than top-down and imposed by outside agents.[16] Roger Mac Ginty describes constructed meanings of the term 'local' and argues that it is made, and remade, by everyday actions, 'a system of beliefs and practices that loose communities and networks may adopt'.[17] This line of research is represented by numerous case studies. Öjendal and Ou outline three stands of critical argument.[18] First, that liberal peacebuilding is too crude an approach that is insensitive to local context and fails therefore to actually contribute to conflict resolution and positive peace. Second, that these interventions routinely follow standard templates and are bureaucratised and insufficiently tailored, therefore, to the case at hand. Third, that liberal peacebuilding as a practice is an expression of a hegemonic world order that is itself to blame for many conflicts, and reproduces these inequalities through hegemonic practice and institutionalised hierarchies between a core of powerful states, and a periphery of dependent states. These arguments have been elucidated through case study research. For example, Toby Dodge describes the application of a liberal peace template in Afghanistan and Iraq, where attempts to transform state-society relations failed to stabilise either state.[19] Similarly, with regard to liberal peacebuilding efforts in Sri Lanka, Goodhand and Walton describe how the simultaneous pursuit of conflict resolution, liberal democracy, and market economy had the unintended effect of bolstering the position of domestic hardliners and provoking defensive responses from nationalists.[20]

A quantitative comparative case study by Doyle and Sambanis, on the other hand, has found that international peacebuilding, where it is tailored to conflicts based on certain parameters, can improve the likelihood that a conflict will be resolved and prevent the recurrence of armed violence.[21] The authors identify three parameters of interest: the degree of hostility among warring factions, measured by the number of total deaths and levels of displacement resulting from the civil war; local capacities, that is, the degree of economic development; and international capacity and commitment, where there is a UN presence with a strong peacekeeping mandate. The study found that more extensive peacebuilding efforts that include efforts at political reform are more successful where the civil war was comparatively less costly in human terms. These more extensive peacebuilding efforts also had higher prospects of success where levels of economic development were relatively higher, and where the UN was involved. While levels of economic development and the nature of the conflict are features of a conflict that are given, the observation that more ambitious peacebuilding efforts have better prospects of success when multilateral actors are involved and committed to a significant degree suggests that international liberal peacebuilding can help prevent conflict recurrence, a finding that stands in contrast to some of the critical case study research outlined above.

However, this empirical observation does not address other normative considerations, pertaining to the effect on local actors' agency and the perceived legitimacy of outsiders' involvement in a conflict. A lack of local legitimacy, David Roberts suggests, undermines popular support.[22] Roberts therefore advances the idea of a 'popular peace' that orients the peacebuilding project towards democratically determined priorities that elevate immediate needs of local populations, including access to food, shelter, and in the longer term, secure forms of income. 'Popular peace', Roberts suggests, is 'genuinely participatory, such that the popular will of society determines the nature of the peace to be built'.[23] Similarly, Oliver Richmond suggests that a 'liberal-local hybridity' may constitute a way of addressing the flaws inherent in the liberal peacebuilding agenda.[24]

Another set of critical arguments revolves around burden-sharing. Peacekeeping and peacebuilding are costly financially for those undertaking them, for both international and local actors. The politics of troop contribution serves as an example. In many cases, troop contribution in line with a UN mandate is a protracted process, and state interests play a role in determining the speed at which a mission can be deployed. A utilitarian argument in favour of local participation might suggest that peacekeeping and peacebuilding is more likely to succeed in a way that is also less costly for all intervening parties when it is conducted in unison with local and regional partners. However, this also risks shifting the burden to weaker parties. From a critical perspective, where international actors have begun coordinating their work with local and regional actors, they have done so to shift responsibilities, and thereby costs, to more proximate actors. For example, David Chandler suggests that by promoting the practice of indirect intervention in co-ordination with regional partners, the Responsibility to Protect principle constitutes 'a mechanism for offloading Western responsibility'.[25]

The arguments discussed above, pertaining to local agency, the need for regional partnership, and the legitimacy of peace processes that are driven by local needs have shaped the debate on intervention and peacebuilding among scholars and practitioners. Two very good works describing in much detail the day-to-day problems associated with top-down peacebuilding practice include Séverine Autesserre's and Sarah von Billerbeck's case studies of peacekeeping efforts in the DRC (see Box 5.2).[26]

This discussion is also reflected in many current policy-relevant texts. The first landmark document operationalising the principle of regionalism as enshrined in Chapter VIII of the UN Charter was a study conducted by the UN in 1999, *Cooperation Between the United Nations and Regional Organizations/Arrangements in a Peacekeeping Environment: Suggested Principles and Mechanisms*.[27] The document suggested that the end of the Cold War had strained the peacekeeping resources of the UN, but encouraged collaboration with regional organisations also on the grounds of better expertise about local affairs and the availability of a local organisation to take over at the end of a mission, providing an exit strategy for UN peacekeeping operations. The report repeatedly emphasised the primary responsibility of the Security Council, and that regional organisations must keep the Council informed; demonstrating that the principle of subsidiarity did not, at that point and from the UN's perspective, frame international multilateral peacekeeping operations. Duplication and competition among organisations should be avoided, the report suggested.

The theme is reflected in more recent policy-relevant texts. For example, the 2019 report of the Secretary-General on the implementation of General Assembly resolution 71/243 on the development of the UN system highlights the need for a comprehensive approach to development, humanitarian action, and peacebuilding, and promotes the distribution of resources in a way that ensures that 'country programmes are anchored in regional contexts, take into account relevant cross-border dimensions and benefit from the large expertise that sits in regional hubs'.[28] A report of the Secretary-General on strengthening the partnership between the UN and the AU on issues of peace and security in Africa, where about half of the UN peacekeeping operations are presently employed, outlined partnerships in peacekeeping operations as well as with regard to projects funded by the UN to enhance transitional justice mechanisms and justice sector reforms, among other programmes.[29] A partnership between the two organisations, the

Box 5.2 The Conflict in the Democratic Republic of Congo (DRC), 1994–2003

Following the Rwandan genocide in 1994 and the flow of refugees to the DRC, a conflict erupted in the DRC that would become known as Africa's first world war. It followed decades of authoritarian rule under Mobutu after the DRC became independent in 1965. The DRC is a country rich in natural resources, a feature understood to explain the proxy war that was fought out in its territory when the conflict escalated. As a consequence of the Rwandan genocide, about two million refugees crossed the border into the DRC, among them many Hutu militias responsible for the genocide in Rwanda. This resulted in conflict spill-over and attacks against Tutsi in the DRC. Rwanda's Tutsi government became involved, backing rival militias that also fought government forces. The Mobutu government was overthrown in 1997, but the conflict did not cease but drew in further states including Uganda, Angola, Namibia, and Zimbabwe. It is estimated that about five million lives were lost in the conflict. The UN's presence there, the United Nations Organization Mission in Democratic Republic of the Congo (MONUC, established in 1999, and replaced by MONUSCO in 2010) was perceived by critical analysts as ineffective, a consequence of its inability to truly comprehend the local conflict. Two seminal studies by Séverine Autesserre and Sarah von Billerbeck outlined these problems in detail. Autesserre describes an international culture of peacekeeping with its own beliefs about local conflict and its causes, that was out of step with local perceptions. Foreign peacekeepers had limited local knowledge, limiting their ability to effectively protect the civilian population. Another critique pertains to the inability of peacekeepers to respond robustly in the face of violence targeting civilians – a common theme echoed in many other cases. The involvement of local actors, Billerbeck suggests, provides legitimacy but may be perceived by foreign peacekeepers as inhibiting an effective response to the conflict. The critical literature suggests that the absence of bottom-up peacebuilding approaches that prioritise the settlement of local disputes through a locally-driven peacebuilding process explains the UN's peacekeeping failure in the DRC. For several years after the end of the war in 2003, fighting continued in the east of the country, with Kigali and Kinshasa backing rival factions. Violent conflict continues in the DRC, and the humanitarian situation remains dire, particularly in Kasai province.

report suggests, 'ensures better coordinated, coherent and effective initiatives to prevent, resolve and manage the increasingly complex peace and security challenges in Africa'.[30] At an institutional level, the UN's Department of Political and Peacebuilding Affairs developed regular 'desk-to-desk' dialogues to improve channels of cooperation with the AU, EU, OAS, and OSCE.[31]

Overall, therefore, the trajectory has been one of increasing international recognition of the role of local ownership and responses that are led or guided by regional partners – not just in theory, but also in practice. It is likely therefore that regional organisations will play an increasingly prominent role in peacekeeping and peacebuilding as well as humanitarian action in the future. Whether these changes will help defuse the critical arguments about hegemonic practices, however, remains to be seen.

UN Reform Proposals

Reform of the United Nations system has been a long-standing policy discussion, following the recognition of the need to better reflect a changing international distribution of power in the UN's key institutions. Security Council reform has been at the heart of the debate, and is especially important given the central role of the Council as the body responsible for addressing issues that threaten international peace and security. Security Council reform is usually associated with formal changes to the structure of the Council. Reform proposals can address the size of the Council as well as the veto power of the members of the Security Council. Discussions may revolve around whether the veto should exist at all and if so, how the power to veto decisions made by the Council should be distributed among Council members. Reform proposals may also address changes in the working methods of the Council, including its procedures – for example, guidelines on best practices for situations in which states should abstain from using their veto. Reform proposals may also address the ways the Council interacts with other bodies and civil society organisations.[32]

There have been various reform proposals of the UN Security Council, however, the Council has only been reformed successfully once, in 1963.[33] This reform expanded the Council to include ten, rather than six, non-permanent members, following an expansion in the number of UN member states. In 1992, after the end of the Cold War, Security Council reform was revisited once again and General Assembly resolution 47/62 invited member states to submit proposals. However, the great number of proposals received required the formation of a working group. The working group proposed the *Razali Plan*, named after Razali Ismail of Malaysia, chairman of the working group. The plan proposed an expansion of the Council by an additional five permanent and four non-permanent seats, including permanent seats for less economically developed states.

Since then, several other proposals have followed. In 2003, a high-level panel report by Kofi Annan proposed two models for reform, for an expansion in the number of seats, and for changes in the duration of Council membership for some seats, respectively, and in either case increasing the Council membership to 24 members. In 2005, the G4 (the Group of Four, consisting of Brazil, Germany, India, and Japan) plan proposed increasing the size of the Council to 25 and again ensuring regional representation. Like the other plans, it did not entail veto powers for new permanent members or non-permanent seats. The 'Uniting for Consensus' plan was a response to the G4 plan and while it supported the idea of increasing the size of the Council to 25, it suggested that new seats should be non-permanent, and called for restrictions on the veto power of permanent states.

Under the Ezulwini Consensus, AU member states endorsed the Responsibility to Protect principle, but suggested regional organisations were best placed to take decisions, although Security Council authorisation should be sought.[34] Under the Ezulwini Consensus, the Council would expand to 26 members, with two permanent seats for Africa, including the power to veto.[35]

However, none of the proposals discussed above is, at present, supported by the permanent five members, or a two-thirds majority of states. Therefore, there have been several proposals for a 'responsibility not to veto' (RN2V), preceded by a long history of thought on the matter of veto restraint.[36] In November 2005, Costa Rica, Liechtenstein, Jordan, Singapore, and Switzerland (the 'Small Five', or 'S5'), circulated a draft resolution on the prevention of the use of the veto in cases of genocide, crimes against humanity, and violations of international humanitarian law. The plan, by contrast to the preceding proposals, envisions no change to the structure of the Council, rather it addresses its working methods, placing particular emphasis on voluntary abstention from the exercise of their power to veto. As a result of the crisis in Syria, in which the Security Council has been deadlocked once again, the idea of 'veto restraint' gained traction. The idea is now supported by numerous states and NGOs, including one permanent state on the Council, France. Meanwhile, the ICISS included the proposal its report, *Responsibility to Protect*. The concept was considered for inclusion in the World Summit Outcome Document of 2005, but given objections by China, Russia, and the United States, was not included in the final document. Since then, the S5, with the support of other states, have continued to press for the adoption of this principle by the Council.

In September 2015, the Accountability, Coherence, and Transparency (ACT) Group, consisting of 27 member states, circulated a draft for a 'Code of Conduct Regarding Security Council Action Against Genocide, Crimes Against Humanity or War Crimes'.[37] The Code of Conduct was aimed at the Security Council in its entirety, including non-permanent members, promoting timely and decisive action by the Council, promoting the formalisation of the principle in a General Assembly resolution. The ACT Code was launched in October 2015, and has garnered the support of 117 member states. Supportive states commit to 'not vote against a credible draft resolution before the Security Council on timely and decisive action to end the commission of genocide, crimes against humanity or war crimes, or to prevent such crimes'.[38] However, of the permanent members of the Council, only two – the United Kingdom and France – have so far signed the Code of Conduct.

Given the difficulties in reform the Council and its working procedures, alternative proposals have focused on other mechanisms for approving decisive multilateral responses. An alternative route for authorising the use of force is through the 'Uniting for Peace' (UforP) mechanism. The UforP mechanism was laid out in a Security Council resolution of 1950,[39] which states that where the Council 'fails to exercise its primary responsibility for the maintenance of international peace and security … the General Assembly shall consider the matter immediately with a view to making appropriate recommendations to Members for collective measures'. The resolution was adopted following vetoes of the Soviet Union on Council resolutions pertaining to the situation in Korea, where, owing to the absence of the Soviet delegate to the Council the Security Council had been able to take substantive decisions – but was no longer able to do so from August 1950, upon the delegates' return to the Council.[40] It is worth noting, however, that General Assembly resolutions are not binding, in contrast to Security Council resolutions. Still, the mechanism allows the General Assembly to discuss an issue pertaining to international peace and security in a special session, and permits the Assembly to make recommendations on responses to such situations. It has, as yet, not been utilised to authorise the use of force; and opinions differ on whether such authorisation would be lawful. The UforP mechanism can also be invoked though a procedural vote of the Security Council, for which nine supporting votes are required, and no veto is possible. A second mechanism for invoking the UforP is through a simple majority vote of the General Assembly calling for special session. Once a special session has been called, the Assembly can then make recommendations on an issue through a two-thirds majority vote. To date, the General Assembly has called ten special sessions under the UforP mechanisms and passed numerous resolutions.[41]

A recent crisis situation that has seen the Council deadlocked by veto has been the crisis in Syria, where Russia and China have vetoed 12 draft resolutions on issues including civilian protection and the use of chemical weapons, including three resolutions authorising measures under Chapter VII of the UN Charter. The justifications for the use of the veto by Russia and China were that both states objected to military intervention and the measures might result in regime change in Syria. The UforP mechanism, Yasmine Nahlawi suggests, might have offered an alternative avenue of expressing the collective will of UN member states for responding to the crisis, and any recommendations articulated by the Assembly would have enjoyed a great degree of legitimacy, given the requirement of a two-thirds majority for the passing of a substantive resolution.[42] Still, the Assembly's authorisation of the use of force has been a more contentious issue. General Assembly resolutions are non-binding, and permanent members of the Security Council have a vested interest in maintaining the Security Council as a sole body able to legitimately authorise the use of force.[43]

The question of Security Council reform – and, especially in the absence of such reform, alternative mechanisms of authorising a wide repertoire of measures for responding to crisis situations – is likely to remain salient and debated themes in the future, particularly when crises emerge and robust collective responses that are able to effectively address the problem are not forthcoming. It may be too soon to tell whether the Assembly will take more robust action in future, becoming active on a greater range of issue pertaining to peace and security where the Council is inactive or unable to reach a decision. It may be that, if concrete reforms of the Council, as outlined above, are not realised in the foreseeable future, the General Assembly will feature more prominently.

As we have seen, Security Council reform, alternative avenues for authorising response measures, and the campaign for the RN2V are parallel initiatives that all aim to accomplish better coordination of global responses to urgent political and humanitarian crises, as well as improved representativeness. RN2V and UforP have emerged because of the structural issues affecting the Security Council's ability to respond, as well as the absence of Council reform that also addresses the issue of the power to veto. With such reform being unlikely, it remains to be seen whether the permanent five members will continue to have sufficient leverage, given changes in the global distribution of power, over other member states to prevent collective responses through the Assembly, in the absence of a Council that is able, and willing, to provide security for populations around the world. Every successive crisis will continue to put the body to the test. Where it is perceived as outdated and unable to respond and rise to present challenges, others may begin to step in.

The UN and Structural Prevention Efforts

Direct prevention efforts – that is, immediate responses to conflict and humanitarian emergency employing the full spectrum of available measures by a host of actors including states, the UN, and civil society – aim to prevent the loss of life by halting killing and violence and mitigating the worst humanitarian effects of conflict. However, for preventing conflict, civilian deaths, and humanitarian crisis, structural prevention efforts are required. International actors including states and international bodies play important roles with regard to structural prevention. 'Structural prevention', essentially, falls into two categories. First, efforts to prevent conflict and humanitarian emergency by bringing about structural changes that make them less likely, such as addressing inequalities, the promotion of positive peace, democracy and good governance. Second, efforts related to the implementation of policies and institutionalisation of practices that promote reliable response mechanisms to conflict and humanitarian emergency when they emerge. When we refer to structural prevention efforts in this context, mostly we are referring to the institutionalisation of prevention.

In recent years, policymakers have put substantial efforts into institutionalisation of atrocity prevention within the UN system.[44] Two primary avenues have been pursued for strengthening the protection regime in structural ways. First, through a strengthening of international institutional capacity for supporting states in meeting their primary Responsibility to Protect through improving state capacity and promoting the rule of law, and, secondly, a crimes-based approach oriented towards strengthening the institutions associated with international criminal justice, in response to suspected violations of human rights and international humanitarian law. Several institutions, in particular, have begun institutionalising protection responsibilities in recent years. These include, in addition to the Security Council and the General Assembly, the Secretariat and the Human Rights Council. The promotion of norms and the institutionalisation of direct prevention practices is conducted by permanent offices at the Secretariat, including the Office on Genocide Prevention and the Responsibility to Protect. The office engages with member states and civil society organisations, and in recent years has promoted the conceptual development of R2P and promoted protection norms. The office also draws up the annual reports of the Secretary-General on R2P, coordinates the General Assembly's annual Informal Interactive Dialogue on the Responsibility to Protect, and provides early warning for emerging crises, as well as engaging in behind-the-scenes preventive diplomacy. The Situational Awareness Briefings of the Secretariat alert the Security Council to situations of concern. The Department for Peacebuilding and Political Affairs (DPPA) is a principal body for the coordination of the UN's responses to ongoing crises and peacebuilding after conflicts have ended.

Another body, the UN Peacebuilding Commission (PBC), was established following the World Summit of 2005 as a subsidiary body to the UN's Economic and Social Council (ECOSOC) and the UN Security Council. Its role is to aid the recovery and rebuilding after conflict has ended, through Disarmament, Demobilisation, and Reintegration (DDR), political and economic reforms, and the support of transitional justice mechanisms, a role all the more significant given that a majority of civil wars are recurring wars where a state has relapsed into conflict. Given that the 'responsibility to rebuild' is a core responsibility within the wider R2P framework as conceptualised by the ICISS, the PBC occupies a central role with regard to the UN's structural prevention efforts, notwithstanding that owing to the body's status as subsidiary to two organisations, its functioning has been hampered by confusion and duplication.[45]

Another recent initiative is Sustainable Development Goal (SDG) number 16, 'peace, justice, and strong institutions'.[46] The initial proposal for the inclusion of this goal had included reference to the term 'security', but middle income states objected to the inclusion of the term on the grounds that it might facilitate interference in the sovereign affairs of states.[47] Targets associated with this goal include broad aims, such as reducing violence; the promotion of the rule of law; the promotion of representative decisions-making at all levels; and strengthening the participation of developing countries in institutions of global governance. The 12 targets listed under SDG 16 also include more specific objectives, such as ending trafficking and all forms of violence against children; a significant reduction in the flow of illicit arms; and the provision of a legal identity, including birth registration, for all by 2030. SDG 16 reinforces rights enshrined in the International Covenant on Civil and Political Rights (ICCPR) and differs in this regard to other SDGs, which are anchored in the International Covenant on Economic, Social and Cultural Rights (ICESCR). As with the Responsibility to Protect principle, SDG 16 does not create new legal obligations, but strengthens existing legal obligations. Language associated with SDG 16 has been adopted in General Assembly and Security Council documents, as well as in reports of the UN Secretary-General documents, and has, to some degree, been successfully institutionalised within the UN system, although the record has been mixed. The greatest influence of SDG 16 has been with regard to the work of the United Nations Development Programme (UNDP). A joint programme by the Department of Political Affairs (DPA) and UNDP focuses on building national capacities for conflict prevention. Funding problems have limited progress on SDG 16, and current projections suggest that it is unlikely to SDG 16 targets will be achieved on time. There are 23 indicators for the SDG 16; however, measuring these is difficult, owing, in part, to limited availability of data. Nevertheless, in spite of these problems, SDG 16 suggests further institutionalisation of the wider protection agenda, providing another means of operationalising structural prevention.

In sum, the record of the UN in promoting structural prevention efforts has been mixed. On the one hand, the language of protection and responsibility is being used more widely, in a range of contexts, and there has been measurable progress with regard to institutionalisation, reflected in the creation of the post of Special Adviser on R2P and the annual report of the Secretary-General on R2P, as well as the annual informal, interactive dialogue on R2P at the General Assembly. Inclusion of the protection agenda in the work of the peacebuilding apparatus of the UN, as well as the inclusion of peace, justice, and strong institutions as a Sustainable Development Goal suggest the wider protection agenda has gained traction across the UN system, also with regard to structural prevention broadly conceived; prevention that addresses issues that increase the risk of conflict and violence. On the other hand, funding problems and inability to monitor progress constitute ongoing obstacles in the implementation of structural prevention.

The preceding discussion has shown that, in spite of the limitations outlined above, the UN is a significant actor in the domain of civilian protection and humanitarian relief – not only with regard to high-level politics at the Security Council, but also with regard to the mainstreaming of the protection agenda in the day-to-day activities of the UN's affiliated bodies. The UN plays an important role in coordinating collective responses where these are possible, as well as through its policy work and the role of the Secretariat and its offices, acting as the world's conscience and an independent voice speaking out on issues of humanity's greatest concern. After having surveyed the role of states and regional organisations and the UN in Chapters 4 and 5, respectively, the next chapter now turns to the role of civil society organisations in advancing the protection agenda and institutionalising protection practices. The United Nations Office for Partnerships supports the meeting of SDG Goals, including Goal 16, through partnerships between the private sector and foundations and serves as an operational interface. Similarly, OCHA, the UN's humanitarian agency, works in partnership with civil society organisations.

Summary

- The UN may be conceptualised as an actor, or as an arena. When conceptualising the UN as an actor, the bodies and offices based in New York (the UN Secretariat, the Security Council, the UN Office on Genocide Prevention and the Responsibility to Protect) and Geneva (the United Nations Human Rights Council) are perceived as having independent agency. By contrast, the UN understood as an arena is no more than the sum of its constituent parts. In this understanding, influential states decide UN policy, and the UN's offices and bodies (such as the UN Secretariat) have little or no actual influence.
- Numerous authors have flagged that the practice of protection constitutes a form of paternalism. Local involvement in conflict response and mitigation, as well as regional support for a host of peacekeeping and peacebuilding activities have been suggested as possible remedies.
- The outdated institutional architecture of the UN has been made responsible for the inability of states to work through the UN in pursuit of humanitarian objectives in an effective way, inhibiting the development of a robust normative framework. Numerous Security Council reform proposals have been tabled. One of these suggests that the Council has a Responsibility Not To Veto (RN2V).
- Various UN bodies promote the structural prevention of conflict and support immediate responses to acute human protection crises. Structural prevention entails addressing factors that make conflict and humanitarian disaster more likely in order to prevent conflicts from happening in the first place; and building institutional capacity for rapid responses to emerging crises when conflicts do occur.

Questions for Reflection

- *Does the UN have agency with regard to conflict management and crisis response?*
- *What are the advantages and disadvantages of regionally-driven protection responses?*
- *Can robust protection norms emerge despite the institutional shortcomings of the UN?*
- *Can the UN succeed in strengthening structural prevention efforts in light of weakening global disengagement from multilateral cooperation?*

Further reading

- Butchard, P.M. (2020): *The Responsibility to Protect and the Failures of the United Nations Security Council* (Oxford: Hart).

- Foley, Conor (2018): *UN Peacekeeping Operations and the Protection of Civilians: Saving Succeeding Generations* (Cambridge: Cambridge University Press).
- Foot, Rosemary (2020): *China, the UN, and Human Protection: Beliefs, Power, Image* (Oxford: Oxford University Press).
- Gill, Peter (2016): *Today We Drop Bombs, Tomorrow We Build Bridges: How Foreign Aid Became a Casualty of War* (London: Zed Books).
- Lischer, Sarah Kanyon (2005): *Dangerous Sanctuaries: Refugee Camps, Civil War, and the Dilemmas of Humanitarian Aid* (Ithaca and London: Cornell University Press).
- Lowe, Vaughan, ed. (2010): *The United Nations Security Council and War: The Evolution of Thought and Practice since 1945* (Oxford: Oxford University Press).
- Mac Ginty, Roger (2011): *International Peacebuilding and Local Resistance: Hybrid Forms of Peace* (Houndmills, Basingstoke: Palgrave).
- Tistounet, Eric (2020): *The UN Human Rights Council: A Practical Anatomy* (Cheltenham: Edward Elgar Publishing).

Notes

1 Melissa T. Labonte, 'Whose Responsibility to Protect? The Implications of Double Manifest Failure for Civilian Protection', *The International Journal of Human Rights* 16, no. 7 (1 October 2012): 982–1002.

2 Martin Binder, 'Paths to Intervention: What Explains the UN's Selective Response to Humanitarian Crises? – Martin Binder, 2015', *Journal of Peace Research*, 16 July 2015.

3 Michael Gilligan and Stephen John Stedman, 'Where Do the Peacekeepers Go?', *International Studies Review* 5, no. 4 (1 December 2003): 37–54.

4 Andrea L. Everett, *Humanitarian Hypocrisy: Civilian Protection and the Design of Peace Operations* (Ithaca and London: Cornell University Press, 2018).

5 Limpho A. Heywood and Sadiki Maeresera, 'Analysis of the United Nations – African Union Hybrid Peace Support Operations in Darfur', *Journal of African Union Studies* 8, no. 2 (1 August 2019): 119–34, https://doi.org/10.31920/2050-4306/2019/8n2a7; Anup Phayal, 'UN Troop Deployment and Preventing Violence Against Civilians in Darfur', *International Interactions* 45, no. 5 (3 September 2019): 757–80, https://doi.org/10.1080/03050629.2019.1593161.

6 Neil Narang, 'Forgotten Conflicts: Need versus Political Priority in the Allocation of Humanitarian Aid across Conflict Areas', *International Interactions* 42, no. 2 (14 March 2016): 189–216, https://doi.org/10.1080/03050629.2016.1080697.

7 Sarah S. Stroup and Wendy H. Wong, 'Leading Authority as Hierarchy among INGOs', in *Hierarchies in World Politics*, ed. Ayşe Zarakol (Cambridge University Press, 2017), 175–97; Alexander Cooley and James Ron, 'The NGO Scramble: Organizational Insecurity and the Political Economy of Transnational Action', *International Security* 27, no. 1 (1 July 2002): 5–39.

8 Dapo Akande and Emanuela-Chiara Gillard, 'Conflict-Induced Food Insecurity and the War Crime of Starvation of Civilians as a Method of Warfare: The Underlying Rules of International Humanitarian Law', *Journal of International Criminal Justice* 17 (2019): 753.

9 Sandesh Sivakumaran, 'Arbitrary Withholding of Consent to Humanitarian Assistance in Situations of Disaster', *International & Comparative Law Quarterly* 64, no. 3 (July 2015): 501–31, https://doi.org/10.1017/S0020589315000184.

10 A good discussion of these principles can be found in Ed Schenkenberg van Mierop, 'Coming Clean on Neutrality and Independence: The Need to Assess the Application of Humanitarian Principles', *International Review of the Red Cross* 97 (2015): 295–318.

11 Andreas Øien Stensland and Ole Jacob Sending, 'Unpacking the "Culture of Protection": A Political Economy Analysis of OCHA and the Protection of Civilians', Security in Practice (NUPI, 2011), 16.
12 Alfred Maizels and Machiko K. Nissanke, 'Motivations for Aid to Developing Countries', *World Development* 12, no. 9 (1 September 1984): 879–900, https://doi.org/10.1016/0305–750X(84)90046-9.
13 Philip Cunliffe, 'The Responsibility to Protect: The Rise of Liberal Authoritarianism', *Handbook of Critical International Relations*, 3 February 2020.
14 David Chandler, 'The Responsibility to Protect? Imposing the "Liberal Peace"', *International Peacekeeping* 11, no. 1 (1 March 2004): 59–81, https://doi.org/10.1080/1353331042000228454.
15 Hanna Leonardsson and Gustav Rudd, 'The "Local Turn" in Peacebuilding: A Literature Review of Effective and Emancipatory Local Peacebuilding', *Third World Quarterly* 36, no. 5 (4 May 2015): 825–39, https://doi.org/10.1080/01436597.2015.1029905.
16 Elisa Randazzo, 'The Paradoxes of the "Everyday": Scrutinising the Local Turn in Peace Building', *Third World Quarterly* 37, no. 8 (2 August 2016): 1351–70, https://doi.org/10.1080/01436597.2015.1120154.
17 Roger Mac Ginty, 'Where Is the Local? Critical Localism and Peacebuilding', *Third World Quarterly* 36, no. 5 (4 May 2015): 840–56, https://doi.org/10.1080/01436597.2015.1045482.
18 Joakim Öjendal and Sivhouch Ou, 'The "Local Turn" Saving Liberal Peacebuilding? Unpacking Virtual Peace in Cambodia', *Third World Quarterly* 36, no. 5 (4 May 2015): 929–49, https://doi.org/10.1080/01436597.2015.1030387.
19 Toby Dodge, 'Intervention and Dreams of Exogenous Statebuilding: The Application of Liberal Peacebuilding in Afghanistan and Iraq', *Review of International Studies* 39, no. 5 (2013): 1189–1212.
20 Jonathan Goodhand and Oliver Walton, 'The Limits of Liberal Peacebuilding? International Engagement in the Sri Lankan Peace Process', *Journal of Intervention and Statebuilding* 3, no. 3 (1 November 2009): 303–23, https://doi.org/10.1080/17502970903086693.
21 Michael W. Doyle and Nicholas Sambanis, 'International Peacebuilding: A Theoretical and Quantitative Analysis', *American Political Science Review* 94, no. 4 (n.d.): 779–801.
22 David Roberts, 'Post-Conflict Peacebuilding, Liberal Irrelevance and the Locus of Legitimacy', *International Peacekeeping* 18, no. 4 (1 August 2011): 410–24, https://doi.org/10.1080/13533312.2011.588388.
23 Roberts, 415.
24 Oliver P. Richmond, 'Becoming Liberal, Unbecoming Liberalism: Liberal-Local Hybridity via the Everyday as a Response to the Paradoxes of Liberal Peacebuilding', *Journal of Intervention and Statebuilding* 3, no. 3 (1 November 2009): 324–44, https://doi.org/10.1080/17502970903086719.
25 David Chandler, 'Book Review Essay: The Paradox of the "Responsibility to Protect": David Chandler Gareth Evans, The Responsibility to Protect: Ending Mass Atrocity Crimes Once and for All. Washington, DC: The Brookings Institution, 2008. 348 pp. Alex Bellamy, Responsibility to Protect: The Global Effort to End Mass Atrocities. London: Polity, 2009. *Cooperation and Conflict* 45, no. 1 (1 March 2010): 134, https://doi.org/10.1177/0010836709352802.
26 Séverine Autesserre, *The Trouble with the Congo: Local Violence and the Failure of International Peacebuilding*, Cambridge Studies in International Relations (Cambridge: Cambridge University Press, 2010), https://doi.org/10.1017/CBO9780511761034; Sarah B.K. von Billerbeck, *Whose Peace?: Local Ownership and United Nations Peacekeeping* (Oxford, New York: Oxford University Press, 2016).
27 United Nations Department of Peacekeeping Operations, 'Cooperation between the United Nations and Regional Organizations/Arrangements in a Peacekeeping Environment: Suggested Principles And Mechanisms', March 1999.
28 United Nations General Assembly, 'Implementation of General Assembly Resolution 71/243 on the Quadrennial Comprehensive Policy Review of Operational Activities for Development of the United Nations System', 2019, 24.
29 United Nations Security Council, 'Strengthening the Partnership between the United Nations and the African Union on Issues of Peace and Security in Africa, Including on the

Work of the United Nations Office to the African Union', Report of the Secretary-General, 2018.
30 United Nations Security Council, 15.
31 United Nations Political and Peacebuilding Affairs, 'Partnerships and Cooperation | Department of Political and Peacebuilding Affairs', https://dppa.un.org/en/partnerships-and-cooperation.
32 A detailed discussion of Security Council reform is provided in Bjarke Zinck Winther, 'A Review of the Academic Debate about United Nations Security Council Reform', *The Chinese Journal of Global Governance* 6, no. 1 (6 April 2020): 71–101, https://doi.org/10.1163/23525207-12340047.
33 These are outlined in Brian Cox, 'United Nations Security Council Reform: Collected Proposals and Possible Consequences', *South Carolina Journal of International Law and Business* 6, no. 1 (2009): 89–128.
34 Thomas Kwasi Tieku, 'A Pan-African View of a New Agenda for Peace', *International Journal* 67, no. 2 (Spring 2012): 373–89.
35 Shashi Tharoor, 'Security Council Reform: Past, Present, and Future', *Ethics & International Affairs* 25, no. 4 (2011): 397–406.
36 John Heieck, 'The Responsibility Not to Veto Revisited. How the Duty to Prevent Genocide as a Jus Cogens Norm Imposes a Legal Duty Not to Veto on the Five Permanent Members of the Security Council', in *Beyond Responsibility to Protect: Generating Change in International Law*, ed. Barnes Richard and Tzevelekos Vassilis, vol. 16 (Cambridge: Intersentia, 2016), 103–22, https://doi.org/10.1017/9781780687483.007; Jean-Baptiste Jeangène Vilmer, 'The Responsibility Not to Veto: A Genealogy', *Global Governance: A Review of Multilateralism and International Organizations* 24, no. 3 (12 September 2018): 331–49, https://doi.org/10.1163/19426720-02403003.
37 United Nations General Assembly and United Nations Security Council, 'Code of Conduct Regarding Security Council Action Against Genocide, Crimes Against Humanity or War Crimes', 2015.
38 'Code of Conduct Regarding Security Council Action against Genocide, Crimes against Humanity or War Crimes', Global Centre for the Responsibility to Protect, https://www.globalr2p.org/resources/code-of-conduct-regarding-security-council-action-against-genocide-crimes-against-humanity-or-war-crimes/.
39 United Nations General Assembly, 'Uniting for Peace', 3 November 1950.
40 Keith S. Petersen, 'The Uses of the Uniting for Peace Resolution since 1950', *International Organization* 13, no. 2 (1959): 219–32.
41 United Nations General Assembly, 'Emergency Special Sessions', General Assembly of the United Nations (United Nations), https://www.un.org/en/ga/sessions/emergency.shtml.
42 Yasmine Nahlawi, 'Overcoming Russian and Chinese Vetoes on Syria through Uniting for Peace', *Journal of Conflict and Security Law* 24, no. 1 (1 April 2019): 111–43.
43 Nicholas Wheeler, 'Operationalising the Responsibility to Protect: The Continuing Debate over Where Authority Should Be Located for the Use of Force', 2008.
44 A comprehensive survey and discussion is provided in Cecilia Jacob, 'R2P as an Atrocity-Prevention Framework: Concepts and Institutionalization at the Global Level', in *Implementing the Responsibility to Protect: A Future Agenda* (Abingdon, Oxon: Routledge, 2020).
45 Srinjoy Bose and Ramesh Thakur, 'The UN Secretary-General and the Forgotten Third R2P Responsibility', *Global Responsibility to Protect* 8 (2016): 343–65.
46 United Nations, 'Sustainable Development Goals', https://www.un.org/sustainabledevelopment/.
47 The origins and institutionalisation of SDG 16 are discussed in Alexandra Ivanovic, Hannah Cooper, and Athena M. Nguyen, 'Institutionalisation of SDG 16: More a Trickle than a Cascade?', *Social Alternatives* 37, no. 1 (2018): 49–57.

6 Humanitarian Organisations and Civil Society

Chapters 4 and 5 discussed the agency of states, regional organisations, and the UN and the legitimacy of protective responses by these intervening actors. Chapter 5 now turns to the role of civil society actors: humanitarian organisations and other civil society actors including human rights organisations. Like for states and international organisations, the work of these non-state organisations falls into two categories: work on policy and the institutionalisation of protective and aid practices; and, second, the provision of immediate aid in crisis situations. Whereas the main scholarly questions with regard to states and international organisations pertain to the degree of their agency, autonomy, influence, and independent decision-making capacity, the main scholarly questions with regard to humanitarian and other civil society organisations pertain – for human rights organisations – to the extent to which their policy work strengthens the human rights and human protection regimes and deters human rights violations and – for humanitarian organisations – the extent to which their responses can, and should, be neutral towards the parties to a conflict in a given protection crisis. This chapter looks, first, at the latter question – the role of humanitarian organisations – and then discusses the role of human rights organisations and concludes with a summary of key changes in the nature of advocacy and relief work in recent years.

Humanitarian Organisations, Aid, and Neutrality

As outlined in Chapter 3, the emergence of human rights-based approaches has changed the range of available policy choices for humanitarian organisations, which are now political actors in their own right with a greater degree of autonomy. Humanitarian organisations are no longer simply providers of relief – provisional shelter, food, and medical treatment and supplies – but also political actors who have begun to attune their policies to the wider impact and longer-term consequences of their actions. However, the degree to which these developments have changed actual humanitarian practice is debatable – while humanitarian organisations have become vocal on human rights questions and seek to demonstrate sensitivity to political context, their practice, arguably, is still very much determined by the humanitarian imperative alone – and rightly so according to some scholars (this will be discussed in more detail in Chapter 8). But different organisations have adopted different policies. What follows below is a brief survey of the ICRC and MSF, both of which dominate the humanitarian aid sector and are respected for upholding principles of neutrality and independence.

DOI: 10.4324/9781003006671-8

The ICRC's headquarters are in Geneva. The organisation is presently active in more than 90 countries and it describes its work as 'neutral, impartial, and independent'.[1] It provides aid to civilians in armed conflict, including in response to natural disasters that occur in the context of armed conflict. Its activities are now comprehensive, spanning traditional tasks such as the provision of humanitarian relief including shelter, food, and medical supplies, as well as sanitation and water supply, support for the private sector and commercial activities in conflict zones, addressing sexual violence, human rights and international humanitarian law advocacy, humanitarian diplomacy, and more recently a virtual reality unit tasked with assessing how virtual reality can be used to educate about international humanitarian law. It is a leading actor for humanitarian diplomacy, whereby it engages in private and confidential dialogue with victims, authorities, and non-state armed groups. It works at different levels with military and administrative staff, as well as other humanitarian and human rights organisations, to bring about better conditions for people affected by conflict and to urge parties to a conflict to adhere to international humanitarian law.[2]

MSF was founded later than the ICRC in 1971, motivated by a desire to implement humanitarian objectives in a way that was sensitive to wider consequences of the provision of aid. MSF describes itself as an 'international, independent medical organisation'.[3] Its work goes beyond the provision of medical aid in the context of armed conflict, including the provision of medical assistance to people affected by epidemics and disasters, as well as people excluded from regular healthcare. MSF provides medical care and emergency relief in more than 70 states and operates a large supply and logistics network. The organisation conducts its work in the spirit of 'ethical reflexivity', meaning that it is more prepared to consider the consequences of a neutral approach and prepared to change its course of action, if a neutral posture is deemed ethically unsupportable.[4] MSF criticised the exploitation of humanitarian relief to support forced relocations in Ethiopia in 1985. Several years later, the French section of MSF ceased operations in then Zaire following the genocide in Rwanda, when perpetrators of the genocide threatened to use the camps as a base for launching attacks against a new government in Rwanda. MSF is committed to 'témoignage', a French term that means 'to bear witness', and regards this as a core responsibility in addition to its medical relief aid. Because MSF spearheaded the movement to promote ethically reflexive humanitarianism, these developments signalled changes in humanitarian practice in which humanitarian aid organisations became aware of the need to consider the ethical consequences of neutrality.

The four core principles upon which humanitarian relief work is premised are distinct from each other and each can be assessed on its own terms.[5] While impartiality and humanity constitute fundamental, general principles of humanitarian relief work, neutrality and impartiality are relational concepts that denote a particular relationship with a client or a principal, respectively. Humanity means that humanitarian action is guided by the objective of alleviating human suffering. Impartiality means that the provision of humanitarian relief should be proportional to need, such that relief is provided where it is needed most. The principle of neutrality suggests humanitarian actors should desist from making political statements. Finally, the principle of independence encompasses political, financial, and operational independence and seeks to ensure that the provision of humanitarian relief is not influenced by considerations other than purely humanitarian ones. At a theoretical level, it is apparent that these principles can contravene each other, and in practice, this results in harrowing dilemmas for humanitarian agencies. For example, the UN acknowledges that it is dependent on funding by its member states, and emphasises the need for operational independence. For some organisations, such as ICRC and MSF that are large, well-respected and attract large volumes of funding by donors, independence can be realised, given that these organisations are in receipt of funding from diverse donors. For smaller organisations that rely on a small number of donors, this is not feasible. Similarly, with regard to neutrality, organisations' ability to operate effectively depends critically on the way they are perceived by all parties to a conflict. On the other hand, where need is higher for one party to a conflict, placating another party by providing relief may infringe on the principle of impartiality, given that aid should be prioritised according to need. Neutrality may also interfere with accountability and justice, when organisations refrain from speaking up about violations of human rights and international humanitarian law by parties to a conflict; thus also failing to help maintain and progress international norms relating to international criminal justice and accountability.

The problem is depicted well in the discussion about the extent to which humanitarian and development aid institutions can and should be independent of donor states and national foreign offices. Donor states may make funding conditional on humanitarians' support for foreign policy priorities, limiting their autonomy.[6] States have numerous reasons for giving aid, and aid can take numerous forms beyond humanitarian aid.[7] State foreign aid can be used as an inducement, aimed at changing the behaviour of recipient states. It can also be used as a threat, where the withdrawal of funding may be threatened in order to influence the behaviour of the recipient state. Aid may be used to fund humanitarian assistance, or infrastructure projects or aid may be fungible, where funding is provided to a recipient state without specification of its purpose. Aid may be disbursed bilaterally, or through multilateral institutions. For states, the advantage of bilateral disbursement is greater control over the use of the funds. In recent years, the number of states participating in foreign aid programmes has increased beyond a group of traditional donor states, and foreign aid has become an international practice. The practice of foreign aid permits states to strengthen their relations with other states, attempt to influence the behaviour of other states, and increases a states' international standing.

From a normative perspective, the critique of the instrumentalisation of foreign aid as a tool of foreign policy is grounded in the humanitarian principle that the provision of humanitarian aid should be based on need, and need alone, not driven by geostrategic and commercial interests. On the other hand, a more pragmatic normative argument suggests that given limited resources of states and non-governmental organisations that depend on funding by states and private donors, aid must necessarily be selective and given that demand for aid surpasses its supply, it matters less that funding is directed where it also aligns with other interests. Furthermore, a realist argument in support of strategic humanitarianism suggests that those responsible for the causes of humanitarian suffering themselves act strategically, bringing about forced migration and threatening to escalate a humanitarian crisis through counterinsurgency or rebel action, so that humanitarians will only accomplish their goals if they adopt similarly strategic tactics and humanitarians should be, Jack Snyder suggests, 'self-consciously political'.[8]

However, it may be possible that even state-funded aid can advance humanitarian principles in a way that is, at least most of the time, principled. Critics may overemphasise the degree to which humanitarian aid is actually driven by private interests.

States may seek to maintain their standing among other states by developing a reputation for impartial assistance. Recent empirical research has found that states' reasons for providing humanitarian aid vary,[9] a finding that is also echoed with regard to intervention decisions.[10]

In articulating policies, humanitarian organisations need to consider whether to adopt human rights-based approaches to humanitarian aid or to adhere to strict interpretations of neutrality. On the one hand, the provision of aid that is not sensitive to conflict dynamics may inadvertently lengthen conflict duration. Several causal mechanisms for this have been proposed in the literature.[11] First, a conflict may be lengthened owing to the provision of material resources needed by parties to a conflict for continued fighting. For example, humanitarian aid organisations may not be able to distinguish between civilians and combatants, inadvertently providing material support to rebel groups. Second, humanitarian safe zones can provide combatants with a space for rest and the recruitment of other combatants. Third, humanitarian relief can lower the costs of continued fighting by making the maintenance of local political support affordable for combatants, lowering the incentive to cease fighting. Fourth, the prolonged provision of humanitarian relief can create a relief industry that incentivises the continuation of the conflict. Local services may cater to the needs of humanitarians, providing a source of income that depends on the aid industry. Fifth, the provision of aid to fighting groups may make it more difficult for belligerents to assess the relative strength of their enemy. The strategic studies literature suggests that incomplete information about capacities makes it more likely that armed factions continue fighting. This is commonly referred to as the 'commitment problem'.[12] By lowering the amount of information pertaining to the strength of either party it may therefore be more difficult for both parties to reach a peace agreement. A fighting party may calculate it has more to win (or less to lose) by continued fighting, and testing the strength and resolve of the opponent, than by laying down their arms.

However, caution is called for in drawing policy conclusions from these theoretical propositions. It would be too quick to jump to the conclusion that humanitarian relief is counter-productive. In some cases, humanitarian aid may not serve to lengthen conflict and even assuming it lengthened a conflict, the relief provided may still lower overall conflict fatalities.[13] Moreover, from an ethical perspective, it is questionable whether standing idly by is ever a viable choice for humanitarians, irrespective of consequentialist calculations.

Still, the acknowledgement that humanitarian action may sometimes have unintended negative consequences has led to increasing interest in strategies for mitigating the risk of negative consequences.[14] In addition to the 'do no harm' principle and human rights-based approaches to humanitarian policy and action, practical measures proposed include steps designed to prevent the instrumentalisation of humanitarian relief by parties to a conflict, including improved methods of accounting for the use of the aid provided. Still, the conundrum is inherent in humanitarian action and humanitarians' purpose remains, in the first instance, to relieve human suffering, all the more so in light of the difficulty of predicting the consequences of the provision of aid. Nevertheless, some humanitarian organisations are more vocal than others. To some extent, 'classic humanitarianism' and the 'new humanitarianism' operate side by side, with some organisations being more vocal, and some remaining silent and maintaining a neutral position. MSF is a good example of an organisation that is more prepared to be vocal on rights violations,[15] but neutrality remains a key principle for all humanitarian organisations.

While the ICRC and MSF are prominent actors in the humanitarian domain, they operate in a complex ecosystem of humanitarian organisations, states, regional organisations, and UN agencies, as will be discussed further on. Therefore, the ICRC and MSF can be understood as key organisations in a broader humanitarian industry that incorporates both state-based and non-state organisations. The boundaries between the two exist in theory more than they do in practice, given pre-existing funding streams and the networked nature of the humanitarian aid industry. A good example is the recent humanitarian response to the conflict in Yemen, where the ICRC has engaged in humanitarian diplomacy and where, despite internal debate, organisations have had no choice but to accept funds from wealthy donor states party to the conflict (see Box 6.1).[16] The practice of humanitarians is, to a large extent, dictated by political realities on the ground. Nevertheless, core principles of humanitarianism still guide their work. Many organisations have adopted human rights-based approaches and take responsibility for publicising the plight of the victims of armed conflict and, in some cases, pointing to violations of international humanitarian law by parties to a conflict, but traditional principles of humanitarianism – humanity, impartiality, and neutrality – continue to guide their work. Human rights organisations – surveyed in the following section – do not need to negotiate access to affected populations and do not share this constraint.

Human Rights Advocacy and Naming and Shaming

The previous section surveyed ethical and practical dilemmas for humanitarian organisations. The work of human rights organisations has given rise to a different set of issues receiving scholarly attention. While the degree to which humanitarians should remain neutral in a conflict is a debated topic with regard to humanitarian relief work, human rights advocacy groups are not faced with the same dilemmas. Their work is inherently political. Human rights organisations' mandate has two dimensions: first, to promote good international practice in accordance with established human rights norms and international humanitarian law, and, second, to promote the further development of international law to guarantee protections of individuals and groups in peacetime as well as in armed conflict. As such, human rights organisations can call out human rights violations by governments or non-state armed groups. Although human rights organisations are not neutral in that they confront suspected human rights violations, they do so in an impartial way, such that violations of human rights and international humanitarian law of all parties to a conflict are recorded and publicised.

The most well-known human rights organisations are Amnesty International (AI), Human Rights Watch (HRW), and the International Federation for Human Rights (IFHR), all of which were established in the 20th century. The origins of Amnesty International are a good example of the role of individuals and networks in establishing transnational civil society organisations. Similar to the founding history of the ICRC and MSF, AI emerged as a result of norm entrepreneurship of a small number of dedicated individuals that become internationally active and promoted new ideas and approaches to pressing human rights and humanitarian issues.[17] AI began as a network of individuals promoting the recognition of a need for stronger human rights guarantees following an article, in 1961, by a London lawyer, Peter Benenson, about

Box 6.1 Yemen, 2015–Present

Yemen has been described as the world's worst current humanitarian emergency. A large number of civilians have been affected by the direct consequence of armed conflict and the indirect consequences of armed conflict, including displacement, access to clean water and sanitation, as well as food and medical supplies. The crisis is the result of a protracted conflict that intensified with the beginning of the Shia insurgency comprising Houthi and other factions in 2004. Fighting continued in the following years and in 2014, the rebels took control of Sanaa, the capital, and were seeking to take more territory. In response, a coalition of predominantly Gulf Arab states, led by Saudi Arabia, supported by the United States, began an air campaign against the rebels. Civilians have been hard-hit by the conflict as a consequence of bombardment of urban areas and the blockade of goods. Coalition bombings have hit MSF hospitals, WFP trucks, and have damaged the state's logistical infrastructure, compounding the humanitarian crisis. As a consequence, the majority of the population is affected by chronic hunger. A cholera outbreak further worsened the humanitarian crisis. In 2019, 10 million Yemenis were at risk of starvation, and three million were internally displaced. Yemen's economy faced complete collapse and a war economy has emerged. The ICRC responded by working with states in the region and engaged in humanitarian diplomacy on the ground and at the UN in New York. The crisis illustrates the problem humanitarians face when needing to decide whether to remain neutral or speak out against those responsible for violations of human rights and international humanitarian law. In the case of Yemen, states party to the conflict, or providing arms and funds (the US, Saudi Arabia, the UK, France, and the UAE), have also been those states pledging the greatest amount of humanitarian aid. As a consequence, some humanitarian staff have criticised funding of operations through funds made available by states involved in the military operations. Other staff have suggested operations critically depend on this funding and refusing to accept funds would mean ceding neutrality. The ICRC, given its unique history as a strong advocate for the development of international humanitarian law, is at the forefront of humanitarian diplomacy, combining both humanitarian assistance on the ground and humanitarian advocacy. However, the crisis is still ongoing. A power-sharing agreement signed in 2019 has not brought about an end to the conflict, and fighting continues to this day.

six forgotten prisoners in several countries, all nonviolent, who had been imprisoned owing to their political or religious beliefs. The article asked readers to contact Benenson's office and write letters in support of the prisoners' release. The appeal was supported by Louis Blom-Cooper, a prominent attorney, and Eric Baker, an academic, and Secretary of the British National Peace Council. The article, re-published in newspapers around the world, led to the establishment of AI as a charity and the setting up of prisoner adoption groups around the world. At the time, a human rights regime as we know it today was not yet in existence, and AI, among other civil society actors, promoted norms and principles associated with the present-day human rights regime. By 1964, the organisation had brought about the release of prisoners in Ireland, East Germany, and other states and, in the same year, AI received consultative status at the UN ECOSOC, which awarded observer privileges in the Council. One of AI's volunteers was Irish diplomat Sean MacBride, who was simultaneously Secretary-General of the International Commission of Jurists, and who led the establishment of a coalition of human rights organisations prior to the 1968 UN International Conference on Human Rights in Tehran. AI aided the emergence of the regime by publicising occasions on which there was a difference between existing human rights agreements and practices by state actors. AI's mission is to report human rights violations and press for the release of political prisoners and improved conditions in prisons.

The founding history of Human Rights Watch echoes that of AI to some extent, but also differs in significant respects.[18] The very early origins of the organisation can be traced to a group of Soviet dissidents who sought to delegitimise the Soviet government by pointing to human rights violations. The US Helsinki Watch committee, its predecessor organisation, was founded in 1978. The organisation sought to monitor violations of the Helsinki Final Act, an international agreement. Its work was then limited to monitoring abuses against Soviet dissidents. A grant by the Ford Foundation funded its establishment. In the context of the Cold War, the group quickly received significant support from the United States, and in the subsequent decades, HRW grew to a large organisation with global reach. Although the organisation is today a truly global organisation that provides impartial human rights monitoring, its development is therefore intricately tied to Cold War politics. Reflecting this history, the organisation's headquarters are based in the US, and US donors contribute a significant amount of funding. Over the decades, the organisation has developed from one that has relied on country committees monitoring domestic compliance, to one that operations truly globally, although the origins of the organisation means that its strong ties to the US continue to characterise the organisation.

Today, the existence of AI and similar groups like it is taken for granted, but it is worth bearing in mind that not-for-profit civil society organisations, such as AI, HRW, the IFHR, Anti-Slavery International or Protection International, take years to become recognised internationally. The dual role of human rights organisations as advocates for better protections in general and with regard to particular situations of concern have determined the nature of the scholarship on human rights and the role of civil society actors. The scholarship on human rights practice has been focused on three main issues: first, the origins and legitimacy of human rights; second, studies of the history of individual organisations and case-based discussion of their role in ongoing crises; and third, the extent to which the expanding human rights regime compels states and other actors to behave in line with human rights norms. The latter class of questions can itself be subdivided into several types of scholarship: scholarship concerning the influence of the existence of a human rights regime on international practice per se (in other words, whether human rights violations have been reduced as a consequence of the human rights regime); the effect of naming and shaming practices (whether stigmatisation can prevent further human rights violations); and a wide range of questions pertaining to accountability mechanisms (i.e. legal proceedings against suspected perpetrators). Some of the questions pertaining to the origins of the human rights regime, as well as the emergence of human rights groups have been discussed in previous chapters or above, respectively; in what follows below, we now turn to the scholarship on the effects of the emergence of a human rights regime. We will discuss two questions in particular to provide an illustration: first, the role of international activist networks[19] and, second, the empirical assessment of the effectiveness of naming and shaming as a political strategy. The latter question pertains to the extent to which human rights organisations compel governments to abide by human rights and humanitarian law, or the extent to which their monitoring and advocacy work deters potential rights abusers in the first place.

The scholarship on the role of transnational activist networks originates in the 1990s. In a study on the role of human rights networks, Margaret Keck and Kathryn Sikkink described the origins of these networks and outline the mechanisms through which they work.[20] Human rights advocacy networks developed following the Second World War. They consist of parts of intergovernmental organisations, parts of governments, international non-governmental organisations, domestic non-governmental organisations, and private foundations. The main impetus for the growth of these networks has been from civil society, in other words non-governmental organisations and private foundations. With reference to human rights advocacy in Latin America, and a qualitative comparative case study of human rights advocacy in Argentina and Mexico, Keck and Sikkink's influential work suggested that human rights advocacy can be successful at bringing about changes in human rights practice at the domestic level, but that advocacy is in and of itself not a sufficient driver of changing practice – normative change is more likely to occur where the interests of rights advocates also align with material interests of governments that can provide leverage.

However, the constructivist scholarship of the 1990s did not yet engage with quantitative measurement of the relative weight of normative and non-normative factors influencing the behaviour of states and other actors. More recent work has begun to engage with some of these questions, although disentangling an actor's strategic and normative interests is methodologically difficult. Most of this work has been rationalist, premised on fixed assumptions of states' preferences. Working within the rationalist paradigm, scholars have attempted to measure the effectiveness of human rights advocacy. For example, Cullen Hendrix and Wendy Wong have explored the effects of naming and shaming by Amnesty International (AI) using quantitative analysis.[21] Statistical analysis was used in order to shed light on the effect of AI's reporting and publication of human rights violations on domestic practices. The study found that, although the effects are small, naming and shaming does improve human rights outcomes, but not for all states. The authors looked at two forms of rights violations: overt forms, such as capital punishment that are not hidden from the public eye; and covert rights violations, such as torture. Distinguishing between states based on regime type, the authors found that autocracies – regimes without an organised political opposition and free press – are more sensitive to naming and shaming of human rights violations by international actors. While democracies and hybrid regimes cannot practice covert human rights violations to the same extent that autocracies given free press and political opposition, the publicisation of human rights violations by external actors such as AI can impose domestic political costs on governments that would not exist in the absence of international advocacy. However, for democracies and hybrid regimes, the effect on human rights outcomes is less clear-cut – naming and shaming has no significant or negative effects on human rights practices by these states. The authors suggested that political leaders in non-autocracies calculate the political cost of overt human rights violations, and given that international advocacy does not reveal information that is not already in the public domain, does not alter the political calculations of governments. In sum, the evidence suggested that naming and shaming can be a successful strategy under some circumstances, and that regime type matters in assessing this question.

Another study, by Emilie Hafner-Burton, suggested that across cases, human rights violators appear to offset some forms of human rights violations with others in response to naming and shaming by civil society actors.[22] Governments that abuse rights strategically to oppress domestic opposition may use killings or beatings to offset the political costs incurred – such as a reduction in power in direct control – through improved civil and political rights. This is why, Hafner-Burton suggested, naming and shaming is not 'cheap talk' and can help bring about improvements for political rights, but it can have the unintended effect of worsening particular forms of political repression. This is what political scientists refer to as a 'substitution effect'. Thus, scholars within the rationalist paradigm have engaged with regime type as well as overall levels of violations and, finally, the nature of human rights violations, as independent or dependent variables of interest in understanding the conditions under which human rights violations occur and the consequences in terms of the violations observed.

Other works looked at the role of networks and state behaviour. For example, Wotipka and Tsutsui assessed state integration within non-governmental organisations, finding that state integration into networks of non-governmental organisations could positively influence states' human rights treaty ratification,[23] meaning that states were more likely to adopt human rights treaties where they were more exposed to civil society organisations. However, Hafner-Burton and Tsutsui found that treaty ratification and states' actual human rights records are not correlated; in some cases, states ratified human rights treaties in order to deflect attention from a poor human rights record.[24] However, the authors also found suggestive statistical evidence that over time, the emergent global normative framework exerts, through civil society, an independent pull shaping the behaviour of governments, reducing human rights violations. In sum, the relationship between human rights advocacy, naming and shaming, and human rights violations is complex, and while advocacy and naming and shaming can bring about human rights improvements, it is important to distinguish between states' rhetoric and their actual practice; and to account for substitution effects by states (when states adopt other repressive measures in response to naming and shaming).

The Changing Nature of Humanitarian Action

Like many other areas of global politics, the humanitarian domain has undergone a range of profound changes as a consequence of globalisation. Improved travel and communication, a higher volume of trade as a proportion of states' GDP, the global spread of ideas, and more international regulation all characterise the process of globalisation. Against this backdrop, there has been a growth of international organisations and easier communication among humanitarian actors. A wider and increasingly denser logistics network characterises the humanitarian domain. Moreover, there is a greater degree of professionalisation and specialisation of humanitarian actors. Similarly, human rights organisations now typically operate globally with a wide international reach, reflected in their policy as well as in their response to ongoing crises.

Describing the nature of these changes and what they mean for humanitarian action can take various forms. First, a quantitative assessment of the number of relevant actors, for example by counting the increase in international organisations. The changes brought by globalisation are reflected in the data available in the International Yearbook of International Organizations, for example. These indicate profound changes since the end of the Second World War,[25] showing a dramatic increase in the number of NGOs.[26] In 1978, there were 96 human rights INGOs; this number had increased to 170 in 1998 and had reached 499 by 1998. Overall, three quarters of the organisations were founded during the last quarter of the 20th century, after the end of the Cold War. The greater number of organisations reflects a growing demand for regulation and governance at the global level, as a consequence of a greater number of issues affecting more than one state.

However, it is worth looking not only at the number of institutions but also at the nature of humanitarianism in a globalised world, and whether it has changed not only in the size and scope of the operations associated with humanitarianism but also whether there have been qualitative changes in the way international actors conduct humanitarian responses today. Some of these changes may be the result of the changing nature of conflict and institutions' need to adapt to these. For example, the UNHRC has had to adapt its work to the fact that internally displaced persons (IDPs) make up a greater proportion of displaced people than they have in the past.[27] Other changes, as outlined below, stem from the effects of globalisation itself (such as better communication, or the capacity to operate transnationally). However, some of the institutional changes and international practices may reflect changing attitudes about the roles and responsibilities of international actors including states, international organisations (IOs), and non-governmental organisations (these responsibilities will be discussed in further detail in Chapters 7, 8, and 9).

Although the changes brought by globalisation have been profound as will be outlined below, in some respects, the work of humanitarian actors remains unchanged, and it is worth bearing this in mind when thinking about the changing nature of humanitarianism. In assessing the degree and nature of the changes that have occurred in the humanitarian sector, it is worth distinguishing between core functions and purpose of humanitarian organisations, the wider institutional environment within which these organisations function, and the practices associated with humanitarianism and how, if at all, these practices have shifted in recent decades. The record, as outlined below, is mixed: the purpose of humanitarian action has not changed, but practices associated with humanitarianism, principles associated with it, as well as institutions and the broader institutional environment have all undergone profound changes. A complex network of organisations and comprehensive logistical structures now characterise the humanitarian aid industry. Present-day humanitarian agencies have established channels of cooperation with governments, local authorities, and other organisations as well as the private sector. A closer look at each of these changes shows what these changes mean in practice.

First, organisations now operate in a complex ecosystem of organisations that engage with governments and other NGOs.[28] This ecosystem consists of local and international non-governmental organisations, UN organisations, faith-based organisations, local governments, aid departments of donor governments, local security forces, including the police, international security forces, for example peacekeepers, private donors, think tanks and universities, businesses, and local public services. An actor network map, using data from the International Yearbook for International Organizations, provides a visualisation of humanitarian actors and their interactions (Box 6.2).[29] The network map shows that the vast majority of actors whose work also comprises humanitarian activities work with more than one other organisation. It also shows that some organisations function as 'hubs', with disproportionately greater influence in the humanitarian domain. These include the ICRC, the OAS, WFP, and the AU. The map also illustrates that some organisations have strong connections with other organisations. For example, the ICRC cooperates closely with the AU and ECOWAS, whereas OAS and WFP have close ties, and a third cluster of organisations includes, among others, OCHA, the OSCE, AI, and Save the Children. In sum, the map shows that there now exists a comprehensive, highly networked ecosystem of humanitarian actors with a high degree of specialisation.

The growth of organisations and the increasingly networked structure of humanitarian actors has also brought about changes in the global humanitarian funding landscape. In recent years, funding appeals for humanitarian emergencies have increased exponentially, but only about half of the requested funding is received by humanitarian agencies.[30] This results in competition for scarce resources, and organisations are forced to accept funds that are 'earmarked', in other words, designated for a particular purpose, even though this reduces their performance as they are more restricted in their ability to employ the funds to maximise their utility and achieve best possible humanitarian outcomes.[31] In recent years, a separate strand of research, drawing on management science, has begun employing game theory – modelling of strategic interactions in a given system – for understanding behaviour of actors in the humanitarian domain.[32] This line of research is facilitated by an abundance of data that is now available to researchers, including data provided by organisations themselves as well as data made accessible by the Humanitarian Data Exchange hosted by OCHA, which permits the application of quantitative methods including quantitative modelling, in addition to traditional approaches employing qualitative methods.[33]

Modern technology has altered the practice of humanitarianism, bringing with it both opportunities and new dilemmas.[34] 'Digital humanitarianism' may have the advantage of increasing humanitarian effectiveness and efficiency through use of new information and communication technologies. For example, crisis mapping that draws on aggregated data drawn from numerous sources may provide better and more accurate information about the nature and magnitude of unfolding crises. Advanced algorithms can help predict conflict dynamics. Mobile networks and web-based applications including mobile money can help facilitate the provision of aid in remote and inaccessible areas. Public-private partnerships that bring together governments and firms to work on a common objective can help bring about synergies and increase efficiency. However, the shift to digital humanitarianism brings about a transformation of the humanitarian aid and relief sectors, and these changes are salient both in terms of policy and politics. For example, while the use of technology associated with 'digital humanitarianism' is touted as a means of better reaching those most in need, it also facilitates 'remote humanitarianism' that is dislocated from the relief context and thus may mean that humanitarians are less able to appreciate the immediate needs of beneficiaries, as well as the lived experience and political realities on the ground. Similarly, while a wider range of data permits more accurate crisis mapping and more detailed information for vulnerable populations, the collection and processing of this

Box 6.2 A Network of Humanitarian Actors

Every node in this diagram represents a humanitarian-oriented international organisation. A link from one node to another indicates that an actor has referenced another as a partner in the Yearbook of International Organizations (using data drawn from the International Organization Codebook). The size of a node represents its *betweenness centrality*. Larger nodes suggest more 'hub-like' qualities, where organisations have a greater number of links to other nodes, i.e. they exhibit high connectivity, and have fewer similarities with other nodes, i.e. lower substitutability. These nodes can be placed in 'communities' of densely connected nodes using a modularity algorithm. A modulation-maximising algorithm yields the following communities: (1) UNHCR, Save the Children, Amnesty International, HRW, OSCE, OCHA, Oxfam; (2) ICRC, AU, ECOWAS, ASEAN, IGAD, and NATO; and (3) OAS and WFP.

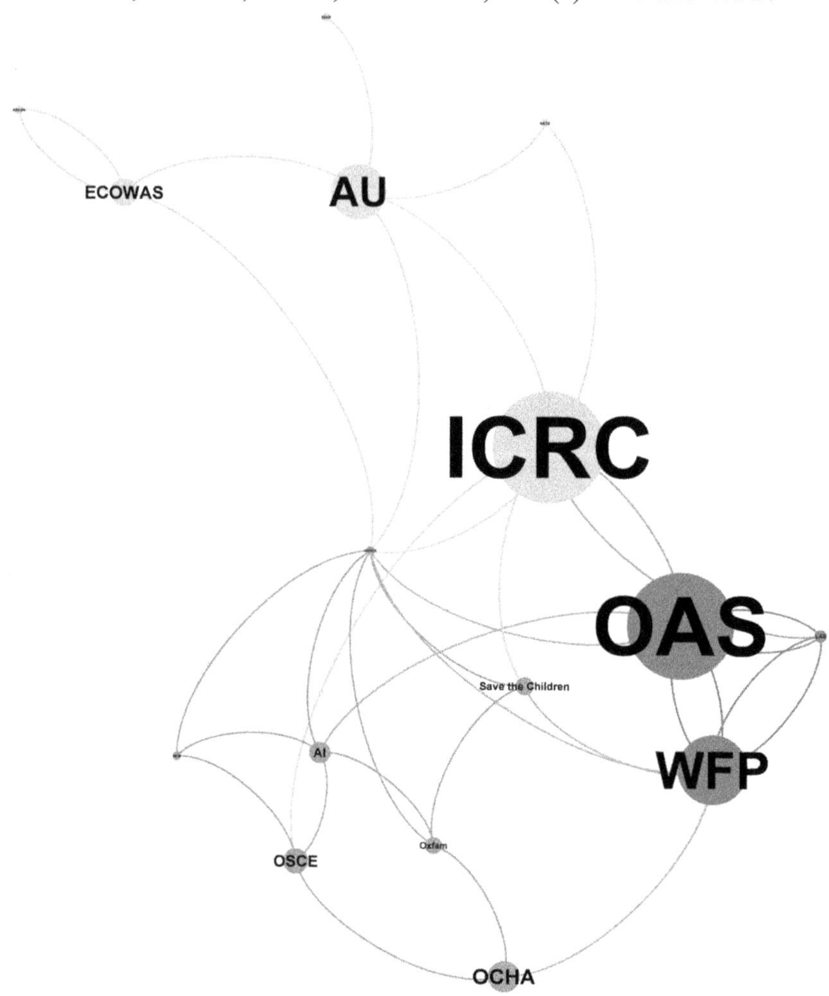

Box 6.3 Haiti 2010

The case of Haiti is a good illustration of the heightened strain placed on countries that are affected by both political unrest and natural disaster. Haiti, a state in the Caribbean, has been independent since 1804 after freeing itself from French colonial rule. Following decades of rule of the Duvalier family until 1986 and a brief period of government by the National Council of Government (CNG), Jean-Bertrand Aristide came to power in 1990 but was ousted in a military coup in September 1991. When economic sanctions were ineffective in restoring democratic rule in Haiti, the UN Security Council authorised the deployment of a civilian mission to monitor human rights, MICIVIH in 1993, and, following the expulsion of the UN presence a peacekeeping operation to restore democratic rule. When Aristide was ousted once again several years later in 2004, the UN authorised the deployment of another peacekeeping operation, the UN Stabilisation Mission in Haiti (MINUSTAH). Throughout history, Haiti has regularly been affected by storms, hurricanes, and earthquakes, and in January 2010 a large earthquake brought a humanitarian emergency to a country already under strain by political instability. The country was struck by a second earthquake in October. Ten months after the first earthquake, a cholera outbreak resulted in over 8,000 deaths and many more hospitalisations in a country of then about 10 million. UN peacekeepers were responsible for bringing the disease to Haiti following an emergency redeployment of peacekeepers from Nepal in the aftermath of the earthquake. Overcrowding, lack of access to clean water and sanitation facilities facilitated the spread of the disease. The outbreak led to protests against the UN peacekeeping force. Moreover, there were allegations of sexual violence and exploitation by UN peacekeepers. The case illustrates the changes that humanitarian action has been subject to in recent decades; even though its success in accomplishing its goals may have been questionable, the UN's approach was one that focused on peacebuilding understood as the strengthening of local institutions, in other words a bottom-up peacebuilding process. Social media and text messaging were used to coordinate the humanitarian relief response, reflecting the growing role of technology in coordinating international responses. In summary, the international response to humanitarian emergency in Haiti may be an example of 'resilience humanitarianism', although the critique of classical humanitarianism and peacekeeping practice remained salient.

data also carries a risk of exploitation and misuse. Better communications technology facilitates improved communication among humanitarians, donors, governments, and beneficiaries, but social media and mass communications can also be misused to spread inflammatory and discriminatory speech. Partnerships with private firms may increase efficiency in the provision of aid and relief, but 'neoliberal humanitarianism', critics suggest, may also result in the economic exploitation of vulnerable populations most in need. Finally, while 'remote humanitarianism' may facilitate access to vulnerable populations that might otherwise be difficult to reach, it may make populations that cannot be reached remotely invisible for digital humanitarian mapping, leaving these populations without access to aid.

The key changes in the humanitarian sector and its associated practices can therefore be summarised as follows: there are many more international organisations than there have been in the past, operating in a complex ecosystem of organisations spanning both the private and public sectors, in other words comprising organisations that work for a profit, organisations that do not make a profit from humanitarian action, as well as governments providing international aid. These practices are now well established and a small number of organisations, particularly OCHA and the ICRC, are placed at the centre of aid networks, responsible for coordinating humanitarian action and, particularly with reference to the 'new humanitarianism', aggregating, analysing, and disseminating data. Given this, the organisations at the core of the humanitarian network have disproportionate leverage in the humanitarian domain. Technological advances of recent years have meant that humanitarian operations have aided the growth in scale of humanitarian operations. This transformation has changed the nature of humanitarianism. Many of the features of present-day humanitarian action are reflected in the international responses to recent humanitarian emergencies, such as Haiti (see Box 6.3).[35] However, the changes should not be overstated. Principles of humanity, impartiality, and neutrality still underpin the ethos of humanitarian aid and relief work and still constitute central standards against which humanitarians' work is assessed. Like in many other fields, therefore, technology has had a profound impact but has not necessarily altered the essence of humanitarian practice itself.

However, some recent scholarship challenges the notion of continuity and suggests that a paradigmatic shift has occurred, with a new era for humanitarianism having begun. For example, Dorothea Hilhorst observes a shift to 'resilience humanitarianism', which is characterised by several features.[36] First, 'resilience humanitarianism' does not, as opposed to 'classical' humanitarianism, understand crisis as a situation unlike normality, with a binary between peace and crisis. Resilience humanitarianism is focused on societies and their ability to cope in crisis situations that are themselves becoming the norm, owing to climate change. The second key feature of resilience humanitarianism is that it regards local institutional structures as continuous through situations of crisis and its aftermath, which can be a drawn-out period given protracted crises and the increasing awareness of the interrelatedness of peacebuilding and conflict prevention, and humanitarian responsibilities. International humanitarian actors have a permanent, institutionalised presence with a high degree of professionalisation and premised on an assumption that crises occur and reoccur in different locations. The key difference is that classical humanitarianism regards humanitarian action as occurring in an emergency situation that is clearly bounded and distinct from peace time, whereas resilience humanitarianism regards humanitarianism as a permanent institution and recognises institutional continuity within states and views domestic institutions as primarily responsible for crisis management, with support from international humanitarian actors, where necessary.

In terms of magnitude, empirical observations suggest the case is clear: the nature of humanitarianism has undergone profound change. However, if we look at practices of humanitarianism, the answer is less clear-cut. On the one hand, institutions have changed and adapted to a new environment in a globalised world and the changing nature of conflict. Humanitarianism is now underpinned by organisations, domestically and internationally, that run routine operations and can respond swiftly to urgent crises. These organisations operate in a complex network of organisations with specialised tasks. But their core function and purpose remain the same, and the essence of humanitarian protection has not changed; although definitions of what constitutes a 'crisis' vis-à-vis normality is beginning to occupy thinkers in the field.

Summary

- Traditionally, humanitarian relief operates on the principles of neutrality and impartiality. Yet doing so also means remaining silent on human rights abuses by de facto or de jure authorities. In some cases, the provision of humanitarian relief may strengthen a party to a conflict politically or militarily.
- Naming and shaming is a form of stigmatising of human rights-violating actors by other international actors including human rights organisations. It is one tool available to international actors for responding to human rights violations, mass atrocities, and inadequate responses by authorities to domestic humanitarian emergencies. However, naming and shaming is not a hard form of enforcement such as prosecution or military intervention.
- Organisations such as Human Rights Watch or Amnesty International operate internationally. Their work falls into two broad categories: immediate responses to human rights violations on the one hand, and longer term, structural human rights advocacy.
- The humanitarian relief industry has changed in recent decades. It has grown and it has become more differentiated. Equally, a greater number of policy approaches is now represented among humanitarian actors. Still, some aspects of humanitarian relief work have remained unchanged.

Questions for Reflection

- *Should humanitarian relief organisations maintain neutrality throughout a conflict?*
- *How successful is naming and shaming as a strategy of human rights advocacy?*
- *Have human rights organisations helped advance the consolidation of the international human protection regime?*
- *To what extent has the role of humanitarian relief changed in recent years?*

Further reading

- Ahmad, Ayesha and Smith, James (2018): *Humanitarian Action and Ethics* (London: Zed Books).
- Becker, Jo (2012): *Campaigning for Justice: Human Rights Advocacy in Practice* (Stanford: Stanford University Press).
- Coyne, Christopher J. (2013): *Doing Bad by Doing Good: Why Humanitarian Action Fails* (Stanford: Stanford University Press).
- Hopgood, Stephen (2006): *Keepers of the Flame: Understanding Amnesty International* (Ithaca and London: Cornell University Press).

- Kumar, Rajeesh (2019): *The International Committee of the Red Cross in Internal Armed Conflicts: Is Neutrality Possible?* (Singapore: Palgrave).
- Meier, Patrick (2015): *Digital Humanitarians: How Big Data Is Changing the Face of Humanitarian Response* (New York and London: Routledge).

Notes

1 'International Committee of the Red Cross', Page, International Committee of the Red Cross, 3 October 2013, https://www.icrc.org/en.
2 Hugo Slim, 'Humanitarian Diplomacy: The ICRC's Neutral and Impartial Advocacy in Armed Conflicts', *Ethics & International Affairs* 33, no. 1 (Spring 2019): 67–77, http://dx.doi.org.libproxy.ucl.ac.uk/10.1017/S0892679418000904.
3 'Médecins Sans Frontières (MSF) International', Médecins Sans Frontières (MSF) International, accessed 28 December 2020, https://www.msf.org/.
4 MSF's ethos is outlined in detail, with examples, in Michal Givoni, 'Humanitarian Governance and Ethical Cultivation: Médecins sans Frontières and the Advent of the Expert-Witness', *Millennium* 40, no. 1 (1 September 2011): 43–63, https://doi.org/10.1177/0305829811406037.
5 These are explained well, and summarised with reference to examples, in Ed Schenkenberg van Mierop, 'Coming Clean on Neutrality and Independence: The Need to Assess the Application of Humanitarian Principles', *International Review of the Red Cross* 97 (2015): 295–318.
6 Christopher Lockyear and Andrew Cunningham, 'Who Is Your Constituency? The Political Engagement of Humanitarian Organisations', *Journal of International Humanitarian Action* 2, no. 1 (23 October 2017): 9, https://doi.org/10.1186/s41018-017-0024-1.
7 States' foreign aid practice is discussed in detail in Clair Apodaca, 'Foreign Aid as Foreign Policy Tool', Oxford Research Encyclopedia of Politics, 26 April 2017, https://doi.org/10.1093/acrefore/9780190228637.013.332.
8 Jack Snyder, 'Realism, Refugees, and Strategies of Humanitarianism' in *Refugees in International Relations*, ed. Alexander Betts and Gil Loescher(Oxford: Oxford University Press, 2010).
9 Richard A. Nielsen, 'Rewarding Human Rights? Selective Aid Sanctions against Repressive States', *International Studies Quarterly* 57, no. 4 (1 December 2013): 791–803, https://doi.org/10.1111/isqu.12049.
10 Andreas Krieg, 'Quantitative Analysis', in *Motivations for Humanitarian Intervention: Theoretical and Empirical Considerations*, ed. Andreas Krieg, Springer Briefs in Ethics (Dordrecht: Springer Netherlands, 2013), 123–32, https://doi.org/10.1007/978-94-007-5374-7_4.
11 Neil Narang, 'Assisting Uncertainty: How Humanitarian Aid Can Inadvertently Prolong Civil War', *International Studies Quarterly* 59, no. 1 (1 March 2015): 184–95, https://doi.org/10.1111/isqu.12151.
12 Robert Powell, 'War as a Commitment Problem', *International Organization* 60, no. 1 (2006): 169–203.
13 Narang, 'Assisting Uncertainty'.
14 Normative developments and risk mitigation strategies are described in Dennis Dijkzeul and Kristin Bergtora Sandvik, 'A World in Turmoil: Governing Risk, Establishing Order in Humanitarian Crises', *Disasters* 43, no. S2 (2019): S85–108, https://doi.org/10.1111/disa.12330.
15 Tim Allen and David Styan, 'A Right to Interfere? Bernard Kouchner and the New Humanitarianism', *Journal of International Development* 12, no. 6 (2000): 825–42.
16 Slim, 'Humanitarian Diplomacy'; Jeannie Sowers and Erika Weinthal, 'Humanitarian Challenges and the Targeting of Civilian Infrastructure in the Yemen War', *International Affairs* 97, no. 1 (2021): 157–77.
17 The emergence of Amnesty International is summarised in Ann Marie Clark, *Diplomacy of Conscience: Amnesty International and Changing Human Rights Norms* Princeton: Princeton University Press, 2001).

18 HRW's history and the Cold War context of its emergence are discussed at length in Peter Slezkine, 'From Helsinki to Human Rights Watch: How an American Cold War Monitoring Group Became an International Human Rights Institution', *Humanity: An International Journal of Human Rights, Humanitarianism, and Development* 5, no. 3 (2014): 345–70, https://doi.org/10.1353/hum.2014.0026.

19 Margaret E. Keck and Kathryn Sikkink, 'Transnational Advocacy Networks in International and Regional Politics', *International Social Sciences Journal* 51, no. 159 (1999): 89–101.

20 Margaret E. Keck and Kathryn Sikkink, 'Human Rights Advocacy Networks in Latin America', in *Activists beyond Borders*, Advocacy Networks in International Politics (Ithaca, New York: Cornell University Press, 1998), 79–120.

21 Cullen S. Hendrix and Wendy H. Wong, 'When Is the Pen Truly Mighty? Regime Type and the Efficacy of Naming and Shaming in Curbing Human Rights Abuses', *British Journal of Political Science; Cambridge* 43, no. 3 (July 2013): 651–72.

22 Emilie M. Hafner-Burton, 'Sticks and Stones: Naming and Shaming the Human Rights Enforcement Problem', *International Organization* 62, no. 4 (2008): 689–716.

23 Christine Min Wotipka and Kiyoteru Tsutsui, 'Global Human Rights and State Sovereignty: State Ratification of International Human Rights Treaties, 1965-2001', *Sociological Forum* 23, no. 4 (2008): 724–54.

24 Emilie M. Hafner-Burton and Kiyoteru Tsutsui, 'Human Rights in a Globalizing World: The Paradox of Empty Promises', *American Journal of Sociology* 110, no. 5 (1 March 2005): 1373–1411, https://doi.org/10.1086/428442.

25 Kiyoteru Tsutsui and Christine Min Wotipka, 'Global Civil Society and the International Human Rights Movement: Citizen Participation in Human Rights International Nongovernmental Organizations', *Social Forces* 83, no. 2 (2004): 587–620.

26 'The Yearbook of International Organizations | Union of International Associations', accessed 20 February 2021, https://uia.org/yearbook.

27 B.S. Chimni, 'Globalization, Humanitarianism and the Erosion of Refugee Protection', *Journal of Refugee Studies* 13, no. 3 (1 September 2000): 243–63, https://doi.org/10.1093/jrs/13.3.243.

28 This is described in detail in Alexander Betts and Louise Bloom, 'Humanitarian Innovation: The State of the Art', Occasional Policy Paper, OCHA Policy and Studies Series (United Nations Office for the Coordination of Humanitarian Affairs, 2014).

29 Network analysis compiled by Christina Qiu using data from the International Yearbook of International Organizations. The modularity algorithm used was first presented in Vincent D. Blondel et al., 'Fast Unfolding of Communities in Large Networks', *Journal of Statistical Mechanics: Theory and Experiment* 2008, no. 10 (October 2008): P10008, https://doi.org/10.1088/1742-5468/2008/10/P10008.

30 Paul B. Spiegel, 'The Humanitarian System Is Not Just Broke, but Broken: Recommendations for Future Humanitarian Action', *The Lancet*, 8 June 2017, https://doi.org/10.1016/S0140-6736(17)31278-3.

31 Arian Aflaki and Alfonso Pedraza Martinez, 'Donations in Humanitarian Operations: Earmarking, Competition, and Joint Fundraising', SSRN Scholarly Paper (Rochester, NY: Social Science Research Network, 1 October 2020), https://doi.org/10.2139/ssrn.3705595.

32 Luke Muggy and Jessica L. Heier Stamm, 'Game Theory Applications in Humanitarian Operations: A Review', *Journal of Humanitarian Logistics and Supply Chain Management* 4, no. 1 (2014): 4–23.

33 Gyongyi Kovacs et al., 'Research Methods in Humanitarian Logistics', *Journal of Humanitarian Logistics and Supply Chain Management* 9, no. 3 (2019): 325–31.

34 Kristin Bergtora Sandvik et al., 'Humanitarian Technology: A Critical Research Agenda', *International Review of the Red Cross* 96, no. 893 (March 2014): 219–42, https://doi.org/10.1017/S1816383114000344.

35 The history of peacebuilding efforts and the international emergency response to the earthquake of 2010 are discussed in Laura Zanotti, 'Imagining Democracy, Building Unsustainable Institutions: The UN Peacekeeping Operation in Haiti', *Security Dialogue* 39, no. 5 (1 October 2008): 539–61, https://doi.org/10.1177/0967010608096151; Julie Dugdale, Bartel Van de Walle, and Corinna Koeppinghoff, 'Social Media and SMS in the Haiti

Earthquake', in *Proceedings of the 21st International Conference on World Wide Web*, WWW '12 Companion (New York, NY, USA: Association for Computing Machinery, 2012), 713–14, https://doi.org/10.1145/2187980.2188189; Komlan Agbedahin, 'The Haiti Cholera Outbreak and Peacekeeping Paradoxes', *Peace Review* 31, no. 2 (3 April 2019): 190–98, https://doi.org/10.1080/10402659.2019.1667568.

36 Dorothea Hilhorst, 'Classical Humanitarianism and Resilience Humanitarianism: Making Sense of Two Brands of Humanitarian Action', *Journal of International Humanitarian Action* 3, no. 1 (10 September 2018): 15, https://doi.org/10.1186/s41018-018-0043-6.

Part III

Responsibilities

7 Prevention

Part two of this book has described the emergence of international actors responsible for humanitarian protection. Chapters 4, 5, and 6 discussed the role of states, regional organisations, the United Nations, and humanitarian and human rights organisations. These chapters described academic debates about some empirical questions – for which answers can only be found through the collection of data, such as statistical measurement, or interviews – about the record of humanitarian protection actors. Relevant practices and norms related to the emergence of these actors and their responsibilities were discussed. These chapters concluded with a summary of the literature on remaining challenges and protection gaps. These chapters also briefly touched on ethical dilemmas and policy questions.

Part three builds on and deepens the discussions in the preceding chapters, focusing on the responsibilities of the actors described in previous chapters. Chapters 7, 8, and 9 adopt a constructivist lens for understanding the emergence of the humanitarian protection regime, its norms, rules, and practices, as well as the formation of responsibilities, duties, and obligations. International practice and the (changing) interpretations of state actors are again relevant here, as they shape actors' perceptions about who is responsible, and which kinds of actions are the responsibility of individual actors, as well as criteria and conditions determining roles and responsibilities. While the humanitarian protection regime has developed rapidly in recent years, some norms remain contested, and the chapters of the final section of this book will place particular emphasis on normative contestation. These chapters will also address policy dilemmas that arise as a consequence of the fact that the practices associated with the humanitarian protection regime are in flux, and, given the soft nature of international law, responses to violent conflict, mass atrocities, and humanitarian need are typically contextually determined, highly variable, and contingent upon the support of powerful states.

Chapter 7 surveys three distinct humanitarian protection practices that do not involve the use of force: preventive diplomacy, humanitarian diplomacy, and sanctions. While these measures are not necessarily non-coercive – some forms of diplomacy, including sanctions, aim to exact a cost on the targeted actor, rather than offer an incentive with a view to persuading them – none of these measures involves the use of force or civilian or humanitarian personnel on the ground in conflict zones (the latter will be the subject of Chapter 8). While preventive diplomacy is associated with the onset of armed conflict, diplomacy, mediation, and sanctions can be implemented at any point in the conflict cycle. Peacebuilding efforts – rebuilding a society following an armed conflict – are discussed in Chapter 9. Peacebuilding comprises conflict resolution and the post-war reconstruction of a state's physical infrastructure and political,

DOI: 10.4324/9781003006671-10

economic, and social institutions. However, peacebuilding should also be seen as a form of structural conflict prevention. Given that a large number of conflicts recur, peacebuilding, including political and economic reforms as well as criminal justice and reconciliation, is of significant importance.

Preventive Diplomacy

Preventive diplomacy is the practice of employing persuasion to prevent conflicts from occurring or escalating if they have already begun. As such, it is part of the broader cluster of practices associated with conflict prevention and mitigation, including the monitoring of conflict, its containment, and the assessment of risk factors that can make conflict more likely or intensify it.[1] Preventive diplomacy can entail the deployment of humanitarian observers, political and fact-finding missions, as well as the deployment of Special Envoys. Generally, when practitioners speak of preventive diplomacy, what is meant is measures short of the use of force. Often these measures are non-coercive and centred on soft power and persuasion. They are adopted to avert the imminent escalation of violence or armed conflict. Following the end of the Cold War, however, with the increase in the number of internal conflicts, preventive diplomacy has expanded conceptually to encompass early action to prevent armed conflicts within states, and a range of international actors, including both state and non-state actors, may be involved in preventive diplomacy. Today, the UN is often a key actor.[2] International efforts to prevent further violence in the aftermath of Kenya's elections of 2007, as well as the international responses to the post-electoral crisis in The Gambia, 2017, serve as some recent examples (see Boxes 7.1 and 7.2, respectively) for preventive diplomacy by states and other actors.[3]

Preventive diplomacy as a practice of states has its origins in the Cold War era, emerging from the desire to prevent disputes among states. The UN has, over the decades, developed and refined the practice of preventive diplomacy.[4] The UN's first Secretary-General, Tryve Lie, charted the path to the UN Secretary-General's provision of good offices during times of crisis, and it was during Lie's era that the Secretary-General received powers of investigation. The Secretary-General also acquired the right to provide an assessment to the Security Council on whether a situation constituted a threat to, or breach of, international peace and security – significant given the legal implications of this wording. Lie also established the practice of deploying observers in sensitive situations. Lie's work was subsequently continued by Dag Hammarskjold, who introduced the role of Special Representatives. Former Secretary-General Ban Ki Moon built on these foundations, promoting a strengthening of the Department for Political Affairs.[5] Today, the UN can draw on a wide network of bodies and agencies, including the UN's Special Political Missions which also engage in preventive diplomacy.

However, the role of the UN varies across cases. Sometimes the role of the UN is more limited, and with states leading on preventive diplomacy efforts.[6] Generally, states remain key actors, particularly great powers and regional powers that hold sway over global and regional politics. A state's foreign policy interests will determine its position on a particular crisis, and in many cases, the role of the UN may be delimited to that of facilitator for preventive diplomacy, rather than taking on a more central role. However, in these circumstances, the provision of good offices by the UN is still crucial for the smooth functioning of preventive diplomacy. For example, in the case of Lebanon, the

Box 7.1 The Case of Kenya, 2007–2008

The post-electoral crisis in Kenya of 2007–2008 is a good example of a successful mediation effort. The presidential elections led to a close result between the two leading candidates. Raila Odinga, the candidate of the Orange Democratic Movement (ODM) had a small lead over Mwai Kibaki, the candidate of the Party of National Unity (PNU). However, there was a widespread perception that the count had been manipulated in favour of Kibaki. Protests by ODM supporters soon degenerated into violence including killing, looting, and rape. In late January, reprisal attacks targeted ethnic groups traditionally supportive of the ODM. The crisis caused a significant number of deaths and there was evidence of systematic, pre-planned ethnic violence. The number of displaced people rose sharply, and Kenya's economy threatened to collapse. The case was widely viewed as the first case of 'R2P prevention'. An international mediation conducted by the African Union Panel of Eminent Personalities, led by former UN Secretary-General Kofi Annan, supported by the UN and other actors, brought about an end to the crisis. The political context was favourable (Kenya is of strategic significance as it hosts UN headquarters and several agencies, and is a logistical hub for regional humanitarian support), promoting a swift resolution. The National Accord of 28 February 2008, establishing a power-sharing agreement, finally brought the violence to an end. The mediation team had been sponsored by the African Union and led by a skilled mediation team including of Kofi Annan, Benjamin Mkapa, former Tanzanian president, and Graça Machel, former Mozambiquan Minister of Education. The mediation team had received technical support from the UN as well as the Centre for Humanitarian Dialogue, based in Geneva. Using a building-block approach, the mediators sought consensus on issues that were more readily resolved, building confidence among both parties, before moving to more challenging issues. A coalition of more than 30 civil society organisations, Kenyans for Peace with Truth and Justice, supported the mediation efforts. International donors (the US, the UK, the European Commission, Japan, and the World Bank) supported the mediation by urging both sides to acknowledge the elections results had been disputable, and donors were in contact with the mediation team and coordinated their strategy. At one point throughout the negotiations, donor states stated their foreign aid was under review. Travel bans on senior political figures from both parties increased the pressure further. In February, then American Secretary of State Condoleeza Rice warned of further punitive steps if the mediation failed to make progress. The case is described in the literature as a case that illustrates best practice with regard to timely and robust international responses.

UN served an important role in that it facilitated cohesion among Security Council members. While the UN had little leverage, it played an important role as an impartial facilitator.[7] In other crises, however, the UN has played a much more substantial role. For example, in the case of Malawi – regarded as a good example of preventive diplomacy – the UN Envoy played a key role as impartial intermediary.[8]

Box 7.2 The Case of Gambia, 2016–2017

The international responses to the post-electoral crisis of 2016–2017 can be described as either preventive diplomacy, or *coercive diplomacy*, given that the incumbent President Yahya Jammeh, unwilling to cede power following the elections of 1 December 2016, was threatened with military intervention. In defence of democracy, and seeking to set an example deterring future attempts at subversion, ECOWAS responded swiftly and with robust measures to the crisis. The case, similarly to the response in Kenya a decade earlier, was seen as a successful, co-ordinated international response to the crisis. There were no casualties, and the president-elect, Adama Barrow, took office after taking an oath of office in neighbouring Senegal, where he had taken refuge following the elections. Barrow had called on international actors – ECOWAS, the AU, and the UN – to intervene. While the UN did not authorise military intervention or Chapter VII measures, the Security Council passed a resolution on the crisis, S/RES/2337, in the same year. Jammeh had come to power in a military coup in 1992, and was running for the fifth time. Jammeh's regime had been accused of human rights violations, with reports of enforced disappearances, detentions without trial, extra-judicial killings, sexual abuse, and torture. International responses to these crimes had been limited to condemnation and efforts to isolate the regime. While there had been little hope for free and fair elections in December 2016, an economic crisis prior to the elections had weakened domestic support for the regime, and there was minimal evidence of malpractice during the elections. Having been defeated by Adama Barrow, Jammeh conceded defeat, but retracted his acceptance a week later, citing voting irregularities. Following local unrest, including street protests, ECOWAS dispatched a mediation team made up of President John Dramani of Ghana, President Muhammadu Buhari of Nigeria, and President Ernest Bai Koroma, then President of Sierra Leone, as well as the UN Special Envoy for West Africa and the Sahel, and the former ECOWAS Commissioner, Mohammed Ibn Chambas. The mediation was supported by UN regional offices and the Department for Political Affairs. ECOWAS threatened to use force in case Jammeh continued to refuse to accept the elections outcome, and a regional military force was drawn up in Senegal. On 17 January, ECOWAS pronounced an ultimatum, and the Security Council's resolution of 21 December recognised Barrow's victory. Jammeh was engaged in the negotiations over the terms of his departure – a feature of the mediation process that was controversial given the allegations of human rights violations during his tenure. Jammeh finally decided to relinquish power, and went into exile in Equatorial Guinea at the end of January 2017. However, Equatorial Guinea is not a party to the Rome Statute and therefore extradition to the ICC is unlikely. While the case, like the responses to the post-electoral crisis in Kenya a decade earlier, was celebrated as an exemplary international response to a volatile political situation threatening to escalate into wider conflict, it is worth noting that the conditions, as in the case of Kenya, were favourable to a swift resolution of the crisis, particularly given that Senegal favoured change in government given the situation over the Casamanca region. The case was also exemplary in that international actors implemented peacebuilding measures following the crisis, through a Peacebuilding Fund, a security sector reform project, and the deployment of international advisers to support the new presidency.

In recent years several regional organisations have institutionalised mechanisms for mediation through provision of permanent good offices or ad hoc responses to crisis situations. For example, the ASEAN Regional Forum is dedicated to preventive diplomacy, although it is a purely deliberative forum.[9] The ARF has a formalised approach to preventive diplomacy and strict adherence to sovereignty norms inhibits decisive diplomatic preventive action. Other regional organisations with preventive action bodies include NATO, which has established the Comprehensive Crisis and Operations Management Centre, and the AU's Peace and Security Council, as well as the AU's Panel of the Wise.[10] Within the APSA, the Panel of the Wise (PoW) has an advisory role, and preventive diplomacy is its main responsibility. Furthermore, African Regional Economic Communities (RECs) have become increasingly important actors with regard to conflict prevention.[11]

A regional organisation that has historically played a significant role with regard to preventive diplomacy is the OSCE.[12] It is by definition a soft security institution as it cannot impose sanctions or threaten the use of force. The OSCE emerged as a significant actor during the Cold War and retains its relevance today. With a clear division of labour between its predecessor organisation, the CSCE, and the EEC, the predecessor organisation of the EU, the CSCE was responsible for political affairs, while the EEC was responsible for economic affairs. However, the EU has expanded eastwards and taken on a wider range of political functions. During the 1990s, the OSCE helped defuse crises in Estonia, Latvia, and Crimea. More recently, however, Russia's criticism about the OSCE's Office for Democratic Institutions and Human Rights (ODIHR), which Russia perceives as biased against former Soviet states, has impacted the organisation's work. From the early 2000s, Russia has begun sending its own elections observers. Given its waning influence, the OSCE has been less able to help address recent conflicts, including those in Nagorno-Karabakh, South Ossetia, and Transdniestria.

While numerous regional organisations have adopted mediation and preventive action as formal tasks, other organisations may have no dedicated offices but still be actively engaged in preventive action on an ad hoc basis. For example, the Arab League has no formalised conflict response mechanism, but has engaged in preventive diplomacy in recent crises, including crises in Syria and Yemen.[13]

While preventive diplomacy describes measures short of the use of force, these are not necessarily limited to persuasion through positive incentives. States may threaten the use of military force or threaten to impose costs through sanctions, as a form of coercive diplomacy. For example, the AU invoked Article 4(h) of its Constitutive Act in response to the crisis in Burundi, issuing an ultimatum for the acceptance of the deployment of peacekeepers for civilian protection in December 2015.[14] In doing so, the AU went further than it had with regard to other crises, where it had suspended member states, or imposed targeted sanctions in response to unconstitutional changes of government. Although the threat was not realised, the example illustrates how diplomacy may be used for compellence.

Although the practice of preventive diplomacy is ubiquitous and a range of actors are involved, neither states, nor the UN have developed standard operating procedures for early warning and preventive action.[15] On the one hand, this means states and other actors retain flexibility to move swiftly in response to crises – on the other hand, the lack of institutional memory and agreement on standards and principles for early action may slow international responses, and make relevant bodies vulnerable to the charge of politicisation. Despite these challenges, the practice of preventive diplomacy is an important part of the international humanitarian protection regime.[16]

Humanitarian Diplomacy

Humanitarian diplomacy emerged as an academic field of study in its own right in the early 2000s.[17] The emergence of this field of study reflects the growing significance of the humanitarian protection regime built on an increasingly robust normative architecture and a complex network of associated institutions at the international, regional, and state levels. *Humanitarian diplomacy* can be defined as the practice of negotiating for access to populations affected by armed conflict for the provision of humanitarian relief. The term also encompasses negotiations for access to affected populations to provide civilian protection. Both state and non-state actors may engage in humanitarian diplomacy. Humanitarian diplomacy is about persuading state leaders and other decision-makers (such as the leadership of non-state armed groups) to grant access to civilian populations, and/or to respect international humanitarian law and international human rights law.

A range of actors may become involved in humanitarian diplomacy, broadly conceived, but their roles and responsibilities differ. States pursue humanitarian objectives through their foreign and defence apparatus, while non-governmental organisations conduct humanitarian diplomacy when they require access to populations affected by armed conflict. Traditionally, humanitarian diplomacy has been associated with the work of non-governmental organisations. For the latter, formal negotiations for access is only part of their humanitarian diplomacy work. Civil society organisations have played an important role in advancing a separate form of diplomacy: *humanitarian public diplomacy*. Save the Children, established by Eglantyne Jebb and Dorothy Buxton during First World War, serves as an early example.[18] The two sisters, in response to impact on civilians, particularly children, of British blockades during the war, put out advertisements in newspapers to raise funds for humanitarian relief efforts, as well as in an effort to change public opinion and influence policy.

Increasingly, however, states play a more prominent role with regard to humanitarian diplomacy. States may use diplomacy in a range of ways, but there is an important distinction between humanitarian diplomacy and *humanitarian foreign policy*.[19] While humanitarian diplomacy is conducted to improve outcomes for populations most in need, humanitarian foreign policy can be defined as the use of foreign policy tools, including diplomacy, to advance humanitarian objectives. Traditionally, states' foreign policy has been influenced by humanitarian considerations, where it has been in their interest to do so and levels of humanitarian assistance also say much about bilateral relations between states. For example, when Australia – traditionally an important humanitarian actor, and an important force promoting the Responsibility to Protect principle – provided aid to Indonesia after the Tsunami of 2004 and the earthquake of 2005 in Sumatra, a large Indonesian island, it was able to strengthen bilateral relations. Although Australia had supported Indonesia's independence from the Netherlands in the late 1940s, relations were strained in the 1960s when Indonesia opposed the creation of Malaysia, resulting in the *Konfrontasi*, a diplomatic and military confrontation, which the Indonesian leadership perceived as a Western attempt to thwart anti-colonist forces in Southeast Asia. Australia's humanitarian response helped rebuild trust among the two states.

The development and consolidation of the humanitarian protection regime has meant that concerns for the protection and well-being of civilian populations – including those in other jurisdictions – are a high-priority foreign policy interest. While states have always been morally compelled to act in the face of humanitarian crisis, and such action undoubtedly has always augmented a state's esteem among its peers in the international arena, the emerging humanitarian protection regime has led to firmer expectations about appropriate responses. The structure of the normative regime is such that a state gains esteem among states when it is seen not only to participate in humanitarian action, but also to actively promote protection norms. This may be reflected in advocacy more generally, but also in a state's responses to individual crises. As a consequence, states may feel more compelled to participate in humanitarian action, even when doing so is costly to them in material terms or interferes with other interests. For example, governments may feel obliged to increase their levels of humanitarian aid, if other states are seen to be providing greater levels of aid. This also means that states incur greater reputational costs when their actions are not perceived as in line with protection norms and principles. Where a state directly violates these principles, it must expect sanction through loss of influence in international fora, or implications for bilateral relations with other states seeking to disassociate themselves. For example, China's response following Typhoon Haiyan in the Philippines was perceived by other states as grounded in bilateral tensions over the South China Sea, given that levels of aid were comparatively lower than those of other large economies. Moreover, a growing number of states are reframing their foreign policies, to address protection issues more directly. A recent example is Turkey, which is increasingly pursuing humanitarian objectives in its foreign policy.[20]

States also play an important role with regard to track two diplomacy. Much of humanitarian diplomacy occurs through informal networks. 'Track two' mediation is when, in addition to formal mediation to facilitate a resolution of a conflict, representatives of parties to a dispute come together informally to promote conflict resolution and post-conflict reconciliation. As a pre-fix to 'humanitarian diplomacy', 'track two' implies informal negotiations to achieve humanitarian objectives. For different reasons, parties to a conflict may prefer 'track two' over 'track one' humanitarian negotiation.[21] States may prefer track two humanitarian diplomacy over formal negotiations, so as not to confer legitimacy on non-state actors by recognising their de facto authority over a given territory. In turn, rebel organisations may prefer to engage directly with 'track two' mediators, in whom they may have more trust than state actors when the conflict is between a state and one or more insurgent groups. These 'track two' mediators may comprise former government officials, academics, faith-based organisations, or non-governmental organisations.

In sum, humanitarian diplomacy can connote a range of actions by states and humanitarian organisations. These can be very formalised, such as the public diplomacy campaigns run by non-state actors or the funding decisions of states, but they also rely heavily on quiet diplomacy and negotiations, including through informal networks of influential individuals and groups, so-called 'track two' humanitarian diplomacy. 'Humanitarian diplomacy', narrowly conceived, is about negotiating the terms of access to populations in need and the mitigation of humanitarian suffering, but in its broader conceptualisation, humanitarian diplomacy may refer to a wide range of actions short of the use of force. While the concept is fairly new and usually associated with the end of the Cold War and the changing nature of armed conflict and the need to access civilian populations caught in the crossfire of war, humanitarian diplomacy as a practice is not new. Still, the emergence of the humanitarian protection regime, with its associated norms and principles, has also influenced humanitarian diplomacy as a practice that is today understood as a habitual and regulated practice of an elaborate network of actors including the UN, states, and humanitarian organisations.

Targeted Sanctions

Sanctions – the imposition of (often economic) costs on a state whose behaviour the sender seeks to modify – have been used as a foreign tool for many decades, although their efficacy has been questioned. The scholarly consensus is that blanket sanctions, that is, economic sanctions directed at the economy of the target state, rarely bring about policy changes, yet they typically inflict great human costs.[22] For this reason, states have begun focusing sanctions on particular actors, rather than impose sanctions that place a burden on a state's entire economy. As an instrument available to states under the UN Charter and through the Security Council, generally sanctions constitute a Chapter VII instrument – a means of enforcing international law, without the consent of the host government. Sanctions have been used to attempt to compel a state – the so-called 'target' state – to change their policies and actions. States impose sanctions upon actors, both state and non-state, involved in terrorism, the proliferation of nuclear weapons technology, as well as human rights violations.

Recent examples of targeted sanctions addressing human rights violations include financial sanctions against Serbian leaders during the 1990s, travel and financial bans on Sudanese and Janjaweed leaders, and the freezing of assets of Gaddafi and his supporters.[23] Given that targeted sanctions are a fairly recent instrument for confronting actors responsible for human rights violations, there is limited literature discussing the empirical record of the effectiveness of these measures. However, there are several reasons for why sanctions are hypothesised to work, or not to work.[24] A proposed causal explanation for why sanctions could work is their effect on perpetrator perceptions about the costs associated with continuing atrocities. Moreover, they may also impose reputational costs through public condemnation internationally. However, sanctions regimes may be ineffective if they cannot be monitored and enforced effectively. Powerful individuals targeted by sanctions may be able to evade sanctions by making use of their influence, or by using their diplomatic immunity.[25]

Although targeted sanctions can target specific actors more precisely, they may still curtail humanitarian responses. The imposition of targeted sanctions requires states participating in a sanctions regime to ensure no individual or organisation makes available economic resources to persons or legal entities specified by the regime.[26] These restrictions may affect the work of humanitarian organisations, making it more difficult for these organisations to carry out their work. For example, humanitarian relief organisations may be liable for taxes in a target state, or may be required to cover the costs of travel for individuals placed on a sanctions list to allow them to participate in negotiations for access to populations affected by armed conflict. Humanitarian organisations may also be required to pay registration fees to be able to operate within a state, or checkpoint fees to access certain territories. Humanitarian relief may contravene a sanctions regime, moreover, where individuals associated with terrorism may be among the beneficiaries of relief efforts to civilian populations. Therefore, states have begun including *humanitarian exemptions* to avoid imposing costs on civilians. These explicitly permit certain types of humanitarian aid.

There are different types of targeted sanctions regimes. Types of targeted sanctions include asset freezes, travel bans, visa restrictions, arms embargoes, financial restrictions, as well as restrictions on the trade or transportation of specified commodities, typically diamonds, timber, oil, charcoal, and luxury goods. Where targeted sanctions are aimed at individuals, they target those who are responsible for violation of international law, as well as members of an elite that supports and benefits from a regime that is in violation of international law. Among the most frequently used types of targeted sanctions are arms embargoes and travel bans.

Institutional learning at the UN Security Council has encouraged the formalisation of sanctions regimes, characterised by the existence of systematic procedures, a common and well-defined sanctions vocabulary, and standardised humanitarian exemptions. This formalisation was brought about upon the initiative of four key states, Switzerland, Germany, Sweden, and Greece, who took the lead in refining international practice through a series of coordinated initiatives.[27] The first initiative, the Interlaken (Interlaken is a town in Switzerland) process, took place in the late 1990s and aimed to improve the effectiveness of financial sanctions. This was followed by the Bonn-Berlin process, which addressed two instruments, travel bans and arms embargoes, in the late 1990s, developing model Security Council resolutions. The Stockholm process was conducted jointly with the Uppsala University's Department for Peace and Conflict Resolution. Finally, in the mid-2000s, a Greek initiative worked on ways of improving the general effectiveness of UN sanctions.

Given the burden to the civilian populations of the target state, targeted sanctions have been developed as an instrument to attempt to avoid harming civilians that may be negatively affected by comprehensive sanctions. Targeted sanctions can be applied with more precision to affect specific individuals and legal entities, as a means of promoting compliance with international law. UN sanctions have multiplied and diversified after the end of the Cold War and a key trend has been towards 'individualisation'.[28] While the trend has been towards individualisation, targeted sanctions have not replaced comprehensive sanctions altogether, and there exists a continuum of sanctions regimes ranging from more comprehensive sanctions regimes to more targeted sanctions regimes that target specific bodies or individuals. Increasingly, sanctions regimes have become more rules-based and formalised. This formalisation is expressed through a shared sanctions vocabulary, helping to clarify common definitions associated with sanctions, as well as fewer opportunities for the exercise of political discretion when implementing sanctions.

Similarly, there have been several thematic foci of the Security Council that have promoted the development of a regime to govern the practice of sanctions.[29] The first is the work by states, at the UN, to protect children affected by conflict, spearheaded by a series of presidential statements starting in the late 1990s. The Council stated its preparedness to use targeted sanctions in S/RES/1539, where parties to a conflict recruited child soldiers. In 1999, Security Council resolution 1265 was the first of a series of resolutions on the protection of civilians in armed conflict, and Security Council resolution 1296 stated states' 'readiness to consider … appropriate steps' to do so. Finally, the first resolution on Women, Peace, and Security was resolution 1325, and resolution 1820 referred to 'appropriate steps' that could be taken to protect the security of women and girls.

Regional organisations play an increasingly important role with regard to the practice of international sanctions for humanitarian protection purposes, as they do for all other instruments available to states.[30] Regional organisations have applied sanctions against individual member states or third parties. There are several ways in which regional organisations have utilised sanctions. Regional organisations may implement sanctions decided by the UN Security Council, or supplement sanctions imposed by the UN. Sanctions imposed by regional organisations may precede sanctions imposed by other actors, or coincide with them. An example for the latter is the AU's sanctions on Central African Republic (CAR) and Guinea-Bissau, where the AU requested that the UN make these sanctions universal. But regional organisations may also impose sanctions independently and autonomously, although the only regional organisation to have done so to date is the EU. While sanctions regimes supported or led by regional organisations may serve to reinforce their efficacy, dual-track sanctions may raise questions around complementarity. Different sanctions regimes may stipulate different prohibitions, and these may be incongruent or contradictory. Moreover, some regional organisations are more amenable to sanctions as a coercive tool for effecting policy change in a target state than others. ASEAN, for example, is more sceptical, having refused to include a sanctioning mechanism in its 1998 Charter, and having repeatedly called for the lifting of EU and US sanctions pertaining to the situation in Myanmar. The EU, by contrast, has adopted an international security agenda and has actively pursued the formalisation of sanctions. As of 2020, the EU Council adopted a global human rights sanctions regime.[31] This framework facilitates the targeting of actors, both state and non-state, involved in or responsible for human rights violations, and, significantly, it applies worldwide. According to the framework, travel bans or asset freezes can be used to target the perpetrators of human rights violations. Sanctions may be imposed following a proposal by a member state or the High Representative of the EU for Foreign Affairs and Security Policy, and the Council is responsible for establishing and reviewing sanctions regimes. For the time being, regional organisations vary with regard to their use of sanctions – whether the imposition of sanctions will be a key responsibility of regional organisations around the globe in future remains to be seen.

Policy Choices and Dilemmas

Several dilemmas confront policymakers and practitioners when responding to armed conflict. Crisis diplomacy requires policymakers to weigh the consequences of different courses of action against each other, and determining the best approach. In many instances, a dilemma arises from the need to negotiate, or engage more significantly, with one or more parties that may be implicated in violations of human rights and international humanitarian law. This is a moral problem in and of itself, but there are other implications. Material or immaterial support provided to parties to a conflict may inadvertently strengthen an armed group or a regime implicated in human rights violations, bolstering the group's ability to continue fighting, and prolongating the conflict. There are five distinct policy problems relating to diplomacy and sanctions, which we shall discuss each in turn.

The first of these dilemmas relates to preventive diplomacy and the need to balance immediate consequences with longer-term consequences. When negotiating the terms of a peace agreement, international actors must consider whether to involve one or more parties to a conflict that may be implicated in human rights violations. For example, the mediation that brought about a swift, bloodless end to the post-electoral crisis in The Gambia, in 2017, engaged the incumbent, President Yahya Jammeh, who had been accused of human rights violations, in negotiations about the terms of his departure from office (see Box 7.2). Throughout the crisis, the possibility of ICC prosecution, or at the very least investigations into alleged human rights violations, influenced the negotiations. Jammeh was permitted to leave the country in exchange for relinquishing power, and neither states nor major NGOs called for accountability.[32] The granting of immunity or asylum to sitting heads of state or other officials to facilitate the swift resolution of a conflict had been used in several cases, but more recent scholarly literature and human rights groups are critical of the practice, suggesting it is 'selling justice short'.[33] On the other hand, amnesty was not offered in the case of Syria, which became a protracted conflict, and Jay Butler argues that in some cases, international actors should be prepared to consider this tool, where it is utilised to serve a protective function in line with the Responsibility to Protect principle.[34] Still, international practice suggests a shift away from impunity, with greater expectation that international actors can, and should – through the ICC, regional, or domestic courts – investigate all allegations and prosecute suspected perpetrators of atrocity crimes.

Second, another policy choice relevant actors need to make pertains to the decision to conduct crisis diplomacy quietly, or under the gaze of the international public. The UN Secretary-General, for example, needs to balance speaking out against human rights violations with the possibility that quiet diplomacy may be more likely to bring about positive humanitarian outcomes. This means the Secretary-General and their team must develop what is referred to among diplomats as a 'diplomatic strategy'. For states, diplomatic strategies will be contingent upon a range of factors and may be determined by more than one objective. For humanitarian organisations, objectives are more clearly circumscribed. For the UN and its agencies, the objectives are consistent across cases, but the need to consider the particular circumstances of each case, including political realities, means that the UN's objectives – and hence its diplomatic strategy – will vary. For example, Indonesia has preferred quiet diplomacy on Myanmar, and has not, like the US and the EU, imposed sanctions or targeted sanctions, although the promotion of democracy and human rights are a foreign policy priority for Indonesia.[35] Indonesia's approach is in line with ASEAN's principle of non-interference, which discourages public criticism of other sovereign states as well as the support of rebel groups in other states. While public shaming and sanctions have been ineffective, former President Thein Sein welcomed Indonesian assistance in addressing the plight of the Rohingya.

Third, with regard to humanitarian diplomacy, non-governmental organisations providing humanitarian relief must consider whether, and to what extent, to cooperate with a party that is in de facto control over a territory, and may be implicated in human rights and international humanitarian law violations. In the case of Syria, for example, the majority of relief was delivered to populations in need through the Syrian government, which was responsible for the majority of civilian deaths, strengthening the resilience of the regime by providing resources to it.[36] Generally, there may be a perception of a lack of neutrality in several circumstances.[37] When humanitarian organisations allocate resources to populations most in need, or when they are granted access to affected areas by partisan groups. They may also be perceived as lacking neutrality if they must rely on formal military support for their own security, or if their activities are restricted in ways that advance particular political interests, when local authorities specify the populations to receive assistance, or when humanitarian agencies need to restrict their work to secure areas, rather than operate on the premise of need alone.

Fourth, targeted sanctions may help bring about an end to human rights violations, but targeted regimes may evade sanctions, or, worse, shift the burden of sanctions onto civilian populations, worsening the humanitarian situation for affected populations. Much of the problems relate to the inability of policymakers to predict the consequences of the sanctions and the likelihood of good outcomes and improving the prospects for lasting peace, democratisation, effective humanitarian relief, improving human rights compliance and ending mass atrocities. While some types of smart sanctions can worsen human rights compliance, where they work effectively, targeted sanctions do not harm civilian populations.[38] Smart sanctions have worsened conditions in the case of Cote D'Ivoire, for example. Sanctions had been imposed in Security Council resolution 1572 and subsequent resolutions and comprised an arms embargo, asset freezes, and travel bans. In this particular case, the targeted sanctions were ineffective at constraining the elites they targeted, but led to further repression of political opposition, and encouraged domestic corruption. However, the literature also suggests that these forms of sanctions may be effective when they lower the resources available to leaders for distribution among their supporters, without the possibility of shifting the burden onto civilian populations, for example by reducing public spending. In general, targeted sanctions may be more likely to negatively affect human rights in autocracies with small winning coalitions, where shifting the burden of the sanctions onto the general public through a reduction in public spending is less likely to affect the prospects of remaining in power – but autocracies are also more likely to generate human rights violations through repressive policies.

Finally, another dilemma concerns the use of humanitarian exemptions in sanctions regimes.[39] While exemptions provide legal clarity, critics argue that those organisations that are not included in the exemptions may be more reluctant to provide aid, thereby limiting the extent of aid provided. Furthermore, critics are concerned that the exemption provided may be perceived as an endorsement, affecting organisations' reputation as impartial, neutral actors. While sanctions may be effective, they may also produce overcompliance by private actors and donors, making the work of humanitarian agencies more difficult.[40] For example, banks may refuse to service regions where sanctions are imposed. These and other restrictions may make it difficult for humanitarian agencies to operate in a particular region, precluding humanitarian assistance. Moreover, arms embargoes may limit the importation of dual-use items, items that may be used for the purpose of humanitarian assistance, but that may also be used for other purposes.

Summary

- The practice of humanitarian diplomacy has developed substantially since it came into being with the establishment of the UN and the work of successive generations of UN Secretaries-General. While the institutional architecture has expanded dramatically, the UN still is confronted with limited capacities, and great power politics may define limitations to the influence of the UN and other actors in crisis situations.

- In some situations, quiet diplomacy may stand a greater chance of bringing about an agreement between warring factions or realising protective measures for affected civilians, and allowing international actors to gain access to affected populations. However, quiet diplomacy may also mean refraining from speaking out publicly against the perpetrators of human rights violations.
- States have become major humanitarian actors, and humanitarian justifications have become powerful calls to action. However, critics think it is important for humanitarians to maintain their independence, and for all humanitarian work to be perceived as neutral and impartial.
- Empirical research suggests sanctions are weak instruments for responding to atrocities. Individuals and regimes targeted by sanctions may be able to evade sanctions, or shift the burden of sanctions to other groups domestically. Sanctions may also obstruct humanitarian relief efforts. However, sanctions also send a strong international signal of condemnation.

Questions for Reflection

- *To what extent has the practice of preventive diplomacy changed since the end of the Cold War?*
- *Should the UN, states, and civil society groups ever make use of quiet diplomacy?*
- *When, if ever, is it preferable for states to take the lead on humanitarian diplomacy?*
- *Can targeted sanctions imposed by the Security Council be an appropriate response to a crisis?*

Further reading

- Fabre, Cécile (2018): *Economic Statecraft: Human Rights, Sanctions, and Conditionality* (Cambridge, MA: Harvard University Press).
- Fehl, Caroline (2015): 'Probing the Responsibility to Protect's Civilian Dimension: What Can Non-Military Sanctions Achieve?', in *The Responsibility to Protect and the Third Pillar*,ed. Daniel Fiott and Joachim Koops (London: Palgrave).
- Happold, Matthew (2016): 'Targeted Sanctions and Human Rights', in *Economic Sanctions and International Law*, ed. Matthew Happold and Paul Eden (Oxford and Portland, Oregon: Hart Publishing), chapter 5.
- Iji, Tetsuro (2020): *Multiparty Mediation in Violent Conflict* (London and New York: Routledge).
- Rousseau, Elise and Achille Sommo Pende (2020): 'Humanitarian Diplomacy', in *Global Diplomacy: An Introduction to Theory and Practice*, ed. Thierry Balzacq et al. (Cham, Switzerland: Palgrave), 253–66.
- Sharma, Serena K. (2016): *The Responsibility to Protect and the International Criminal Court: Protection and Prosecution in Kenya* (Abingdon, Oxon: Routledge).

Notes

1 Robert Muggah and Natasha White, 'Is There a Preventive Action Renaissance? The Policy and Practice of Preventive Diplomacy and Conflict Prevention', 2013.
2 Muggah and White.
3 On Kenya, see Noele Crossley, 'A Model Case of R2P Prevention? Mediation in the Aftermath of Kenya's 2007 Presidential Elections', *Global Responsibility to Protect* 5, no. 2 (1 January 2013): 192–214, https://doi.org/10.1163/1875984X-00502004. On The Gambia, see Abdul-Jalilu Ateku, 'Regional Intervention in the Promotion of Democracy in West Africa: An Analysis of the Political Crisis in the Gambia and ECOWAS' Coercive Diplomacy', *Conflict, Security & Development* 20, no. 6 (1 November 2020): 677–96, https://doi.org/10.1080/14678802.2020.1854954; Rebecca Brubaker and Dirk Druet, 'Back from the Brink: A Comparative Study of UN Preventive Diplomacy in West and Central Africa: The Gambia and Gabon' (United Nations University Centre for Policy Research, n.d.).
4 These are described in Bertrand G. Ramcharan, *Preventive Diplomacy at the UN* (Bloomington, Indiana: Indiana University Press, 2008).
5 Richard Gowan, '"Less Bound to the Desk": Ban Ki-Moon, the UN, and Preventive Diplomacy', *Global Governance: A Review of Multilateralism and International Organizations* 18, no. 4 (12 August 2012): 387–404, https://doi.org/10.1163/19426720-01804001.
6 Barry H. Steiner, *Collective Preventive Diplomacy: A Study in International Conflict Management* (Albany, NY: SUNY, 2004).
7 Adam Day, 'Firefighting on Multiple Fronts: Preventive Diplomacy in Lebanon through the Syria Crisis (2011–17)', UN Preventive Diplomacy (United Nations University Centre for Policy Research, 2018).
8 Laurie Nathan, 'UN Preventive Diplomacy and Facilitation of Dialogue in Malawi (2011–12)', UN Preventive Diplomacy (United Nations University Centre for Policy Research, 2018).
9 Emmers discusses the role of the ARF. Ralf Emmers and See Seng Tan, 'The ASEAN Regional Forum and Preventive Diplomacy: Built to Fail?', *Asian Security* 7, no. 1 (28 February 2011): 44–60, https://doi.org/10.1080/14799855.2011.548211.
10 Muggah and White, 'Is There a Preventive Action Renaissance?'
11 A good description of the role of the AU and RECs is provided in Sophie Desmidt, 'Conflict Management and Prevention under the African Peace and Security Architecture (APSA) of the African Union', ed. Bruce Lamont, *Africa Journal of Management* 5, no. 1 (2 January 2019): 79–97, https://doi.org/10.1080/23322373.2018.1563465.
12 The OSCE's role is described in Matthew Levinger, 'Forging Consensus for Atrocity Prevention: Assessing the Record of the OSCE', *Genocide Studies and Prevention* 11, no. 3 (2018): 60–74.
13 Muggah and White, 'Is There a Preventive Action Renaissance?'
14 Nina Wilén and Paul D. Williams, 'The African Union and Coercive Diplomacy: The Case of Burundi', *The Journal of Modern African Studies* 56, no. 4 (December 2018): 673–96, https://doi.org/10.1017/S0022278X18000459.
15 Emmers and Tan, 'The ASEAN Regional Forum and Preventive Diplomacy'.
16 Cecilia Jacob, 'The Status of Human Protection in International Law and Institutions: The United Nations Prevention and Protection Architecture', *The Australian Year Book of International Law Online* 38, no. 1 (12 December 2021): 110–33, https://doi.org/10.1163/26660229_03801006.
17 A good definition of the field, its meaning, scope, and origins can be found in Antonio De Lauri, 'Humanitarian Diplomacy: A New Research Agenda', *CMI Brief* 2018:4 (2018), https://www.cmi.no/publications/6536-humanitarian-diplomacy-a-new-research-agenda.
18 Larry Winter Roeder and Albert Simard, 'A Practical Model for Diplomacy and Negotiation: Steps 4-6 – The Negotiation and Implementation Stages', in *Diplomacy and Negotiation for Humanitarian NGOs*, ed. Jr. Roeder Larry Winter and Albert Simard, Humanitarian Solutions in the 21st Century (New York, NY: Springer, 2013), 51–97, https://doi.org/10.1007/978-1-4614-7113-4_3.

19 A discussion of reasons for states' engagement in humanitarian diplomacy, including examples, is available in Jacinta O'Hagan, 'Australia and the Promise and the Perils of Humanitarian Diplomacy', *Australian Journal of International Affairs* 70, no. 6 (1 November 2016): 657–69, https://doi.org/10.1080/10357718.2016.1220495.
20 Federico Donelli, 'Features, Aims and Limits of Turkey's Humanitarian Diplomacy', *Central European Journal of International and Security Studies* 11 (5 October 2017): 59–83.
21 Donelli.
22 Robert A. Pape, 'Why Economic Sanctions Do Not Work', *International Security* 22, no. 2 (1997): 90–136, https://doi.org/10.2307/2539368.
23 Matthew Krain, 'The Effect of Economic Sanctions on the Severity of Genocides or Politicides', *Journal of Genocide Research* 19, no. 1 (2016): 88–111.
24 These are summarised in Krain.
25 Larissa Van den Herik, 'The Individualization and Formalization of UN Sanctions', in *Research Handbook on UN Sanctions and International Law* (Cheltenham: Edward Elgar, 2017), 1–18.
26 A good discussion of sanctions regimes and humanitarian exemptions is provided in Katie King, Naz K. Modirzadeh, and Dustin A. Lewis, 'Understanding Humanitarian Exemptions: UN Security Council Sanctions and Principled Humanitarian Action', in *Working Group Briefing Memorandum* (Harvard Law School Program on International Law and Armed Conflict Counterterrorismand Humanitarian Engagement Project, 2016), https://dash.harvard.edu/handle/1/29998395.
27 These are described in detail in Sue E. Eckert, 'The Evolution and Effectiveness of UN Targeted Sanctions', in *Research Handbook on UN Sanctions and International Law*, ed. Larissa Van den Herik (Cheltenham: Edward Elgar, 2017), 52–72.
28 Post-Cold War trends are described in detail in Van den Herik, 'The Individualization and Formalization of UN Sanctions'.
29 These are described in Matthew Happold, 'UN Sanctions as Human Rights and Humanitarian Law Devices', in *Research Handbook on UN Sanctions and International Law*, ed. Larissa Van den Herik (Cheltenham: Edward Elgar, 2017), 125–46.
30 The role of regional organisation is discussed in Mirko Sossai, 'UN Sanctions and Regional Organizations: An Analytical Framework', in *Research Handbook on UN Sanctions and International Law*, ed. Larissa Van den Herik (Cheltenham: Edward Elgar, 2017), 52–72.
31 'EU Adopts a Global Human Rights Sanctions Regime', https://www.consilium.europa.eu/en/press/press-releases/2020/12/07/eu-adopts-a-global-human-rights-sanctions-regime/.
32 Mark Kersten, 'Could Yahya Jammeh End Up at the International Criminal Court?', *Justice in Conflict* (blog), 23 January 2017, https://justiceinconflict.org/2017/01/23/could-yahya-jammeh-end-up-at-the-international-criminal-court/.
33 'Selling Justice Short', Human Rights Watch, 7 July 2009, https://www.hrw.org/report/2009/07/07/selling-justice-short/why-accountability-matters-peace.
34 Jay Butler, 'Amnesty for Even the Worst Offenders', *Washington University Law Review* 95, no. 3 (n.d.).
35 ASEAN's non-interference principle, and Indonesia's foreign policy is described in Mohamad Rosyidin, 'Reconciling State's Sovereignty with Global Norms: Indonesia's Quiet Diplomacy in Myanmar and the Feasibility of the Implementation of Responsibility to Protect (R2P) in Southeast Asia', *Global Responsibility to Protect* 12, no. 1 (17 February 2020): 11–36, https://doi.org/10.1163/1875984X-01201003.
36 Carsten Wieland, *Syria and the Neutrality Trap: The Dilemmas of Delivering Humanitarian Aid through Violent Regimes* (London: I.B. Tauris, 2021).
37 Grant Broussard et al., 'Challenges to Ethical Obligations and Humanitarian Principles in Conflict Settings: A Systematic Review', *Journal of International Humanitarian Action* 4, no. 1 (5 September 2019): 15, https://doi.org/10.1186/s41018-019-0063-x.
38 The effectiveness of smart sanctions is discussed in Jiyoun Park and Hyun Jin Choi, 'Are Smart Sanctions Smart Enough? An Inquiry into When Leaders Oppress Civilians under UN Targeted Sanctions', *International Political Science Review*, 26 June 2020, https://doi.org/10.1177/0192512120931957.

39 King, Modirzadeh, and Lewis, 'Understanding Humanitarian Exemptions: UN Security Council Sanctions and Principled Humanitarian Action'.

40 Examples of the ways in which sanctions may impede humanitarian action are provided in Rebecca Brubaker and Sophie Huvé, *UN Sanctions and Humanitarian Action: Review of Past Research and Proposals for Future Investigation* (United Nations University, 2021).

8 Reaction

Chapter 7 discussed the practice of diplomacy and mediation as a responsibility of international actors, discussing the role of policymakers and practitioners working in the background to prevent conflict or mitigate conflict escalation and the consequences for civilian populations. Chapter 8 now turns to the practices of peacekeeping and humanitarian relief, both mechanisms of managing conflict and its consequences on the ground. The origins of peacekeeping and humanitarian action, discussed in depth in Part I, can be traced to the early 20th century. Chapters 2 and 3 have outlined the role of the UN in developing peacekeeping as a practice. Traditional peacekeeping saw the UN act as an impartial arbiter to help keep the peace after parties to a conflict had reached an agreement and laid down their arms. Only gradually, and following numerous setbacks, most notably failures in Rwanda and Srebrenica, did UN peacekeeping adapt to permit more robust responses to conflict to allow UN peacekeepers to intervene proactively to protect civilian populations. Today, UN peacekeeping is typically a comprehensive, multifaceted practice involving a wide range of actors, both civilian and military. While the UN continues to be a leading actor, it is worth noting that regional organisations, as outlined in Chapter 4, have become significant actors. Both the AU and the EU have conducted their own peacekeeping and conflict prevention missions. Likewise, humanitarian action has become a highly organised activity comprising numerous state-based and non-state actors.

This chapter takes a closer look at the contemporary practice of peacekeeping and humanitarian action, what it entails, and the rules and norms associated with this form of responding to ongoing conflict. States have drawn their conclusions from previous crises and, in conjunction with norms advocacy and policy reform, international peacekeeping efforts have become highly regulated forms of social practice. Similarly, humanitarian relief is routinely orchestrated among several actors within a network. This chapter will discuss the literature on peacekeeping successes and failures, and perceptions about weaknesses and tabled proposals for how these weaknesses can be addressed to provide more effective protection to at-risk populations. With regard to humanitarian action, this chapter will take a closer look at the concept of 'do no harm', and humanitarian action in practice. The final part of this chapter turns to some ethical dilemmas and normative questions that routinely arise in the context of international peacekeeping and humanitarian aid. These questions relate to the norms underpinning international intervention; the unintended consequences of the provision of humanitarian aid; and the motives that guide decision-making on intervention.

DOI: 10.4324/9781003006671-11

International Peacekeeping

International peacekeeping as a practice has undergone some major changes in recent decades, but with regard to some essential features, it has remained fairly unchanged. The following section will discuss changes and how they have impacted the practice of peacekeeping. Importantly, the changes have not been limited to the practice as such – the way practitioners and scholars think about, conceptualise, and assess peacekeeping as such has changed substantially in recent years. We will now look at some changes with regard to the way scholars and practitioners think about peacekeeping, and then the implications for the practice of peacekeeping.

The study of peacekeeping as a practice has grown substantially in recent years. Reflective of this trend, the journal *International Peacekeeping* was established after the end of the Cold War, with the first issue appearing in 1994. In its foreword, Brian Urquhart, former UN Under Secretary-General for Special Political Affairs and the principal architect of UN peacekeeping,[1] suggested there had been 'little systematic chronicling of peacekeeping operations in a form that is accessible to the interested public' in the past.[2] This has now changed, with peacekeeping having become established as a field of research. There is now a substantial body of scholarship engaging with a range of questions, including questions around the conditions under which peacekeeping can be successful in protecting civilians, ending conflicts or shortening their duration, and positive peace. The Oxford Handbook of United Nations Peacekeeping was first published in 2015, and is another valuable reference resource covering central concepts related to peacekeeping, as well as its history.[3] Generally, it is difficult to assess the effectiveness of peacekeeping as a practice of international actors – the *Oxford Handbook* dedicates a whole chapter to this problem.[4] When discussing peacekeeping success, blanket assessments about the successes and failures of the UN have been common. Against which objectives is a peacekeeping mission assessed? These can vary from assessing missions based on their own aims as per their mandates, or extraneous indicators, such as whether the operation helped bring about an end to the conflict,[5] whether it has helped limit levels of violence,[6] or positively influenced the capacity of international actors to provide relief. However, these assessments are complicated by the fact that it is difficult to know the counterfactual – what would have occurred if international actors had not intervened. Recent advances in research employing quantitative methods is helping to shed light on some of these questions, but overall the field continues to rely on qualitative research and in-depth case study to identify the causal relationships that are important for understanding the conditions under which peacekeeping operations succeed, and the conditions under which they fail to succeed in mitigating conflict, protect civilians, and support local peacebuilding processes.

The scholarship on peacekeeping reflects the transformations that have occurred with regard to its practice. This scholarship engages with the norms that govern the expectations of international actors with regard to the conditions under which peacekeeping is considered appropriate, the way peacekeeping operations are conducted, the aims and scope of present-day peacekeeping operations, and their mandates. Present-day peacekeeping operations are routinely equipped with a Chapter VII mandate, authorising robust measures, including the use of force.[7] Traditionally, peacekeeping had been defensive in nature, constituting a neutral force to monitor peace agreements reached by parties to a conflict. Examples of these types of missions include the UN

Truce Supervision Organization (UNTSO) of May 1948 to observe the ceasefire agreements, or the UN Military Observer Group in India and Pakistan, which was tasked with reporting on violations of the ceasefire. The Council has deployed peacekeeping missions regularly since the end of the Cold War, and in recent years, there has been a shift to an emphasis on civilian protection. Examples of missions tasked with civilian protection include the UN Mission in Sierra Leone (UNAMSIL), authorised by Resolution 1270 of 1999, which had an explicit mandate for civilian protection. In 2000, the Report of the Panel on United Nations Peace Operations, also known as the Brahimi Report, was published. Today peacekeeping operations are routinely equipped with a wider mandate, peacekeeping operations are more complex, and peacekeepers are increasingly also combatants.

Contemporary peacekeeping operations are multidimensional, and their tasks include facilitation of the political peacebuilding process, and support for DDR, as well as the support of electoral processes. Multidimensional peacekeeping operations have three main objectives: first, the traditional objective of providing security; second, the provision of humanitarian assistance; and, third, political objectives.[8] They seek to go beyond the traditional roles of monitoring a ceasefire and providing civilian protection, to address longer-term peacebuilding objectives. Civilian peacekeepers are made of both international and national staff and are engaged in a range of tasks including mission leadership, liaising between uniformed staff and local actors, language assistance, and administrative support. This broader mandate of contemporary peacekeeping operations has, in turn, prompted new research into the consequences of multidimensional peacekeeping in the longer term for 'peacekept' states, although there are again significant challenges of assessment (the tasks associated with longer-term peacebuilding will be discussed in more detail in Chapter 9).[9] An example of a multidimensional peacekeeping operation is the UN Stabilisation Mission in Haiti (MINUSTAH), a long-running UN peace operation that was in place between 2004 and 2017. The mission's mandate encompassed the restoration of security, the strengthening of domestic institutions including judicial institutions, and the promotion of human rights. The mission also included a Gender Unit, and indeed, contemporary peacekeeping operations are all now routinely equipped with gender focal points.[10] However, in recent years the proportion of civilian roles within peacekeeping operations has fallen, reversing a growth trend in the early 2000s.[11]

Similarly, significant changes have occurred with regard to the financing of peacekeeping operations more generally. While the expenditure for peacekeeping grew dramatically after the end of the Cold War,[12] and the UN still deployed approximately 95,000 peacekeepers in 2020, there has been a 23 per cent budget reduction since 2015.[13] Whether or not this is a trend pointing to declining significance of UN peacekeeping, or a temporary trend, remains to be seen. Undoubtedly, regional organisations are becoming increasingly relevant first responders to crisis situations. Still, the current reduction of resources provided by states to UN peacekeeping does not necessarily signal the overall decline of UN peacekeeping practice, given the continued demand for conflict resolution and protection responses at the global level.[14] What is required, Carayannis and Weiss argue, is a 'Third UN' if the organisation is to remain relevant in a post-COVID world in which funding is even scarcer.[15] This can be achieved, the authors suggest, by more budgetary resources being provided not only by governments, but also by philanthropies.

Finally, the role of technology has had an important impact on international peacekeeping, particularly in the context of the COVID-19 pandemic which has acted as a catalyst for many changes.[16] For example, the UN has had to identify a core set of tasks that need to be carried out, including the protection of civilians, the provision of humanitarian assistance, and the protection of key infrastructure. Most of the civilian functions of multidimensional peacekeeping forces were being carried out remotely during the pandemic, and both civilian and uniformed staff were working from their homes or mission accommodations. The pandemic promoted the digitalisation of all planning and support tasks. While these changes may have had a positive impact with regard to efficiency, the consequences were devastating with regard to local ownership as a lack of internet availability meant a loss of input from national staff. As a consequence, the UN has been working to improve its communications and data infrastructure; all changes that are bound to influence the way the UN will operate in future.

As the above discussion has shown, international peacekeeping has undergone some major changes, particularly in the context of developments brought by the COVID-19 pandemic. Peacekeeping operations today are routinely equipped with robust mandates and are comprehensive in scope and with regard to their objectives. The increasing significance of peacekeeping as a practice is reflected in the growth of scholarship on UN peacekeeping. At the same time, the global pandemic may affect funding for peacekeeping in the medium term. Moreover, general trends, including increasing urbanisation and the changing distribution of power at the international level, with the increasing role played by the BRICS, will undoubtedly affect UN peacekeeping in the future.[17] In sum, the practice of peacekeeping has changed substantially since the end of the Cold War, bureaucratically, politically, as well as with regard to the political economy of peacekeeping. It is, however, a robust institution of international society – one unlikely, despite the contraction in overall funding levels, to disappear in future.

Humanitarian Relief

The practices that make up the field of humanitarian action today have been subject to profound changes in recent decades, both with regard to the international norms and thinking in the policy world, as well with regard to the means and modes of delivering humanitarian relief to civilians and non-combatants affected by conflict. However, the question remains, as before with regard to peacekeeping, whether this changed landscape for humanitarian action is significantly and qualitatively different to humanitarian action throughout the 20th century, after humanitarian action emerged in a formalised form in the first half of the 20th century. We would expect humanitarianism to have constituted a new kind of practice if some of its essential features had changed. As outlined in previous chapters on the origins of humanitarianism and the actors, both state and non-state, associated with this practice, one of the essential features of humanitarian action is that it has always been premised on the principle of neutrality. Human rights-based approaches have become increasingly important, and the work of states, as Chapter 4 outlined, has grown more significant in the sphere of humanitarian action as the funding provided by states has become an important source of resources for the civil society organisations co-ordinating the relief; but states are also important humanitarian leaders in their own right, with states increasingly couching their own foreign policy objectives and actions in humanitarian terms and tied to broader human security and development objectives. The role of technology has become more salient in the way humanitarian action is coordinated and the way that relief is delivered. There are, however, other ways in which the field has been changing, and it is worth looking in some more detail at the changes outlined earlier, as well as some other recent changes.

Human-rights based approaches to humanitarian action have emerged fairly recently. These approaches espouse traditional principles of impartiality and humanity, but they are not politically naïve and prepared to depart from the principle of neutrality where it serves the interest of defending and promoting human rights.[18] However, to what extent these approaches have changed humanitarian practice is debatable. Humanitarian action has always been political, as illustrated in the case of the Biafra conflict, described in Chapter 2. Ample literature now points to the ways in which human rights-based approaches inform and shape the international discourse on humanitarian action.[19]

In any given conflict humanitarian actors are confronted with hard choices around whether, or not, to work in what Anderson describes as 'tainted circumstances'.[20] Tainted circumstances are situations in which humanitarians must engage with corrupt government officials or warlords who manipulate aid, for access to affected populations, or, worse, with de jure or de facto authorities who are themselves implicated in political violence and violations of human rights and international humanitarian law. In such situations, humanitarian organisations must ask themselves whether they are making themselves complicit in the crimes committed by sustaining the activities of the authority whose support is required. There are two dimensions to this problem that are worth exploring separately. The first of these pertains to the symbolic nature of the act of withdrawing or refusing to engage, and the broader normative implications; the second pertains to the immediate consequences for affected populations. With regard to the former, withdrawal or refusal to engage in tainted circumstances sends a powerful signal internationally and to affected groups that international relief actors will not allow themselves to be silenced and are prepared to speak out against human rights violations, strengthening the international human rights and protection regimes through 'naming and shaming' and stigmatisation. Yet, on the other hand, it also suggests that a particular organisation, or the humanitarian sector more broadly, is less wedded to the principle of political neutrality and, in the eyes of the relevant authorities and armed actors, less trustworthy. This may also complicate the work of humanitarians, who may be more at risk in conflict situations. Anderson suggests two ways of addressing these problems. First, organisations might engage in quiet critique rather than public condemnation, where individual aid workers share their experiences and thoughts among each other in informal settings. However, questions remain around the extent to which armed actors are sensitive to informal, off-the-record criticism, particularly when official naming and shaming strategies are already known to be a weak tool to compel human rights compliance. Another way of resolving this problem is what the author refers to as a 'marketplace' of aid providers, each with their own strategies. Where one organisation withdraws, another organisation will fill in the void. In this way, as a collective, the humanitarian aid sector will both provide the needed relief, but will also send a strong symbolic gesture. While some organisations are free to apply more pressure on the government at the risk of expulsion, other organisations prefer not to speak out publicly.

Research by Marte Nilsen surveyed the approaches of several organisations. The research takes a closer look at the case of Myanmar, which had been subjected to sanctions throughout the 1990s. With the opening up of the regime aid activity has been ongoing since 2008. Since then, humanitarians have been continuously confronted with the perennial question of whether to cooperate with the regime, or confront it, as well as the need for access to affected populations. Nilsen found that there are three types of organisations. First, organisations that operate on strict principles of neutrality and make few political statements. By contrast, a second group of organisations is prepared to speak out to confront national authorities and to hold international donors accountable. A third group of organisations is more prepared to work with moderate, reform-minded elements of governments to both maximise access to affected populations, as well as to promote reforms leading to better human rights compliance.[21]

A study on the provision of humanitarian aid in South Sudan illustrates the problems, particularly where there is no clear distinction between emergency relief and development aid.[22] Local NGOs avoided close collaboration with local authorities implicated in human rights violations committed in the conflict. At the same time, the organisations operated in a context where humanitarian work was integrated with longer-term development aid, reflective of a conscious policy-effort to integrate peacekeeping, humanitarian aid, and development within more comprehensive post-conflict reconstruction and statebuilding efforts. These efforts are no longer simply about medical emergencies, but also about transforming conflicts. Where the provision of humanitarian relief is coupled with longer-term development objectives, the avoidance of engagement with local authorities can be detrimental to the work of these organisations. In a detailed study of humanitarian development aid in the Jonglei State in South Sudan, Drazkiewicz describes how neutrality was used by NGOs as a justification for bypassing local authorities. Following the peace agreement, however, the NGOs were not involved with emergency assistance. Organisations were engaged in projects that included the development of local infrastructure and offering vocational training, tasks requiring close engagement with local actors.

Other important changes are the result of global power shifts: the impact of geopolitical changes and the greater proportion of material power and economic wealth held by the emerging powers, the BRICS states and importantly, China.[23] While the liberal international order, underpinned by the UN, the Bretton Woods system, and the international human rights regime, has facilitated the coordinated pursuit of humanitarian and human rights objectives through the institutions associated with this order, the growing political influence and economic affluence of China and other emerging powers means that the international political economy of aid may be beginning to change.

For example, a recent report by the US-China Economic and Security Review Commission suggests that while China has increased its involvement with multilateral humanitarian assistance in recent years, its participation in humanitarian assistance has been driven by political considerations.[24] While China responded to the Nepal earthquake in 2015 with a large force, performing a range of disaster relief activities, China's army only coordinated bilaterally with Nepal's army, rather than through the Multinational Military Coordination Center, as is usual for the coordination of multilateral assistance missions. Moreover, China declined to participate in several UN-sponsored conferences and training for humanitarian assistance missions, perhaps signalling that it is less invested in the existing global institutional humanitarian response mechanisms established by leading Western states. China has been critical of Western human rights advocacy,[25] and China's humanitarian development aid is attached to fewer conditions.[26] These developments could signal future structural shifts in the humanitarian action landscape. It may be that new multilateral systems for the coordination of aid will emerge in future – systems within which China is pivotal – or, alternatively, that China will play a more prominent role in pre-existing multilateral fora.

Finally, humanitarian practice has become more self-reflective and critical and more prepared to re-think the principles that inform its practice. The recipients of aid or protection need first to be recognised as 'vulnerable', and understanding the politics of labelling is therefore crucial.[27] 'Humanitarianism always controls as it cares', Lewis Turner suggests, and vulnerability as a concept can be understood both as an analytical tool, as well as itself a politicised concept.[28] In parallel with developments in academic work, where traditional conceptions of gender and 'vulnerability' are being questioned, organisations involved in delivering humanitarian relief in complex emergencies have begun to rethink the way they conceptualise humanitarian need and groups of beneficiaries. Increasingly there has been recognition among humanitarian actors that the traditional perceptions about groups of beneficiaries – traditionally women, children, the elderly, as well as people with disabilities – exclude men, who as a group may face particular threats in political crisis situations. For example, in 2016 the IRC found that the vulnerability of Syrian men in Lebanon had been overlooked, even though a majority of Syrian men in Lebanon limited their movements and only a small minority had received assistance. More generally, however, the academic impetus provided by critical scholars has prompted humanitarian actors to think about the relationship between aid and control, and the role of aid dependency in a post-colonial world and the way in which the dynamics of caritative action perpetuate existing power inequalities and disempower aid recipients.

These arguments are embedded in more general arguments about the need to decolonise interventionist practices associated with post-conflict statebuilding. Critical scholars point out that the institutions and practices associated with liberal interventionism and the humanitarian relief industry regard humanitarian emergency as a permanent condition – there is always some crisis, somewhere, that requires international intervention.[29] The system as such depends on the perpetual recurrence of humanitarian crisis and, as a form of remedy, liberal interventionism has institutionalised and normalised the use of force. In a detailed case study on Mozambique,[30] Meera Sabaratnam describes the problems – both ethical and practical – of liberal intervention practices and international donors' 'political need to insert oneself into the narrative'.[31] Moreover, liberal interventions prioritise the needs of the interveners over those of the beneficiaries. Although donors have extensive monitoring and evaluation systems in place, there is no accountability for failed intervention. Sabaratnam refers to these practices as 'politics of disposability', a system within which interveners are rewarded and suggesting that 'the primary purpose of intervention is to provide for [interveners'] … comfort and luxurious lifestyles'.[32] Sabaratnam suggests that real ownership and sovereignty can only emerge by putting in place the material conditions to put an end to chronic aid dependency, while interveners, for their part, must be prepared to cede their moral authority while continuing to provide financial assistance – specifically to cede control.

These ideas have been echoed among practitioners, who have attempted to show how humanitarian aid can be delivered in a way that is sensitive to this critique. A 2009 joint report by the Center for Transatlantic Relations and the Global Public Policy Institute, for example, explains what terms such as 'local involvement', 'local participation', and 'local ownership' actually mean in practice, and what the implementation challenges are.[33] For example, 'local ownership', in this context, means the capacity and power 'to set and take responsibility for an agenda and to muster and sustain support for that'.[34] In order to realise this aim, the relevant bodies must be rooted in the target state, and represent the interests of ordinary citizens. This, in turn, requires mechanisms of representation. The case of intervention, humanitarian relief and subsequent peacebuilding efforts in East Timor and Cambodia illustrate the way in which international responses can both help build local civil society but may also marginalise local efforts (see Boxes 8.1 and 8.2).[35]

As we have seen, there have been numerous significant developments in the way we think about and practice humanitarian action today. Humanitarian action will always be premised on humanitarian need. However, states' more direct involvement in humanitarian practice, both with regard to funding as well as foreign policy, means that a greater proportion of humanitarian actors than in the past are involved in humanitarian action that is also shaped by more inherently political calculations. For states whose foreign policy pursues objectives that are tied to the promotion of human rights, this may bode well for human rights-based approaches to humanitarian aid. A worrying trend may be the de-coupling of development aid from good governance objectives. On the other hand, humanitarian and longer-term development aid by many traditional donors and organisations now explicitly seeks to empower local actors; a subject we will return to once again in Chapter 9. While humanitarian action has changed in substantial ways, therefore, some things have remained the same and are unlikely to change – and yet other developments are still underway.

Policy Choices and Dilemmas

The changes with regard to peacekeeping and humanitarian practice have thrown up their own respective policy conundrums and academic debates. The first dilemma concerns a debate about military intervention, and the extent to which a degree of pragmatism with regard to the targets of coercion, in a system that is now more – but not completely – permissible to robust protection practice, is condonable. The second policy dilemma (for academics) or hard choice (for practitioners) pertains to the consequences of humanitarian aid when there is a trade-off between short-term amelioration of humanitarian suffering, and the prolongation of conflict and the humanitarian consequences of continued fighting. Third, whether mixed motives for military intervention are permissible. In the following section, we will discuss each of these problems in turn, with examples.

The first dilemma relates to pragmatism. With regard to coercive measures, the problem is twofold: relating to the decision of when to intervene forcefully or implement other coercive measures such as sanctions against norms-violating regimes, effectively adopting a posture of confrontation rather than cooperation with the host government where this is politically feasible at all, and if so, whether to co-operate with the relevant authorities on the ground. Military intervention is costly both

Box 8.1 Peacekeeping and Humanitarian Action in East Timor, 1999–2012

Following over two decades of unrest in East Timor and urged by Australia and the UN to do so, Indonesia authorised a referendum on East Timor's independence. The referendum was held on 30 August 1999. The result of the referendum showed that the population was largely in favour of independence from Indonesia. However, the vote sparked violence by militia groups against homes and public buildings. To stabilise East Timor after Indonesia's withdrawal from the region, as well as to provide humanitarian relief and support longer-term statebuilding efforts, the UN Security Council authorised a humanitarian intervention. INTERFET was authorised by the Security Council in September 1999. The International Force East Timor (INTERFET) was subsequently replaced by United Nations Transitional Administration in East Timor (UNTAET). The mandate of UNTAET included the provision of security and the establishment of local administration, although the focus in the earlier stages of the intervention was on humanitarian relief coordinated by UNOCHA and UNTAET. Other international humanitarian actors included UNHCR, WFP, WHO, the ICRC, and CARE. The peacekeeping operation was led by Australian forces and was supported by numerous other states in the Asia-Pacific region and beyond. The intervention was conducted with the consent of Indonesia, which relied heavily on international donor funding. The intervention constituted the first time the UN gained sovereign authority over a state. The intervention was justified on humanitarian grounds, prompting scholarly debate on whether the intervention signalled regional endorsement of intervention on humanitarian grounds, or whether this case constituted an exception given a very particular set of circumstances. For example, the UN had never recognised Indonesia's claim to the territory, a condition that may have facilitated decisive intervention. In any case, the intervention, humanitarian assistance and state-building actions were criticised by local actors as being insufficiently inclusive and driven by local needs, and the CNRT voiced open criticism. In response, the Community Empowerment Programme was drawn up to promote local participation and bottom-up peacebuilding efforts by helping to draw up local authorities that were democratically elected. Since the initial post-referendum violence, the UN authorised five peacekeeping and political operations in the country. In response to an internal crisis in 2006, which displaced up to 150,000 people, the UN deployed United Nations Integrated Mission in Timor-Leste (UNMIT). UNMIT's final mandate ended in 2012, but the UN and humanitarian agencies remain engaged in the country.

economically and politically, and it is feasibly only where it would not escalate a conflict to the extent that the outcome of the intervention would certainly be worse in humanitarian terms than the not intervening at all. This means that intervention is by definition more likely in states with weak capacities, and less likely in states with greater capacities. While some thinkers believe that pragmatism can be condonable, so

Box 8.2 Peacekeeping and Humanitarian Action in Cambodia, 1992–1993

Cambodia was colonised by France until its independence in 1953. The Cambodian civil war has its origins in the Cold War era. Following a period of unrest and the government's collapse in 1975, Communist forces took over the country – the beginning of Pol Pot and the Khmer Rouge's murderous regime. Populations in major cities were forced to move out of urban areas, causing the death of thousands during the forced marches. Thousands of members of the educated middle classes were executed. The Communist party abolished private property and pursued a policy of collectivisation, through which at least 1.5 million people died as a consequence of starvation, disease, or execution. In December 1978, Vietnam invaded Cambodia and overthrew the regime. However, the UN did not recognise the new government, the People's Republic of Kampuchea (PRK), instead continuing to grant a UN seat to the government in exile. ASEAN had campaigned for the ousted government to retain the seat of Cambodia at the UN, suggesting the PRK was a puppet regime. As a consequence of a lack of international recognition, the PRK was deprived of international aid and development assistance, which weakened the government. Throughout the 1980s, guerrilla forces controlled the refugee camps, and as a consequence, aid funding by the UN bolstered the resistance, demonstrating the way in which aid can influence conflict dynamics. Following Vietnam's withdrawal in 1989, a peace agreement signed in 1991 mandated a UN peacekeeping operation, which was created in 1992. The UN Transitional Authority in Cambodia (UNTAC) supported multi-party elections and the drafting of the new constitution. The UN operation also helped build local civil society and non-governmental organisations. In the 1993 elections, the royalist party won, and a three-party coalition was formed. A legacy of the comprehensive peacebuilding process is the continued presence of UN staff in an advisory capacity. Despite initial peacebuilding success, there has been a decline in political freedom and the Cambodian government has passed new laws targeting civil society. Today, the country continues to receive a large proportion of its national budget from aid by international donors.

long as interventions alleviate humanitarian suffering, others criticise the lack in protection afforded to those who are left without protection and relief.[36]

The case of the AU's and the UN's peacekeeping operation in Sudan serves as an example. The international response to the atrocities committed in Sudan's western region, Darfur, was what Melissa Labonte has described as 'satisficing', as opposed to 'permissive', or 'conservative'.[37] A permissive approach by international actors is one where states choose robust responses to rights violations. Under the conservative approach, by contrast, states are more cautious and fail to respond or limit their responses to condemning the violations. A satisficing approach, on the other hand, is one where states intervene and want to be seen to be doing something in response to large-scale human rights violations and mass atrocities, but where measures are often insufficient or ineffective. In the case of Darfur, for example, the Responsibility to Protect had been invoked and the Security Council authorised UNAMID. Peacekeepers were deployed with the consent of the host government, but the peacekeeping operation struggled on a day-to-day basis in delivering on its mandate, as it required government approval for everyday operations on the ground, and was perceived by both parties to the conflict as lacking impartiality.[38]

Second, and relatedly, policymakers need to consider the problem of mixed motives. While mixed motives are typically perceived as detrimental to the humanitarian cause, as they can draw attention and resources away from the alleviation of humanitarian need or because they may be perceived to lower the threshold for intervention under the guise of humanitarianism, mixed motives can also function to garner support for legitimate humanitarian interventions and some scholars have argued that the motives driving coercive measures are less important than the outcomes these interventions achieve.[39]

For example, when NATO intervened in Libya in 2011, it did so with the authorisation of the UN Security Council and a mandate to protect civilians. NATO's intervention included the establishment of a no-fly zone and aerial attacks against government forces. However, by the end of the year, NATO's support had gone further, facilitating the overthrow of the Gaddafi regime.[40] Alan Kuperman suggested that shortly after the launch of the mission, NATO's objective changed to regime overthrow – even at the risk of exacerbating harm to civilians. NATO's actions, Kuperman suggested, did not contribute to the protection of civilians, given that NATO and its allies provided support to armed rebels who refused peaceful settlement of the conflict. In the aftermath of the intervention, Ramesh Thakur, a commissioner of the ICISS report, suggested that the case illustrated the salience of legitimacy criteria for guiding decisions on UN authorisation and oversight of military interventions.[41] The intervention added to scepticism about a more robust intervention principle among emerging states, and may have meant that some states were more hesitant about invoking the Responsibility to Protect principle and provide a robust Security Council mandate for addressing the conflict in Syria, with serious consequences for Syrian civilians.[42]

The third dilemma practitioners are faced with relates to the unintended consequences of providing humanitarian aid. Humanitarian emergency relief is intended to relieve human suffering by providing medical supplies, food, and shelter. However, the provision of these supplies can impact on conflict dynamics in ways that can be harmful to civilians. Of important policy significance is the recognition in the academic literature on humanitarian aid that aid may lengthen conflict and increase its intensity when it fuels conflict by strengthening both parties.[43] This creates a dilemma: the greater the conflict, the greater the humanitarian need, but supplying more aid may inadvertently worsen an already bad situation.

There are several distinct mechanisms by which humanitarian action can interact with conflict dynamics.[44] First, by providing local welfare, NGOs may provide legitimacy to warlords and rebel movements, while these groups are left with greater resources to purchase arms that, in turn, fuel the conflict. Second, combatants may position themselves near civilians, effectively using civilian populations as shields. For example, Hutu militants set up their camp close to the Chimanga civilian camp in order to stage an incursion into Rwanda. Similarly, the Sudan People's Liberation Army (SPLA) drew on food supplies provided by aid agencies. Third, aid agencies can inadvertently aid either party to a conflict in depopulating certain areas, by transferring civilian populations to 'safe areas'. For example, Mozambique in the late 1980s moved large civilian populations into camps, where they received supplies from humanitarian aid agencies. Doing so allowed the government to attack rebels in depopulated regions of the country. Fourth, by looting humanitarian supplies, belligerents obtain resources that may be sold or bartered to fund the acquisition of arms. This activity is common and has been observed in numerous conflicts, including conflicts in Somalia, Liberia, Sierra Leone, and the DRC. Fifth, governments or warlords may demand bribes or access fees at checkpoints and roadblocks. In other cases, humanitarian relief organisations may be charged extreme currency exchanges, again directly funding the war economy. For example, the government of Sudan charged relief organisations with a currency exchange rate that was about four times above the market rate for converting dollars to Sudanese pounds. However, there is also evidence to suggest that under certain conditions, aid can have positive effects. A recent survey by J. Michael Greig showed that when coupled with mediation efforts, aid can increase the likelihood that a conflict will end.[45]

To conclude, peacekeepers and humanitarians face numerous dilemmas when engaging in humanitarian action. They need to weigh immediate benefits to affected civilians against longer-term costs. While the provision of humanitarian relief and peacekeeping provide immediate relief and protection, aid and intervention can also affect conflict dynamics in ways that deteriorate the humanitarian situation over a longer period of time. Practitioners need also to balance the need for protection and relief with the longer-term normative implications. Each action by interveners sets a precedent for the future and in so doing, can either promote the strengthening of the protection regime, or weaken it. When humanitarians are no longer perceived as neutral, this may affect their ability to access affected populations in the future. When interveners are perceived as pursuing private objectives, rather than the public good of upholding protection norms, this weakens trust in the protection regime. On the other hand, the practice of protection is infused with politics and humanitarian action can be motivated by private objectives as well as the desire to strengthen humanitarianism as a public good, and mixed motives do not necessarily stand in the way of effective humanitarian action.

Summary

- The nature of peacekeeping as a practice has changed in some important ways in recent years. While contemporary peacekeeping missions are more comprehensive and equipped with a more robust mandate, the overall budget for peacekeeping has declined in recent years.
- Human rights-based approaches have influenced the humanitarian aid sector, as have structural changes, including new humanitarian actors, as well as a greater awareness for the unequal relationships underpinning humanitarian work.
- Humanitarians face a range of dilemmas when deciding a course of action in a given case, needing to consider short- and long-term consequences of their actions. This has given rise to a policy of 'do no harm' among humanitarians.
- When contemplating the use of force for humanitarian protection purposes, interveners are confronted with a range of ethical questions and practical dilemmas.

Questions for Reflection

- *Has peacekeeping become a more successful mechanism for conflict resolution and civilian protection?*

- *To what extent have humanitarian aid organisations been successful at implementing human rights-based approaches?*
- *Have humanitarian organisations been able to promote local ownership and bottom-up, rather than top-down approaches to aid?*
- *To what extent has the policy of 'do no harm' influenced humanitarian practice?*
- *When should the Security Council authorise the use of force?*

Further reading

- Ali, Shahla F. (2017): *Governing Disasters: Engaging Local Populations in Humanitarian Relief* (Cambridge: Cambridge University Press).
- Glasman, Joël (2020): *Humanitarianism and the Quantification of Human Needs: Minimal Humanity* (Abingdon, Oxon: Routledge).
- Hultman, Lisa et al. (2019): 'Measuring Peacekeeping Effectiveness', in *Peacekeeping in the Midst of War* (Oxford: Oxford University Press), 25–44.
- Koops, Joachim A. et al., eds. (2015): *The Oxford Handbook of United Nations Peacekeeping Operations* (Oxford: Oxford University Press).
- Mac Ginty, Roger and Jenny H. Peterson, eds. (2015): *The Routledge Companion to Humanitarian Action*. (Abingdon, Oxon: Routledge).
- Nadin, Peter, ed. (2018): *The Use of Force in UN Peacekeeping* (Abingdon, Oxon: Routledge).

Notes

1 'Sir Brian Urquhart Obituary', *The Guardian*, 4 January 2021, http://www.theguardian.com/world/2021/jan/04/sir-brian-urquhart-obituary.

2 Brian Urquhart, 'Foreword', *International Peacekeeping* 1, no. 1 (1 March 1994): p. 6, https://doi.org/10.1080/13533319408413487.

3 *The Oxford Handbook of United Nations Peacekeeping Operations*, *The Oxford Handbook of United Nations Peacekeeping Operations* (Oxford University Press, 2015), https://doi.org/10.1093/oxfordhb/9780199686049.001.0001.

4 Paul F. Diehl and Daniel Druckman, 'Evaluating Peace Operations', in *The Oxford Handbook of United Nations Peacekeeping Operations*, 2015.

5 For example, Jacob Kathman and Michelle Benson, 'Cut Short? United Nations Peacekeeping and Civil War Duration to Negotiated Settlements', *Journal of Conflict Resolution* 63, no. 7 (1 August 2019): 1601–29, https://doi.org/10.1177/0022002718817104.

6 For example, Hanne Fjelde, Lisa Hultman, and Desirée Nilsson, 'Protection through Presence: UN Peacekeeping and the Costs of Targeting Civilians', *International Organization* 73, no. 1 (2019): 103–31, https://doi.org/10.1017/S0020818318000346; Anup Phayal and Brandon C. Prins, 'Deploying to Protect: The Effect of Military Peacekeeping Deployments on Violence Against Civilians', *International Peacekeeping* 27, no. 2 (14 March 2020): 311–36, https://doi.org/10.1080/13533312.2019.1660166.

7 Changes in peacekeeping practice are described in Scott W. Lyons, 'New Robust Peacekeeping', *Proceedings of the ASIL Annual Meeting* 112 (2018): 109–11, https://doi.org/10.1017/amp.2019.12.

8 The features of multidimensional peacekeeping operations are described in Maline Meiske and Andrea Ruggeri, 'Peacekeeping as a Tool of Foreign Policy', in *Oxford Research Encyclopedia of Politics*, 26 September 2017, https://doi.org/10.1093/acrefore/9780190228637.013.462.

9 Richard Caplan, 'The Foundations of a Research Agenda', *International Peacekeeping* 27, no. 1 (1 January 2020): 70–76, https://doi.org/10.1080/13533312.2019.1710376.
10 Megan Dersnah, 'WPS inside the United Nations', in *The Oxford Handbook of Women, Peace, and Security*, 2019.
11 Katharina P. Coleman, 'Downsizing in UN Peacekeeping: The Impact on Civilian Peacekeepers and the Missions Employing Them', *International Peacekeeping* 27, no. 5 (19 October 2020): 703–31, https://doi.org/10.1080/13533312.2020.1793328.
12 Todd Sandler, 'International Peacekeeping Operations: Burden Sharing and Effectiveness', *Journal of Conflict Resolution* 61, no. 9 (1 October 2017): 1875–97, https://doi.org/10.1177/0022002717708601.
13 Katharina P. Coleman and Paul D. Williams, 'Peace Operations Are What States Make of Them: Why Future Evolution Is More Likely than Extinction', *Contemporary Security Policy* 42, no. 2 (3 April 2021): 241–55, https://doi.org/10.1080/13523260.2021.1882802.
14 Coleman and Williams.
15 Tatiana Carayannis and Thomas G. Weiss, 'The "Third" UN: Imagining Post-COVID-19 Multilateralism', *Global Policy* 12, no. 1 (2021): 5–14, https://doi.org/10.1111/1758-5899.12919.
16 These are described in detail in Cedric de Coning, 'COVID-19 Will Change the Way the UN Conducts Peacekeeping Operations in the Future', COVID-19 Brief, n.d.
17 Cedric de Coning, 'The Future of UN Peace Operations: Principled Adaptation through Phases of Contraction, Moderation, and Renewal', *Contemporary Security Policy* 42, no. 2 (3 April 2021): 211–24, https://doi.org/10.1080/13523260.2021.1894021.
18 Fiona Fox, 'New Humanitarianism: Does It Provide a Moral Banner for the 21st Century?', *Disasters* 25, no. 4 (2001): 275–89, https://doi.org/10.1111/1467-7717.00178; Fiona Fox, 'Conditioning the Right to Humanitarian Aid? Human Rights and the "New Humanitarianism"', in *Rethinking Human Rights: Critical Approaches to International Politics*, ed. David Chandler (London: Palgrave Macmillan UK, 2002), 19–37, https://doi.org/10.1057/9781403914262_2.
19 Michael Barnett, 'Humanitarianism Transformed', *Perspectives on Politics* 3, no. 4 (December 2005): 723–40.
20 Mary B. Anderson, 'To Work, or Not to Work, in "Tainted" Circumstances: Difficult Choices for Humanitarians', *Social Research* 74, no. 1 (2007): 201–22.
21 Marte Nilsen, 'Perceptions of Rights and the Politics of Humanitarian Aid in Myanmar', *The European Journal of Development Research* 32, no. 2 (1 April 2020): 338–58, https://doi.org/10.1057/s41287-020-00265-0.
22 A detailed description of the work of NGOs in the context of the merging of humanitarian relief work with longer-term development objectives is provided in Elżbieta Drążkiewicz, 'Neutrality in Foreign Aid: Shifting Contexts, Shifting Meanings – Examples from South Sudan', *Focaal* 2017, no. 77 (1 March 2017): 90–102, https://doi.org/10.3167/fcl.2017.770108.
23 Matthew Southerland, 'The Chinese Military's Role in Overseas Humanitarian Assistance and Disaster Relief: Contributions and Concerns', Staff Research Report (U.S.-China Economic and Security Review Commission, 11 July 2019), https://www.uscc.gov/sites/default/files/Research/USCC%20Staff%20Report_The%20Chinese%20Military%E2%80%99s%20Role%20in%20Overseas%20Humanitarian%20Assistance%20and%20Disaster%20Relief_7.11.19.pdf.
24 Southerland.
25 Suisheng Zhao, 'A Revisionist Stakeholder: China and the Post-World War II World Order', *Journal of Contemporary China* 27, no. 113 (3 September 2018): 643–58, https://doi.org/10.1080/10670564.2018.1458029.
26 David Rieff, 'Humanitarian Politics and the Spectre of Illegitimacy', *Journal of Humanitarian Affairs* 1, no. 1 (1 January 2019): 46–48, https://doi.org/10.7227/JHA.006.
27 A good discussion of the politics of 'vulnerability', with recent examples, can be found in Lewis Turner, 'The Politics of Labeling Refugee Men as "Vulnerable"', *Social Politics: International Studies in Gender, State & Society* 28, no. 1 (1 March 2021): 1–23, https://doi.org/10.1093/sp/jxz033.
28 Turner.
29 Philip Cunliffe, *Cosmopolitan Dystopia* (Manchester: Manchester University Press, 2020).

30 Meera Sabaratnam, *Decolonising Intervention: International Statebuilding in Mozambique* (London: Rowman & Littlefield, 2017).
31 Sabaratnam, 133.
32 Sabaratnam, 134.
33 Beatrice Pouligny, 'Supporting Local Ownership in Humanitarian Action', Humanitarian Policy Paper Series (Center for Transatlantic Relations, Global Public Policy Institute, 2009).
34 Pouligny.
35 General background information on UN peacekeeping operations in East Timor can be found here: 'United Nations Integrated Mission in Timor-Leste (UNMIT)', https://peacekeeping.un.org/mission/past/unmit/. A good summary of critical arguments on the failure to promote local participation during the initial phase of the intervention can be found in Ian Patrick, 'East Timor Emerging from Conflict: The Role of Local NGOs and International Assistance', *Disasters* 25, no. 1 (2001): 48–66, https://doi.org/10.1111/1467-7717.00161; and Tanja Hohe, 'Local Governance after Conflict: Community Empowerment in East Timor', *Journal of Peacebuilding & Development* 1, no. 3 (1 March 2004): 45–56, https://doi.org/10.1080/15423166.2004.681592442113. For a discussion of the extent to which the intervention indicated changing regional attitudes to state sovereignty, see James Cotton, 'Against the Grain: The East Timor Intervention', *Survival* 43, no. 1 (1 March 2001): 127–42, https://doi.org/10.1080/00396330112331343015. For the conflict in Cambodia and regional as well as international responses, see Lee Jones, 'ASEAN Intervention in Cambodia: From Cold War to Conditionality', *The Pacific Review* 20, no. 4 (20 November 2007): 523–50, https://doi.org/10.1080/09512740701672001; Cecilia Jacob, 'Practising Civilian Protection: Human Security in Myanmar and Cambodia', *Security Dialogue* 45, no. 4 (1 August 2014): 391–408, https://doi.org/10.1177/0967010614535831; Kheang Un, 'A Mixed Legacy: The United Nations Intervention in Cambodia', *International Peacekeeping* 27, no. 1 (1 January 2020): 22–28, https://doi.org/10.1080/13533312.2019.1710369.
36 Noele Crossley, 'Conceptualising Consistency: Coherence, Principles, and the Practice of Human Protection', *Global Responsibility to Protect*, forthcoming; Noele Crossley, 'Consistency, Protection, Responsibility: Revisiting the Debate on Selective Humanitarianism', *Global Governance: A Review of Multilateralism and International Organizations*, forthcoming.
37 Melissa T. Labonte, 'Whose Responsibility to Protect? The Implications of Double Manifest Failure for Civilian Protection', *The International Journal of Human Rights* 16, no. 7 (1 October 2012): 982–1002.
38 Noele Crossley, *Evaluating the Responsibility to Protect: Mass Atrocity Prevention as a Consolidating Norm in International Society*, 1st ed. (Milton Park, Abingdon, Oxon; New York, NY: Routledge, 2016).
39 Alex J. Bellamy, 'Motives, Outcomes, Intent and the Legitimacy of Humanitarian Intervention', *Journal of Military Ethics* 3, no. 3 (1 November 2004): 216–32; Noele Crossley, 'Explaining Inconsistency: Motive, Intent, and the Practice of Human Protection', *South African Journal of International Affairs* 27, no. 3 (2 July 2020): 413–32, https://doi.org/10.1080/10220461.2020.1837232.
40 Alan J. Kuperman, 'A Model Humanitarian Intervention? Reassessing NATO's Libya Campaign', *International Security* 38, no. 1 (1 July 2013): 105–36, https://doi.org/10.1162/ISEC_a_00126.
41 Ramesh Thakur, 'R2P after Libya and Syria: Engaging Emerging Powers', *The Washington Quarterly* 36, no. 2 (1 April 2013): 61, https://doi.org/10.1080/0163660X.2013.791082.
42 Justin Morris, 'Libya and Syria: R2P and the Spectre of the Swinging Pendulum', *International Affairs* 89, no. 5 (1 September 2013): 1265–83, https://doi.org/10.1111/1468-2346.12071; Derek Averre and Lance Davies, 'Russia, Humanitarian Intervention and the Responsibility to Protect: The Case of Syria', *International Affairs* 91, no. 4 (1 July 2015): 813–34, https://doi.org/10.1111/1468-2346.12343.
43 Neil Narang, 'Assisting Uncertainty: How Humanitarian Aid Can Inadvertently Prolong Civil War', *International Studies Quarterly* 59, no. 1 (1 March 2015): 184–95, https://doi.org/10.1111/isqu.12151.

44 These are described, with examples, in Wafula Okumu, 'Humanitarian International NGOs and African Conflicts', *International Peacekeeping* 10, no. 1 (1 March 2003): 120–37, https://doi.org/10.1080/714002390.

45 J. Michael Greig, 'Helping without Hurting: Ameliorating the Negative Effects of Humanitarian Assistance on Civil Wars through Mediation', *International Interactions* 47, no. 1 (2 January 2021): 79–106, https://doi.org/10.1080/03050629.2020.1814763.

9 Rebuilding

Chapter 8 discussed humanitarian relief and peacekeeping and the practices associated with immediate international responses to conflict and humanitarian emergency. In recent years, scholars, policymakers, and practitioners have had to agree on ways of measuring successes and failures of direct response efforts and to think about a range of normative questions arising from their implementation. This chapter extends the discussion to the longer-term responsibilities of international actors in the immediate aftermath of armed fighting, although longer-term structural peacebuilding efforts may begin before fighting officially ends. For many states, a ceasefire or the signing of a peace agreement is only the beginning of a long process towards sustainable, lasting peace. Peacebuilding seeks to build the basis for positive peace that goes beyond the mere absence of armed hostilities.

The field of study that concerns itself with the practice of third-party assistance for constructing and supporting lasting peace has come to be known as 'peacebuilding'. Frequently, the prefix 'liberal' is attached, to form the term 'liberal peacebuilding'. 'Liberal peacebuilding' has been the subject of considerable critique over the last 20 years or so. This chapter describes the emergence of liberal peacebuilding in the context of the growing number of internal conflicts after the end of the Cold War.

The practice of peacebuilding encompasses a range of activities. Peacebuilders seek to assist with the transition to a peace economy, to support political reforms and the demobilisation and reintegration of former fighters into a post-conflict society, and to help put in place processes for accountability and criminal justice for war crimes and crimes against humanity.

The Origins of Liberal Peacebuilding

Contemporary peacekeeping practice reflects developing ideas about the role of international actors in supporting post-conflict states in rebuilding after the end of a conflict. The institutional development of the peacebuilding architecture was ongoing as ideas and concepts about peacebuilding were being discussed in academic circles.[1] Although efforts to promote peacebuilding internationally have earlier antecedents, for example the efforts to support the reconstruction of Europe and Japan after the Second World War, post-Cold War peacekeeping approaches were first formulated in the early 1990s. Therefore, the development of present-day peacekeeping practice can be described as the product of three distinct stages: post-Cold War reckoning at institutional and policy levels, and the need to adapt to a changed international political environment and new forms of challenges; the formulation of a liberal peacebuilding

DOI: 10.4324/9781003006671-12

agenda, the articulation of peacebuilding concepts and ideas, and the formation of associated institutions; and, more recently, the 'local turn' in peacebuilding.[2] In this section, we will look at each of these three stages in turn.

The end of the Cold War heralded an era of opportunity for multilateral cooperation not only in the domain of high politics and hard questions of security, but also with regard to cooperation in the fields of international economic assistance and transnational development aid. Against this backdrop, the idea of liberal peacebuilding first emerged in 1992 following the appearance of the terminology in the 1992 United Nations report, 'An Agenda for Peace'. In the report, peacebuilding is defined as 'action to identify and support structures which will tend to strengthen and solidify peace in order to avoid a relapse into conflict'.[3] The report influenced scholarly thinking on the topic, and spurred research in this field. Kofi Annan's reform efforts included designating the Department for Political Affairs (DPA) as the focal point within the organisation for UN peacebuilding efforts. However, the proposal for a peacebuilding unit within DPA was refused funding by the budget committee of the UN General Assembly. Developing states feared the Commission's work might lead to greater interference in the internal affairs of states. Initially, there had been discussions about whether such a Commission would ideally be located within the architecture of the UN, or outside of it.

These ideas were developed further throughout the 2000s. In 2000, the publication of another UN report, the Brahimi Report, signposted the beginning of a new peacebuilding era. The report's objective was to review the record of UN peacekeeping. In the report, the Secretary-General suggested that the UN should be a principal peacebuilding actor. Several years later, in 2005, the UN made a decision to establish the Peacebuilding Commission within its architecture. The Commission is comprised of 31 states, including representatives of the Security Council and the General Assembly, the ECOSOC, leading financial and military contributors to the UN. Several bodies have a right to participate at meetings, although they are not themselves members of the Commission: the World Bank, the IMF, the EU, and the Organisation of Islamic Cooperation. The diverse nature of the bodies represented in the Commission attests to the wide range of tasks associated with present-day peacebuilding practice. The Peacebuilding Support Office (PBSO) supports the PBC.

Over the recent decade or so, a scholarship that has begun to reckon with the legacy of liberal peacebuilding practice and the role of international financial institutions has emerged. This literature has taken a long, hard look at the record of liberal peacebuilding practice, and has shone a light on some of the most glaring failures. The critique, however, was not confined to the world of academe: the 2010 report, 'Review of the United Nations Peacebuilding Architecture'[4] called for greater local ownership of peacebuilding processes, as well as greater involvement of civil society actors. The 'local turn' in peacebuilding has also encouraged the study and recognition of local peacebuilding practice and the role of local civil society actors. Local peace activism and civil society efforts existed long before the 'local turn' – but the change in the discourse facilitated the international recognition of, and support for, these efforts. For example, recent scholarship has explored the role of women's organisations in Myanmar, which for long stretches of the conflict have been operating from outside of Myanmar (see Box 9.1).[5]

More recently, critical self-reflection has led to the surfacing of arguments that are critical of the critical arguments. For example, Thania Paffenholz argues that the

Box 9.1 The Case of Myanmar 1962–Present

Burma, renamed Myanmar in 1989, was a former British colony that was occupied by Japan during the Second World War and became independent in 1948. A military coup in 1962 established a single-party, socialist state. Decades of state repression, in which a military junta suppressed pro-democracy activism, followed. The regime has been accused of human rights violations against ethnic minority groups including the Karen and the Rohingya. More recently, two crises in particular received wide international attention and raised questions about the role of third parties. When in 2008, following havoc wrecked by a cyclone (Cyclone 'Nargis'), which killed tens of thousands and resulted in humanitarian crisis, the government refused access for humanitarian relief efforts, policymakers considered the implications for R2P. At the time R2P was still a relatively new concept. While some international actors including Bernard Kouchner invoked R2P, others were more sceptical, fearing that a widening of the R2P concept in this way might trigger further scepticism about R2P. Today, invoking R2P in complex humanitarian emergencies is less contentious, following years of advocacy emphasising the preventive and supportive nature of international assistance and protection measures under the R2P framework. The second major crisis that once again brought Myanmar to global public attention was the escalation of the Rohingya crisis. The Rohingya, who predominantly live in Rakhine state, have no citizenship rights and are regarded as illegal immigrants by the government. In 2017, thousands of Rohingya fled violence and human rights organisations reported the destruction of local villages and crimes against humanity committed by military forces. One year later, a UN report alleged mass killings had been carried out with genocidal intent. In 2020, a ruling by the International Court of Justice (ICJ) imposed measures against Myanmar. At the court proceedings, the pro-democracy leader, Aung San Suu Kyi, who had been released from house arrest in 2010 and who had been awarded the Nobel Peace Prize in 1991 for her activism, defended the government by claiming that the allegations had been misleading. Her speech surprised human rights activists and tarnished her international reputation. Today, there are approximately one million Rohingya refugees in Bangladesh. The case illustrates the role of civil society in complex, protracted conflicts. Women's groups, in particular, have played an important role and have been active since the 1990s. These groups are committed to the goal of gender equality as a cornerstone of positive peace. Women exiles part of the pro-democracy movement formed women's organisations in neighbouring countries. The Women's League of Burma (WLB), an umbrella organisation, drew more international attention to the conflict. Since 2011, many organisations have moved their operations into Myanmar, with WLB relocating to Yangon in 2017. Women's activism in Myanmar is an example of the way in which women's bottom-up peacebuilding practices can help bridge divides and influence the official peace process. In rural regions, such as Kayah State in the southeast of Myanmar, women have been able to raise awareness through civil society organisations for the effects of development projects such as dams, factories, and mines, as well as arranging dialogue among communities.

'local turn' has encouraged understanding peacebuilding practice in binary terms with regard to distinguishing between the local and the international. This overlooks the role of local elites and overstates local resistance, Paffenholz suggests.[6] To address this problem and to allow for a deeper understanding of the complexity underlying the politicised nature of peacebuilding practice, Paffenholz suggests, scholars should be prepared to add further analytical layers and to avoid a romanticised interpretation of hybrid (i.e. local-international) governance structures. Paffenholz describes how these governance structures can be formed at the expense of pre-existing state structures.

Other scholars criticise the absence of a robust 'responsibility to rebuild' by policymakers. Outi Donovan, for example, suggests that the association of R2P with the use of force has discouraged peace scholars from building on the framework – instead, R2P's preventative dimension has dominated the discourse.[7] The local turn in peacebuilding, moreover, contradicts the core assumptions inherent in a concept postulating international post-conflict peacebuilding responsibility.

Bearing these debates in mind, the following sections now turn to four dimensions of peacebuilding practice: security sector reform (SSR), political reforms, economic reforms, and criminal accountability. Each of these domains bears witness to a developing international discourse that is increasingly aware of the inequalities that perpetuate and sustain the power dynamics that underpin the liberal peacebuilding project, and prepared to challenge it and promote critical re-thinking of the way peacebuilding is practiced in post-conflict spaces.

Spoiler Management, DDR, and Security Sector Reform

SSR encompasses a range of activities designed to improve the institutional security architecture of the state. Thus, SSR encompasses reforms of the armed forces, the police, the ministry of defence and the ministry of internal affairs, of justice and law enforcement as well as, where these exist, private security providers.[8] The term 'Security Sector Reform' was first used in a speech by Claire Short, former UK Secretary of State, in a March 1999 speech at King's College London. Since then, SSR has become a staple term of reference in the academic literature on peacebuilding, and the activities falling under the purview of SSR are commonplace in the context of international, regional, and national efforts to build peace after the end of a conflict. SSR programmes target, in particular, those bodies of the state apparatus that are key for maintaining law and order, specifically the military and the police. The aims of SSR can be manifold, but SSR objectives often include the provision of a greater degree of civil and constitutional control over the military and the police, as well as to promote more efficient utilisation of resources by affiliated bodies. Reforms of the security sector may be necessary to improve trust in these institutions after the end of armed conflict, particularly in situations where military and paramilitary groups have been party to the conflict. Reform of the security sector itself forms an essential part of peace negotiations, as former enemies will vie for inclusion and representation in a post-conflict, reformed security sector. A typical reform policy is a reduction in the size of the military, which at the end of a conflict is greater than a military required during peacetime. Other reforms may seek to improve diversity and representativeness among the ranks of military personnel. However, SSR reform is often externally funded and critical scholarship suggests that these typically seek to implement reforms according to a preconceived template, taking little note of local context.[9] For example, in the case of Burundi the UN and the World Bank were involved in post-conflict peacebuilding efforts that included a DDR programme. However, the programme was implemented in cooperation with the government and failed to engage local civil society actors and the ex-combatants themselves. SSR reforms that are devoid of local participation are less effective, as they receive limited local acceptance.

Spoiler management and DDR are related concepts that take place in conjunction with SSR. Spoilers are the greatest source of risk of conflict recurrence.[10] Spoilers are groups who believe the peace agreement is not in their interest and are prepared to employ violent means to undermine it. For example, spoilers succeeded in Angola in 1992 and in Rwanda in 1994. International actors can mitigate the risk of spoiling by implementing coherent peacebuilding strategies. Whereas some types of spoilers are parties to a peace agreement, some types of spoilers sit outside of a peace process. The number of potential spoilers is important for peacebuilders to consider, as weakening one spoiler might strengthen another. Different types of spoilers pursue different objectives – whereas limited spoilers seek minimal goals, such as the redress of particular grievances, total spoilers seek complete power and typically have radical ideologies. The third type of spoiler, greedy spoilers, has preferences that may be contingent upon calculations of costs and risks. While it is easier to accommodate limited spoilers if their demands can be met and it can be possible to assuage greedy spoilers if their demands are met and they are dissuaded from making greater demands through the imposition of high costs, total spoilers cannot be accommodated. Total spoilers will not be prepared to compromise, and any commitments to a peace agreement are likely purely tactical.

Disarmament, demobilisation, and reintegration (DDR) is a concept encompassing three dimensions. First, the disarmament of parties to a conflict, that is their voluntary (or, in some cases, enforced), ceding of weapons. Sometimes, a compensation is provided for the arms. Demobilisation relates to the decommissioning of the institutional and material support structures of armed groups. Finally, reintegration relates to the return of combatants into civilian society. Some former combatants may resume work in a newly formed security sector. The history of DDR is fairly recent, beginning in the 1980s,[11] but by the late 1990s DDR became common practice. By the late 1990s, the more expansive peacekeeping mandates provided by the Security Council also mean changes for DDR programmes, and an emphasis on the promotion of positive peace. As a consequence, DDR became part of more comprehensive programmes designed to promote reconciliation. DDR programmes have been successful, for example in Mozambique and in South Africa. However, in other cases DDR programmes have not fared as well, failing to collect weapons or demobilise forces. Examples of cases of ineffective DDR programmes are Cambodia and Haiti.

Another example is the case of Timor-Leste, where externally led SSR has had mixed success.[12] On the one hand, some newly introduced institutions have remained effective, but on the other hand, insensitivity to local politics inhibited the success of reforms. The peacebuilding process in Timor-Leste began with a referendum in August 1999. To some extent, the SSR efforts, two decades later, have proved successful, improving the general public's trust in the police forces. This demonstrated the success of the SSR efforts, given that the police had, during the conflict, been associated with state repression. This is all the more so given that elites' abuse of police powers continued after the beginning of the peacebuilding process. Police forces were also colluding with criminal networks, posing further challenges to SSR. The SSR reforms in Timor-Leste were far-reaching; under the auspices of the UN, new military, police, and judicial institutions were established. Under the premiership of Gusmão beginning in 2007, personnel released from the military received a monetary compensation. Initiatives for 'buying peace' extended to other potential spoilers. This included a programme of benefits programme for displaced persons, an expansion of the government's civil service sector, and awarding infrastructure contracts to groups who may not have been unsatisfied by the peace agreement. These policies, however, were a double-edged sword: while they appeased potential peace spoilers and encouraged local ownership, they also increased the power of political elites and in doing so was perceived as constituting a new form of authoritarianism.[13]

Political Institutions and Electoral Reform

Political reform in post-conflict spaces entails institutional changes as well as the implementation of reforms designed to promote democratisation. The field, like that for SSR, is vast. The empirical questions pertaining to what works with regard to the main objectives of preventing recurrence of armed conflict, promoting positive peace, and as a part thereof, the promotion of democratisation, are manifold. For example, whether elections should be held immediately after the signing of a peace agreement, or whether this should be delayed. Another question relates to the nature of the electoral process of elections, and how this is best organised to accomplish a smooth elections process that reinforces the peacebuilding objectives. Normative questions around local ownership play an important role as well. Questions revolve around what can be done to make the political reform process as inclusive as possible and driven bottom-up, rather than top-down; and, from a critical perspective, outsiders' role in helping to facilitate political reform can be scrutinised.

With regard to the empirical and technical questions around political reform, one of the key questions relates to the relationship between the democratic transition and the peace process, and the need to ensure that actions intended to promote democratisation do not threaten the success of the peace process. In particular, there are several issues that practitioners need to consider.[14] First, whether to prioritise short-term gains or longer-term objectives; second, how to promote local ownership of the reforms; third, whether to prioritise legitimacy or efficacy; and, finally, how to create a truly inclusive political system. If peacebuilders fail on important questions of political reform, the outcome may be a return to war or a return to authoritarianism. When considering which groups will be represented in a reformed political landscape, it is important not to exclude any groups as these groups may then not want peace, and become spoilers. For this reason, a more inclusive system stands a greater chance of success. On the other hand, a more inclusive system may also be perceived as one that rewards violent tactics by armed groups. A swift transition to democracy increases the perceived legitimacy of post-conflict reforms, but at the same time, early elections can increase the risk of violence. Since the 1990s and the development of multidimensional peacekeeping, democratisation has been a key part of conflict management.

Empirical research on elections timing has shown that holding elections soon after the end of hostilities increases the risk of conflict recurrence.[15] However, there are some factors that can mitigate this risk, for example, the demobilisation of armed groups, whether a peacekeeping force is present, whether there is power sharing, and whether there are strong institutions. From a policy perspective, early elections are however desirable, given that they legitimise the peacebuilding process and the new political constitution of the post-conflict state. Elections are also a significant milestone in a system transitioning towards democracy and as such are often a condition for the provision of aid by donors. However, the other side of the argument is that peacebuilders should wait until effective political and administrative institutions are in place, so that elections take place in an environment where a return to violence is less likely. This means that there is an effective bureaucracy, an independent judicial system, and free media. Where elections take place early not only is there a risk of conflict recurrence, but there is also a risk that any manipulation throughout the elections process could lock in an unfair advantage in future elections. Early elections may favour recent combatants, who may be more likely to renege on democratic procedures. As in other domains, practitioners are faced with a difficult set of questions both with regard to both their choices as well as the timing of their actions.

There are other questions to consider with regard to the timing and sequencing of electoral processes.[16] Another important question relates to the establishment of a new constitution, specifically, whether a new constitution should be drawn up before or after elections. With early elections, there is a danger that the parties to the conflict will form political factions, rather than the electoral politics being determined by policy-driven parties. Throughout the 1990s, interventions were conducted with the objective of quick elections and a swift departure in mind. Early elections were perceived as a milestone of successful intervention. However, at the same time research has established that it may take two or three decades following a conflict before a state's budget can be funded from tax revenue, rather than the support of international donors. With regard to sequencing, peacebuilders must consider also whether to hold national elections before local elections. Holding national elections first encourages the formation of larger parties, whereas holding local elections first can strengthen regional parties, which can strengthen moderate groups, but which may also strengthen separatists. With regard to promoting positive peace within divided societies, therefore, there are two opinions. One approach is to promote proportional representation and multiparty parliaments. This encourages wide representation. On the other hand, some scholars argue in favour of a 'centripetal' (moving towards the centre) approach that may help break down social divisions, rather than to create a system that reflects these along party lines. This system can help produce broad-based parties.

The type of electoral system that is formed in a post-conflict space matters as well. In a case study on Bosnia-Herzegovina, for example, Belloni discusses the advantages of consociationalism.[17] While some experts believe pre-existing cleavages should be represented institutionally, others promote 'integrative' measures that can limit the importance of these cleavages and promote unity. In the case of Bosnia and Herzegovina, Belloni argues, integrative devices were used within a consociational system. In this case, this approach however served to reify ethnic division. In other cases, decentralisation reforms were implemented in an effort to extend political participation to marginal actors at the regional levels. An example of such an effort is the case of Colombia (see Box 9.2),[18] where a constitutional reform facilitated greater political participation at sub-national level. However, these reforms had the unintended consequence of providing armed groups with state funds.

Box 9.2 The Case of Colombia, 1964–Present

The civil war in Colombia has been a decades-long armed conflict between left-wing rebels, the Revolutionary Armed Forces of Colombia (FARC) and paramilitary fighters backed by the government. The conflict resulted in tens of thousands of deaths and significant humanitarian crisis. The conflict illustrated the complex political economy of intra-state conflict, given the rebels' funding was sourced from the revenue from illegal drug trade. FARC organised politically in the 1980s, leading to the establishment of the Patriotic Union (UP). Sympathisers of the party were targeted by paramilitaries, who were supported by the army, which itself collaborated with drug cartels. A new constitution in 1991 led to political decentralisation, permitting FARC to become part of the political process. However, both the rebels and paramilitaries coerced voters and candidates, illustrating the limitations of electoral reforms in ongoing conflicts. The case also illustrates the peace versus justice debate. In June 2005, the Justice and Peace Law was passed. This law guaranteed lenient sentences for paramilitaries who demobilised. It was criticised heavily by Amnesty International for failing to protect victims of human rights abuses. In 2016, a ceasefire was agreed between the government and FARC. A draft peace agreement was rejected in a national referendum in October 2016. A revised peace deal between the government and FARC was signed in November 2016. In 2017, FARC formally disbanded. Following the peace agreement, FARC turned in all of its registered arms, and President Juan Manuel Santos approved amnesties for former FARC fighters. A UN mission oversaw the disarmament process. However, the reintegration of former combatants proved difficult, as some of the former combatants re-joined dissident groups or criminal networks. Similarly, the rebuilding of democratic institutions proved difficult, as decades of civil war had weakened democratic institutions and practices. Today, the conflict has officially ended, but violence and human rights abuses continue.

Economic Factors

Economic factors play an important role at every stage of the conflict cycle. The presence of poverty and inequality can make conflict more likely; and certain structural economic conditions can inhibit the outbreak of armed violence. During conflict, economies are transformed in specific ways, and some actors may have vested interests involved in sustaining the war economy. These factors must be taken into consideration by local, regional, and international actors engaged in building peace after conflict. Local civil society organisations, state authorities, international donor states, international non-governmental organisations, and regional organisations as well as international financial institutions all play an important role in co-ordinating international responses and bringing about the structural conditions that make conflict recurrence less likely, and that are required for positive peace to emerge.

Economic factors are relevant in understanding the causes of conflict in the first place; hence they are also important in understanding their role with regard to post-conflict reconstruction and peacebuilding. In a seminal article, Paul Collier and Anke Hoeffler investigated the relationship between economic factors and civil war.[19] The authors found that states with a higher per capita income have a lower probability of civil war. This is because, the authors suggested, a population whose income is high has more to lose from war than a population with a lower income – warfare causes economic disruption. Poorer states, therefore, have a higher incidence of violent conflict. Other factors influencing the likelihood of civil war are the existence of natural resources; more natural resources increase the risk of war, but at a higher level, the existence of natural resources begin to decrease the risk of war. Third, the size of a state matters as well. A larger population has a greater risk of civil war. Finally, while highly fractionalised societies are no more war-prone than homogenous ones, there is a higher risk of civil war when society is polarised into two groups. Taken together these four factors provide a good understanding of the economic conditions under which civil war is more likely; a hypothetical country with the least favourable of each of these four conditions would have a 99 per cent risk of civil war. Another cause of conflict may be linked to economic inequality, rather than levels of wealth per se. Horizontal inequality, that is 'inequalities in economic, social or political dimensions or cultural status between culturally defined groups'[20] are one important cause of ethnic or religious conflict, although the vast majority of multi-ethnic or multi-religious societies are not violent.[21] Reducing horizontal inequality can therefore help reduce the likelihood of conflict. For this reason, international financial institutions and donor states investing in post-conflict spaces play an important role in a post-conflict context.

When conflicts are ongoing, a clandestine political economy may emerge. Armed groups may adopt criminal strategies, using illicit trade as funding streams. For this reason, states emerging from internal conflict have a greater prevalence of organised crime and following a peace settlement there is a danger of a 'criminalised peace', a situation where corruption and illicit trade in drugs is rife.[22] For example, in the case of Afghanistan a drug economy emerged that in some regions of the state was organised in a way that contributed to political order, while in some regions it contributed to unrest.[23] The case shows that the relationship between the illicit trade in drugs and conflict is a complex one. For example, in Bosnia networks in illicit trade formed that funded the ongoing war.[24] The clandestine economy of the Sarajevo siege protracted the conflict and although an arms embargo was in place, this was evaded.

There are several key actors in the domain of post-conflict economic reform. These are international donors, international aid agencies, and development banks. Like for political and security sector reform, objectives are both issue specific as well as geared at preserving a fragile peace. The objectives of donor states and other relevant actors involved with transitional administration of a post-conflict state include the physical reconstruction of state infrastructure, economic development that is not adversely affected by policies of rapid liberalisation, for example, an increase in inequality; implementing a fiscal policy that is sustainable; and introducing public spending policies that are both effective and efficient.[25]

Using case studies of post-conflict economic reform in Nicaragua, El Salvador, and Guatemala, Roland Paris argued that economic liberalisation weakened prospects for stable and lasting peace.[26] Towards the end of the Cold War, revolutionary groups attempted to overthrow the government in all three states. Peaceful conflict resolution was achieved in all three states by the late 1990s. Three peacebuilding missions in each of these states were deployed to support the implementation of the peace agreements.

These peacebuilding efforts were largely perceived as successful given that there was no relapse into armed fighting. However, Paris suggested that the liberal policies implemented throughout the peacebuilding process cast doubt over the success of the missions, if the aim is to help bring about positive peace that addresses the causes of the conflict and will last once the peacekeepers have left. The liberal economic policies brought about the enrichment of a very few, at the expense of vulnerable groups in society. Therefore, the international efforts have helped bring about the same conditions that contributed to the violence associated with the conflicts. Paris suggested the record, therefore, is mixed: on the one hand, the liberal policies provided access to political participation and representation, encouraging the ending of armed fighting; on the other hand, by heightening domestic inequalities, they may have inadvertently fuelled the conditions that may threaten a fragile peace.

Justice and Reconciliation

Peacebuilding after the end of a conflict entails political, economic, and security measures. It also entails actions that hold those responsible for violations of international law accountable, and seeks reforms to rebuild, reform, and strengthen judicial institutions in the process of post-war recovery. These types of interventions are intended to realise multiple objectives: first, to punish perpetrators of crimes, promote reconciliation, and provide compensation to victims. Second, in facilitating reconciliation and strengthening judicial institutions, to help prevent conflict recurrence and deter human rights violations. Finally, these efforts also have wider significance. In strengthening protection locally, these efforts also help realise a robust international protection regime. The expanding reach and better implementation of protection norms at domestic, regional, and international levels improve trust in the regime and promote the rule of law.

However, as in other areas, humanitarian protection practitioners are once again confronted with a dilemma, a dilemma referred to by scholars as the 'peace versus justice' dilemma. In a nutshell, the question is whether local and international actors should pursue reconciliation among parties to a conflict, even when one or more groups demand immunity from prosecution for alleged crimes; or whether justice should be pursued without compromise. The latter may pose a challenge not only for reaching a peace agreement, but also for grassroots reconciliation and the reintegration of former combatants into society, particularly where large numbers of civilians were among the perpetrators.[27] For example, in the aftermath of the Rwandan genocide, the Gacaca process attempted to combine punitive and restorative justice mechanisms. In a case study,[28] Max Rettig found that while the process succeeded in bringing more perpetrators to trial, they also exposed resentment and the threat of punishment resulted in deception and silence by those on trial. In some cases, aggrieved individuals saw the trials as an opportunity for revenge. Finally, the process did not prosecute crimes committed by the Rwandan Patriotic Army (RPA).

Local and international peacebuilders are confronted with a range of choices when deciding which approach to take.[29] They need to decide whether to adopt a policy of forgetting, or amnesia and amnesty, whether to prosecute alleged perpetrators, or alternatively whether to make use of a truth and reconciliation process. In South Africa, for example, a Truth and Reconciliation Commission aimed both at revealing the truth, as well as at reconciliation, rather than at truth and justice. By contrast, in the aftermath of the Rwandan genocide, a punitive approach centred on prosecutions was chosen. Scholars arguing in favour of truth commissions, rather than formal prosecutions, suggest that the threat of prosecution may pose a barrier to a ceasefire and the end of the fighting, increasing the costs associated with the end of the conflict as former combatants and those responsible are held to account, which in turn may lead to more human rights violations and atrocities than there would have been had the conflict ended sooner.[30] On the other hand, there are strong arguments for legal accountability. First, they provide a powerful signal to potential future perpetrators of atrocities. Second, they strengthen the rule of law and consolidate international protection practice. Finally, they emphasise the guilt of individual perpetrators, and in doing so defuse the potential for conflict recurrence. In a statistical analysis of 32 cases of civil war between 1989 and 2003, Snyder and Vinjamuri found that trials contribute to ending abuses when there is a robust judicial apparatus.[31] Truth commissions can backfire when there are demands for justice, although the authors found that they can provide political cover for amnesties, that in turn may be successful when their use can ensure the removal from power of spoilers by a new regime. Defining success as both a reduction in human rights abuses as well as securing peace, the authors identified successful cases for a range of approaches. In East Timor and Peru, for example, trials and truth commissions were used; in Mozambique, amnesty only was chosen as an approach; and El Salvador provides an example of a case in which there was both amnesty and a truth commission.

Moreover, protection and peacebuilding practitioners need to consider which jurisdiction or institution is best placed to conduct trials. Where international actors have assisted with the trial of alleged perpetrators, before the establishment of the International Criminal Court (ICC) this has typically been on an ad-hoc basis, such as the International Criminal Tribunal for the Former Yugoslavia or the International Criminal Tribunal for Rwanda. With the Rome Statue, a permanent judicial body to try perpetrators of human rights violations has been created. However, the proceedings of the ICC have been subject to criticism, as the court has been perceived to lack independence from the interests of the Security Council and great powers and narrowly preoccupied with cases in the Global South.[32] On the other hand, proponents suggest that at a practical level, it is an improvement to ad-hoc systems, and at a normative level it has helped the campaign to end impunity.

Consequently, the practitioners are faced with a dilemma – whether to stay true to principle, or whether to permit a degree of pragmatism to allow for an expedient end to the conflict. Once again, questions around timing and sequencing are salient – whether, for example, to prioritise the peace process to provide conditions under which justice and accountability can be pursued more effectively and with fewer risks of conflict recurrence; or whether, conversely, to prioritise justice and accountability with a view to promoting truth and reconciliation, and strengthening the rule of law at the state-level, as well as the international human rights and protection regimes. Moreover, practitioners need to consider whether to adopt one or more mechanisms; and whether these should be led and implemented locally, or whether regional or international organisations should play a leading role, and if so, whether the mechanism should be ad-hoc and tailored to the conflict; or whether cases should be referred to a standing court, such as standing regional courts or the ICC.

A case illustrating the complexity of these issues is the case of transitional justice in Côte D'Ivoire.[33] The case illustrates that coordinating DDR and transitional justice can be difficult, given that victims of the conflict may perceive the reintegration efforts of former combatants as a form of reward for their crimes. In the aftermath of the conflict, the new government implemented several recovery programmes, including the establishment of the Authority for Demobilization Disarmament and Reintegration (ADDR) and the Truth and Reconciliation Commission (CDVR). While the work of these bodies was lauded internationally and pronounced a success by the government, victims' groups and civilians objected that they had been marginalised. While former combatants received support through the DDR process, these groups were still waiting to receive reparations. For this reason, some argue a closer co-ordination between DDR and transitional justice is necessary;[34] although others suggest that this may be difficult to implement and lower the prospects for successful peacebuilding.[35]

Summary

- In the long-term, security sector reform can help stabilise post-war institutions and promote the security of civilians. In the short-term, DDR is a form of post-conflict intervention that seeks to help reduce the security dilemma among former belligerents, build trust among former enemies, and provide former combatants with viable opportunities for subsistence after the end of fighting. However, these efforts may not always be effective.
- Peacebuilders need to carefully consider the timing and sequencing of post-conflict political reform. It is important that political actors implement political reforms at the right time, but also that these reforms are introduced in the right order. Moreover, when considering constitutional reform and reform of the electoral process, policymakers have a range of options, for each of which they must weigh advantages and disadvantages.
- Post-conflict economic reform is another important dimension of peacebuilding. Several cases discussed above have illustrated the complexity of the political economy of civil war situations. Above, we looked at the role of international financial institutions, and the successes and failures of economic liberalisation efforts.
- With regard to post-conflict accountability, there is a 'peace versus justice' dilemma. On the one hand, principled action prioritising trials of alleged perpetrators serves justice and promotes the international human rights regime. At the same time, pragmatic approaches such as the use of amnesties can mitigate the risk of spoilers.

Questions for Reflection

- *Which risks do humanitarian protection actors need to consider when implementing long-term and short-term security policies? How can these risks be mitigated?*
- *Should a new constitution be put into place before a peace agreement, or following a peace agreement? What are the advantages, what are the disadvantages?*
- *Does post-conflict economic liberalisation weaken the prospects for positive peace? Why are some scholars critical of liberal economic reforms?*
- *Which should come first, justice or peace? Which justice mechanisms are preferable, and why?*

Further reading

- Ba, Oumar (2020): *States of Justice: The Politics of the International Criminal Court* (Cambridge: Cambridge University Press).
- Chandler, David (2017): *Peacebuilding: The Twenty Years' Crisis, 1997–2017* (Cham, Switzerland: Palgrave).
- Clark, Phil (2018): *Distant Justice: The Impact of the International Criminal Court on African Politics* (Cambridge: Cambridge University Press).
- Duncanson, Claire (2016): *Gender and Peacebuilding* (Cambridge: Polity).
- Mégret, Frédéric and Immi Tallgren (2020): *The Dawn of a Discipline: International Criminal Justice and Its Early Exponents* (Cambridge: Cambridge University Press).
- Pugh, Michael et al., ed. (2008): *Whose Peace? Critical Perspectives on the Political Economy of Peacebuilding* (Houndmills, Basingstoke: Palgrave Macmillan).

Notes

1 A detailed account of the history of peacebuilding thought and practice can be found in Stephen Ryan, 'The Evolution of Peacebuilding', in *Routledge Handbook of Peacebuilding Routledge*, ed. Roger Mac Ginty (Routledge, 2013), 25–35; Lisa McCann, 'A Discursive Institutionalist Analysis of Global Policy Ideas in the Creation of the United Nations Peacebuilding Commission', *Policy Studies* 35, no. 5 (3 September 2014): 458–83, https://doi.org/10.1080/01442872.2014.946481.

2 Hanna Leonardsson and Gustav Rudd, 'The "Local Turn" in Peacebuilding: A Literature Review of Effective and Emancipatory Local Peacebuilding', *Third World Quarterly* 36, no. 5 (4 May 2015): 825–39, https://doi.org/10.1080/01436597.2015.1029905.

3 United Nations Secretary-General, 'An Agenda for Peace: Preventive Diplomacy, Peacemaking and Peace-Keeping: Report of the Secretary-General', 1992.

4 United Nations, 'Review of the United Nations Peacebuilding Architecture', n.d.

5 For a comprehensive political history of the decades-long conflict, see Nehginpao Kipgen, *Myanmar: A Political History* (Oxford: Oxford University Press, n.d.). For discussion of the role of women's groups in peace activism and bottom-up peacebuilding, see Åshild Kolås, ed., *Women, Peace and Security in Myanmar: Between Feminism and Ethnopolitics*, 1st ed. (Abingdon: Routledge, 2019); Linnéa Blomqvist, Elisabeth Olivius, and Jenny Hedström, 'Care and Silence in Women's Everyday Peacebuilding in Myanmar', *Conflict, Security & Development* 0, no. 0 (2 June 2021): 1–21, https://doi.org/10.1080/14678802.2021.1933031; Magda Lorena Cárdenas and Elisabeth Olivius, 'Building Peace in the Shadow of War: Women-to-Women Diplomacy as Alternative Peacebuilding Practice in Myanmar', *Journal of Intervention and Statebuilding* 15, no. 3 (27 May 2021): 347–66, https://doi.org/10.1080/17502977.2021.1917254. For a discussion of the international responses in the aftermath of Cyclone Nargis, see Julian Junk, 'Testing Boundaries: Cyclone Nargis in Myanmar and the Scope of R2P', *Global Society* 30, no. 1 (2 January 2016): 78–93.

6 Thania Paffenholz, 'Unpacking the Local Turn in Peacebuilding: A Critical Assessment towards an Agenda for Future Research', *Third World Quarterly* 36, no. 5 (4 May 2015): 857–74, https://doi.org/10.1080/01436597.2015.1029908.

7 Outi Keranen, 'What Happened to the Responsibility to Rebuild?', *Global Governance* 22, no. 3 (2016): 331–48.

8 For a description of SSR practice and its origins, see Nadine Ansorg, 'Security Sector Reform in Africa: Donor Approaches versus Local Needs', *Contemporary Security Policy* 38, no. 1 (2017): 129–44; Sarah Detzner, 'Modern Post-Conflict Security Sector Reform in

Africa: Patterns of Success and Failure', *African Security Review* 26, no. 2 (3 April 2017): 116–42, https://doi.org/10.1080/10246029.2017.1302706.
9 For a critical discussion of SSR practice see Ansorg, 'Security Sector Reform in Africa: Donor Approaches versus Local Needs'.
10 For a definition of spoiling, a description of spoiler types, as well as a discussion of spoiler management, see Stephen John Stedman, 'Spoiler Problems in Peace Processes', *International Security* 22, no. 2 (1997): 5–53, https://doi.org/10.2307/2539366.
11 A review of the history of DDR, as well as successes and failures, can be found in Robert Muggah and Chris O'Donnell, 'Next Generation Disarmament, Demobilization and Reintegration', *Stability: International Journal of Security and Development* 4, no. 1 (21 May 2015): Art. 30.
12 Yuji Uesugi, 'Evaluating Security Sector Reform in Timor-Leste: The Triad Hybridity Nexuses', *Asian Journal of Peacebuilding* 9, no. 1 (2021): 111–38.
13 Yuji Uesugi, 'Neo-Authoritarian Peace in Timor-Leste', in *National Security, Statecentricity, and Governance in East Asia* (London: Palgrave Macmillan, 2018), 107–26.
14 Anna Jarstad, 'Dilemmas of War-to-Democracy Transitions: Theories and Concepts', in *From War to Democracy: Dilemmas of Peacebuilding*, ed. Anna Jarstad and Timothy Sisk (Cambridge: Cambridge University Press, 2008), 17–36.
15 For a comprehensive empirical study on the relationship between conflict recurrence and elections see Dawn Brancati and Jack L. Snyder, 'Time to Kill: The Impact of Election Timing on Postconflict Stability', *Journal of Conflict Resolution* 57, no. 5 (1 October 2013): 822–53, https://doi.org/10.1177/0022002712449328.
16 An overview of these is provided in Benjamin Reilly, *Timing and Sequencing in Post-Conflict Elections*, *Building Sustainable Peace* (Oxford University Press), https://oxford.university pressscholarship.com/view/10.1093/acprof:oso/9780198757276.001.0001/acprof-9780198757276-chapter-5.
17 Roberto Belloni, 'Peacebuilding and Consociational Electoral Engineering in Bosnia and Herzegovina', *International Peacekeeping* 11, no. 2 (1 June 2004): 334–53, https://doi.org/10.1080/1353331042000237300.
18 A special issue in the Journal of Conflict Management and Peace Science provides a good overview of recent research in the field of peacebuilding, focusing in particular on the case of Colombia. See especially Thomas E. Flores and Juan F. Vargas, 'Colombia: Democracy, Violence, and the Peacebuilding Challenge', *Conflict Management and Peace Science* 35, no. 6 (1 November 2018): 581–86, https://doi.org/10.1177/0738894218787786; Abbey Steele and Livia I. Schubiger, 'Democracy and Civil War: The Case of Colombia', *Conflict Management and Peace Science* 35, no. 6 (1 November 2018): 587–600, https://doi.org/10.1177/0738894218787780; Sarah Zukerman Daly, 'Determinants of Ex-Combatants' Attitudes toward Transitional Justice in Colombia', *Conflict Management and Peace Science* 35, no. 6 (1 November 2018): 656–73, https://doi.org/10.1177/0738894218788084.
19 Paul Collier and Anke Hoeffler, 'On Economic Causes of Civil War', *Oxford Economic Papers* 50, no. 4 (1998): 563–73.
20 F. Stewart, ed., *Horizontal Inequalities and Conflict: Understanding Group Violence in Multiethnic Societies*, 2008th ed. (Basingstoke: Palgrave Macmillan, 2008), 3.
21 For a discussion of the relationship between horizontal inequality and conflict, see Stewart, *Horizontal Inequalities and Conflict*.
22 James Cockayne, 'Chasing Shadows', *The RUSI Journal* 158, no. 2 (1 April 2013): 10–24, https://doi.org/10.1080/03071847.2013.787729.
23 Jonathan Goodhand, 'Corrupting or Consolidating the Peace? The Drugs Economy and Post-Conflict Peacebuilding in Afghanistan', *International Peacekeeping* 15, no. 3 (1 June 2008): 405–23, https://doi.org/10.1080/13533310802058984.
24 Peter Andreas, 'The Clandestine Political Economy of War and Peace in Bosnia', *International Studies Quarterly* 48, no. 1 (2004): 29–51.
25 Richard Caplan, 'Economic Reconstruction and Development', in *International Governance of War-Torn Territories: Rule and Reconstruction* (Oxford: Oxford University Press, 2005).
26 Roland Paris, ed., 'Nicaragua, El Salvador, and Guatemala: Reproducing the Sources of Conflict', in *At War's End: Building Peace after Civil Conflict* (Cambridge: Cambridge University Press, 2004), 112–34, https://doi.org/10.1017/CBO9780511790836.009.

27 Lyn S. Graybill, 'Pardon, Punishment, and Amnesia: Three African Post-Conflict Methods', *Third World Quarterly* 25, no. 6 (1 September 2004): 1117–30, https://doi.org/10.1080/0143659042000256922.
28 Max Rettig, 'Gacaca: Truth, Justice, and Reconciliation in Postconflict Rwanda?', *African Studies Review* 51, no. 3 (December 2008): 25–50, https://doi.org/10.1353/arw.0.0091.
29 Donna Pankhurst, 'Issues of Justice and Reconciliation in Complex Political Emergencies: Conceptualising Reconciliation, Justice and Peace', *Third World Quarterly* 20, no. 1 (1 February 1999): 239–55, https://doi.org/10.1080/01436599914027.
30 A review of the literature is provided in Jack Snyder and Leslie Vinjamuri, 'Trials and Errors: Principle and Pragmatism in Strategies of International Justice', *International Security* 28, no. 3 (1 January 2004): 5–44, https://doi.org/10.1162/016228803773100066.
31 Snyder and Vinjamuri.
32 Kirsten Ainley, 'The International Criminal Court on Trial', SSRN Scholarly Paper (Rochester, NY: Social Science Research Network, 10 August 2011), https://papers.ssrn.com/abstract=2928183.
33 Jessica Moody, 'Reaching for the Impossible?: Coordinating DDR and Transitional Justice in Post-Conflict Côte d'Ivoire', *International Peacekeeping* 28, no. 1 (1 January 2021): 110–33, https://doi.org/10.1080/13533312.2020.1850281.
34 Chandra Lekha Sriram and Johanna Herman, 'DDR and Transitional Justice: Bridging the Divide?', *Conflict, Security & Development* 9, no. 4 (1 December 2009): 455–74, https://doi.org/10.1080/14678800903395999.
35 Phil Clark, 'Bringing Them All Back Home: The Challenges of DDR and Transitional Justice in Contexts of Displacement in Rwanda and Uganda', *Journal of Refugee Studies* 27, no. 2 (1 June 2014): 234–59.

10 Conclusion

This book has set out to provide an introduction to the field of humanitarian protection, a practice entailing a wide range of measures that can be implemented to prevent human rights violations and respond to humanitarian suffering during armed conflict. The book described international efforts to promote protection principles and the origins of the humanitarian protection regime. Humanitarian crises are complex emergencies. While they are not always brought about by political conflict, in many cases they are made more complicated by it. A wide definition of human protection recognises the multifaceted, complex nature of humanitarian crisis,[1] and sits comfortably beside a conceptualisation of security as *human security*, that takes as its starting point the structural and immediate needs of individuals and communities as a basis for scholarship and practical action.

Understanding humanitarian protection is only possible in conjunction with understanding the causes of *human insecurity*. Security and insecurity are themselves constructed and contested meanings, as the discussion at the beginning of this book sought to illustrate. While some conceptualisations of security focus on political factors, regime type, and civil liberties, other conceptualisations show the significance of structural factors and understand security as autonomy, the absence of structural violence, and inequality.

Both conceptualisations can be identified in positivist empirical research and both are also reflected in policy approaches to humanitarian protection. For example, regime type has been found to be a significant determinant of a state's human rights record as human rights violations are less likely to occur in an open, democratic political regime.[2] Liberal systems of governance that are representative provide opportunities for political participation and protect minority groups. By contrast, clientelist, authoritarian political regimes rely on violent means of repressing dissent. For this reason, democratisation features as part of longer-term peacebuilding efforts. At the same time, vertical and horizontal inequalities have been the subject of empirical research,[3] and long-term peacebuilding efforts have sought to take on board the policy recommendations from this body of literature.

Building on the definitions and approaches explored at the beginning of this book, subsequent chapters have described the relevance and responsibilities of state and non-state actors. These actors are routinely confronted with difficult choices and policy dilemmas. Protection responsibilities of states were codified with the articulation of the Responsibility to Protect principle. The principle recognised states' primary responsibility to protect their populations. It also recognised a secondary responsibility of states collectively to assist states in meeting this protection responsibility and

DOI: 10.4324/9781003006671-13

to take the responsibility upon themselves if all else fails. However, while this seems straightforward enough in theory, the implementation of this principle can be fraught with difficulties in practice. For example, humanitarian protection responders face hard choices when engaging with governments that may be implicated in violations of fundamental rights. As a community, the society of states must navigate the boundary between 'assistance' and the acquisition of protection responsibilities by third parties. This boundary is opaque, interpretations vary, and decisions may be contested.

The implementation of protection measures carries its own risks and challenges. Interveners must protect non-combatants caught in the line of fire. Sometimes non-combatants are used as civilian shields, such as in Sri Lanka, Iraq, or Yemen,[4] and sometimes securing access to vulnerable populations means coordinating actions with one or both belligerent parties. The protection of displaced people and refugees searching for safety is a practice imbued with politics, requiring the consent of those with effective control over a given territory, or their patrons – be they rebels, governments with a questionable human rights record, or a government with a given set of economic, strategic, and security interests. International society is premised on norms and principles that do not compel or constrain the behaviour of its citizens in a way that is comparable to the rule of law at the domestic level. As a consequence, urgent crises for which international constituents of international society ought to be able collectively to determine principles and best practices for effective response are highly politicised, preventing the sober, rational and needs-based collective response these situations so desperately require.

The political story of the origins, practice, and responsibilities of humanitarian protection has been the story of this book. And while it has been an agonising and often tragic story, it is not one that ends without hope for the future. As the first part of this book – *Origins* – showed, the story of international humanitarian protection is one of a growing sense of collective responsibility and the formation of an increasingly complex network of global, regional, and domestic institutions. A wide range of actors are today habitually engaged in the protection of vulnerable populations – described in detail in part two of this book, *Actors*. The practices associated with international responses to conflict and complex humanitarian emergencies are described in part three – *Responsibilities*. This chapter now revisits the core themes of the book, before ending with a reflection on the strengths and weaknesses of the present protection regime, remaining challenges, and the road ahead.

Origins, Actors, Responsibilities: Principles and Practice

The discussion in previous chapters illustrated that the field of humanitarian protection is one fraught with dilemmas and difficult choices. Norms and complex regimes are meant to help break down these dilemmas, by charting an appropriate course of action under a given set of circumstances. However, some of the principles underpinning the protection regime are contested, making the implementation of protection norms and the effective provision of protection and relief, already a difficult undertaking on purely practical grounds, all the more challenging.

A fundamental problem, as illustrated in *Origins*, is norm contestation with regard to the meaning of state sovereignty and its conditionality. The question relates to constitutive norms of international society; what it means to be a *state*. The interpretation of statehood and the conditions under which it should yield to other principles is now a less contentious issue than it has been in the past, but is still of relevance in understanding relations among states and the arguments they make in justifying responses to humanitarian protection crises at the UN and within other diplomatic fora and in statements intended for international audiences.

Another dilemma, discussed in more detail in Part II, *Actors*, and Part III, *Responsibilities*, relates to the role of proximate versus distant protection interveners. The trend in recent years has been to encourage greater engagement of local actors, including national authorities and regional institutions. 'Local ownership' has become a catch-all term in this regard. Relatedly, scholars and policymakers have promoted the idea of bottom-up preventative and restorative actions, that are driven, or at least significantly informed by, civil society and grassroots organisations. The need to locate authority and determine who is responsible are problems that occupy jurists, diplomats, defence staff, UN civil servants, and humanitarian practitioners working in acute crisis situations. These questions are both theoretical and practical. They relate to fundamental rights and humanitarian principles, as they do to day-to-day decisions in specific circumstances.

However, the contested nature of sovereignty and intervention itself, and the role of the international versus the local, broadly conceived, are not the only examples of questions over which there has been much debate. When responding to acute crisis situations, a recent trend among policymakers has been to emphasise the importance of prevention.[5] However, others have suggested this should not draw attention away from hard questions about coercive measures, nor should it lower perceptions of the responsibilities of international actors after a conflict has ended.[6] When is the right time to intervene forcefully if the objective is to save as many lives as possible? This is a dilemma because knowing what would have happened if another course of action had been chosen is difficult.

Another dilemma, one relevant for humanitarian action, peacekeeping, mediation, and criminal justice, concerns the level and depth of engagement with parties to a conflict. Should protection agents be prepared to engage with an authority implicated in human rights violations if doing so helps mitigate conflict, end it altogether, or to obtain access to affected populations? This central question – of whether to adopt a principled approach, or whether to allow a degree of pragmatism – is an ethical conundrum that lies at the heart of many questions relating to the practice of protection.[7] A similar question emerges with regard to justice and accountability at the end of a conflict – should amnesties ever be offered in return for peace? For the sake of peace and inter-communal reconciliation, should a post-conflict reconciliation plan ever sacrifice criminal prosecution, in favour of restorative justice mechanisms? In the realm of post-conflict state-building, similarly, should elections precede the drafting of a new constitution, or should a stable state that can guarantee free and fair elections come first?

For some of the questions, a consequentialist approach drawing on empirical observation can offer some guidance – what works to, say, prevent further civilian casualties, or further outbreak of armed fighting. Other questions require engagement with a range of arguments; these questions are difficult to answer because the answers depend on core values and diverse perspectives. A common thread running through many of these questions relates to the degree to which respect for rights – *human rights* – ought to be an absolute guide to principled humanitarian protection. A principled position in defence of human rights in all circumstances would point to similar types of answers to the questions raised above. For example, such a position would suggest it is *never* right to make pragmatic choices: to be prepared, in principle, to engage with human rights violating governments, rebels or warlords to gain access to affected populations; to help to run development projects that benefit wider society, but may legitimate a norms-violating government; to secure a peace agreement with the support of armed factions that have committed war crimes; to provide amnesties in exchange for disarmament; or to prevent spoiling of a peace process by armed factions by providing financial incentives. Those inclined to allow a greater degree of pragmatism – to consider other valued things, such as peace, stability, and security; or to prioritise the protection of lives saved now over the strength of human rights and protection norms designed to protect in perpetuity – are more likely to prefer to make an informed judgement after considering the context of each individual case.

Theoretical arguments on both sides have been discussed in the academic literature.[8] For pragmatists, a flexible approach, where it is well-intentioned and enacted in good faith with the protection ethos, can help alleviate suffering while drawing attention to protection gaps and creating greater awareness for collective responsibilities.[9] Indeed, an inflexible approach invoking good principles in the wrong circumstances may itself contradict the protection ethos. For example, the invocation of 'local ownership' for justifying early withdrawal from a post-conflict state constitutes a misuse of the local ownership principle when early withdrawal undermines any prospect of stability for local populations; similarly, invoking the 'inclusiveness' principle to justify engagement with radical groups for strategic purposes may constitute a subversion of the inclusiveness principle.[10]

A protection regime that leaves scope for tailor-made responses that take note of the specific context of the crisis may be advantageous, given that every crisis is different. On the other hand, stable practices are constitutive for emerging norms and norms consolidate where there is intersubjective agreement on an appropriate course of action.[11] The degree to which international audiences share a common perception about the circumstances under which responsibilities shift to third parties and international actors have a responsibility to take more robust measures, therefore, can be taken as a yardstick for measuring the strength of the protection regime.

The aim of this book has not been to provide firm answers to the wide array of ethical questions that arise in the context of humanitarian protection; rather, to provide the reader with the tools required to come to their own conclusions. In what follows below, we now turn to the question of the conditions under which the responsibility should fall to third parties and the measures they should choose to respond to urgent protection crises.

Assistance, Suasion, Compellence, and Humanitarian Protection

Chapters 1 and 2 outlined the process of the development of the human rights regime and its associated institutions. The establishment of the United Nations at the end of the Second World War established the institutional context for the development of the human rights regime and the campaigning for the recognition of responsibilities for enforcing these rights that came later, towards the turn of the century. These efforts were crucial in advancing the recognition of individual and group rights as inalienable, and enforceable internationally. In so doing, the formation of these institutions also provided a basis for confronting governments for failures to protect individuals and groups from violations of human rights. This created a conundrum for state practice, given that state sovereignty and territorial integrity were granted special status in the UN Charter, in order to prevent inter-state war, as well as, in a post-colonial context, to prevent illegitimate violations of national sovereignty.

In order to reconcile the principle of state sovereignty with human rights, the drafters of the ICISS report suggested conceptualising sovereignty as a form of responsibility. In the context of the policy debates on humanitarian intervention in the 2000s, emerging scholarship suggested that since antiquity, sovereignty had always, in fact, been understood as entailing, and being contingent upon, the discharge of protection responsibilities.[12] These ideas built on the conceptual work of Francis Deng in the context of IDP protection in the 1990s. Having drafted the Guiding Principles on Internal Displacement, Deng identified a 'primary duty and responsibility to provide protection and humanitarian assistance to internally displaced persons'.[13] This formula provided a starting point for further thinking about ways in which the principle of state sovereignty could be reconciled with human rights protection, leading to the articulation, in 2009, of a 'three pillars' approach to the implementation of the Responsibility to Protect principle, outlined in a report of the UN Secretary-General.[14] The report suggested that the Responsibility to Protect was, in the first instance, the responsibility of the state concerned. Only where a state was unable to meet its protection responsibilities, did the responsibility to assist fall to international actors. Where a state was still unable to protect, or unwilling to do so, did the Responsibility to Protect shift to international actors entirely. In those cases, international actors could employ coercive measures as a last resort.

These developments signalled a clear departure from the traditional interpretation of state sovereignty and a greater preparedness to challenge state authorities with regard to human rights violations. However, the departure from state sovereignty as absolute sovereignty also required international consensus on the conditions under which state sovereignty should yield to protection norms. This required, in particular, a closer look at threshold criteria for international intervention employing force.[15] It required, moreover, identifying the appropriate authority for establishing whether these threshold criteria have been met. While many legal analysts maintained that the right authority was, and remained, the Security Council as determined by the UN Charter, others called for alternative mechanisms of authorising humanitarian intervention where there was a just cause for doing so, but the Security Council was deadlocked due to a veto by one of the permanent members of the Council.[16] In any case, these discussions indicated a departure from a global attitude that was not prepared to confront systematic violations of rights, and where invocation of justification for intervention on human rights grounds was rare, even in cases where intervention could have been justified on these grounds, as Nicholas Wheeler illustrated vividly in his seminal book, *Saving Strangers*.[17]

However, the UN has not been the only venue where a more robust stance on human rights has emerged in recent years. Chapters 3 and 4 took a closer look at the role of states, and regional organisations, respectively. Some states played a leading role in the advocacy for the R2P principle, as outlined in Chapter 3. Regional organisations, as Chapter 4 illustrated, are playing an increasingly important role. In the field of peacekeeping, hybrid forms of peacekeeping, operations conducted jointly by the UN and regional organisations was trialled in the case of Darfur and UNAMID. But regional organisations such as the AU, the Arab League, and the OSCE are becoming increasingly important independent human security actors. In the field of international criminal justice, similarly, both trends have affected international practice. The emergence of the ICC has promised an end to impunity for grave crimes, and at the same time, regional courts have been created. While the emergence of regional courts has promoted local engagement and ownership, it has also, therefore, meant greater institutional fragmentation of the protection regime. As a consequence, some feared this would pave the way for 'forum shopping'.[18] Again, the advantages and disadvantages of greater regionalisation aside, these developments show that sovereignty is increasingly perceived as a responsibility, and greater preparedness, regionally and internationally, to confront systematic human rights violations.

These trends are also reflected in the ever-growing tasks of the United Nations and its affiliated bodies, as Chapter 5 showed. The number of peacekeeping operations has grown, and these have become increasingly complex, notwithstanding a recent decline in funding for peacekeeping. Similarly, peacekeeping operations are today routinely equipped with a Chapter VII mandate, authorising them to use force, where necessary, to implement the mission's protection objectives. Recent crises have seen the routine invocation of the R2P principle, suggesting that the idea that there is a collective responsibility to protect has taken root. The case of Libya served as an example. Although the intervention was criticised subsequently, giving rise to fears of a 'swinging pendulum'[19] for support for the R2P principle, it also served to promote engagement with questions surrounding the implementation of protection mandates, and led to the articulation of the RWP principle.

Moreover, the idea that more needs to be done to promote the idea of collective protection responsibilities, and at the same time the recognition that the use of force carries its own risks, ushered in a long phase of conceptualising responsibilities for preventing conflict and humanitarian emergency in the first place. The Secretary-General's report on the subject was an important step forward.[20] These efforts, particularly around structural prevention efforts, were closely connected to an emerging body of scholarship on the causes and prevention of violent conflict that has developed into a research field seeking to understand, also, the role of a range of international actors, including international organisations, international financial institutions, and non-governmental organisations, in applying political and diplomatic pressure, providing economic incentives through donor funding, or economic deterrents through the threat of sanctions, as well as, in the case of civil society actors, the capacity to name and shame. Focus on each of these dimensions shows the simultaneous awareness of the capacity to coordinate and cooperate with a range of actors and assist state authorities in meeting protection responsibilities; while also signalling greater awareness of a range of policy options with greater coercive potential, such as sanctions, short of the use of force.

Chapter 6 looked at the role of civil society, in particular the role of humanitarian organisations in filling protection gaps. In this context, Chapter 6 also looked more closely at the position of international relief organisations towards the governments and other groups with de facto control over territories these groups require access to in order to provide humanitarian relief to affected populations. While some organisations are historically more wedded to a more stringent interpretation of the principle of neutrality – the ICRC is an example – other groups, such as the MSF, are more willing to confront state authorities and other groups that may be implicated in war crimes and crimes against humanity. The chapter discussed the role of other types of civil society organisations – human rights organisations – whose role is, essentially, to be confrontational. The core task of these groups, such as Amnesty International and HRW, is to call out human rights violations and draw attention to such violations internationally, in an effort to name and shame human rights perpetrators and in so doing, deter further human rights violations and increase the costs of would-be human rights violators in future, in this way strengthening the human rights and international protection regime.

In the realm of preventive diplomacy, as discussed in Chapter 7, these questions are particularly pertinent. Preventive diplomacy encompasses measures short of the use of force. While preventive diplomacy may refer to positive incentives such as financial inducement and the promise of development funding, they may also refer to coercive measures such as the threat of sanctions, or the threat of the use of force. In this sense, preventive diplomacy encompasses measures that are co-operative, but also measures that are more confrontational and seek to hold responsible actors to account. With regard to humanitarian diplomacy narrowly defined, a practice associated with negotiating access to affected populations for the provision of humanitarian relief, the question is not so much whether to confront authorities with questionable human rights records, but whether to co-operate with such authorities in the first place. Doing so risks legitimating such authorities, as well as providing resources that sustain their power and may prolong a conflict. However, the broader conceptualisation of humanitarian diplomacy also entails general and specific foreign policy objectives by states, as well as the actions of the UN Secretariat in response to individual crises. States may be in a position to use their influence in other areas, for example, trade, bilateral agreements, and military alliances, to leverage their power with regard to individual crisis situations in pursuit of humanitarian objectives. Where humanitarian diplomacy is pursued in a way that seeks to compel or deter through the threat of, or imposition of, costs, humanitarian diplomacy may be perceived of as a tool that can be used to confront actors where they have failed to discharge protection responsibilities.

Chapters 8 and 9 extended the discussion further, looking at the practice of peacekeeping, humanitarian relief efforts, and post-conflict peacebuilding and the policy choices and dilemmas routinely confronting practitioners. Chapter 8 showed that the UN Security Council has adopted different approaches in responses to different cases, sometimes using more robust measures, at other times using softer measures.[21] This raises questions about the degree of politicisation of international responses to situations in which civilians are at risk. In some cases, states' other interests may come to bear on a decision of whether to confront a regime more directly, or whether to avoid direct confrontation and instead employ soft means of policy and persuasion. While mixed motives may help spur states into action, including through action through the Security Council, the danger of politicised decision-making, i.e. decisions that are made not on consideration of humanitarian need alone, is twofold: that protection principles are misused in pursuit of other objectives that in turn may harm civilians directly, such as the consequences of armed fighting; or have other negative consequences for local populations, such as a loss of agency and longer-term economic hardships in the aftermath of conflict. On the other hand, where a reliance on political will results in a failure to respond where a decisive response is called for, outcomes for affected populations may be calamitous, as the case of Rwanda showed.

Remaining Challenges and the Road Ahead

There are three clusters of challenges for the humanitarian protection regime. First, there are those challenges that relate to the development of the regime and the norms underpinning it. This relates to international law but also customary practice and the principles that a range of actors have found a consensus on and deem appropriate in guiding international responses to conflict and humanitarian emergencies. Second, there are those challenges that relate to the institutionalisation of protection norms. This means mainstreaming protection norms into institutions that already exist, or, alternatively, creating new institutions at the international, regional, and state levels. Finally, there are those challenges that relate to ongoing crises and how best to address them. Current trends point to developments that may pose challenges, but there are also positive developments helping to promote the protection regime.

First, a recent trend discussed is the increasingly significant role of states in the realm of humanitarian diplomacy.[22] States conduct diplomacy to different ends, and in this context, it is important to distinguish between humanitarian diplomacy and humanitarian foreign policy. States have always considered humanitarian needs in the conduct of their foreign policy but increasingly, conflict resolution and responses to humanitarian needs rank very highly among states' foreign policy interests. The normative shift has been such that responses to humanitarian needs are perceived as states' duties, particularly for those states with high capacities for rapid response and the financial resources to assist with longer-term peacebuilding and post-conflict development. This can mean that states' policies may attract criticism when funding levels in response to humanitarian crisis are lower than expected and do not match the contributions of other states, particularly where this is deemed the consequence of politicised decision-making. It also means states face closer scrutiny with regard to overall humanitarian and development aid funding levels and are more susceptible to domestic and international criticism when they make sharp reductions to their funding levels. This overall shift in expectations with regard to the roles and responsibilities of states for short term as well as long-term assistance means that both at the normative level, as well as in terms of the institutionalisation of protection norms, significant advances have been made.

Second, consequences for funding have affected peacekeeping as well. With a large reduction in peacekeeping expenditure, it remains to be seen whether this suggests a decline in the significance of UN peacekeeping, or a temporary trend. With the rising importance of regional organisations with regard to rapid response to crisis situations, this may signal a larger shift away from the centrality of the UN Security Council in future crises. Although peacekeeping is likely to remain as a significant international practice in the future, multilaterally coordinated action may be more fragmented regionally in the future, and regional powers may play an increasingly important role with regard to authorisation and the provision of economic and material resources as well as operationally in the implementation of local peacekeeping operations.

Third, the development of unilateral sanctions mechanisms, specifically, the Magnitsky Act with its broader implications for protection practice. The Act was enacted in 2012 and named after a Russian tax lawyer who had been imprisoned and died in custody after being denied medical treatment.[23] The Act was drawn up with the aim of regulating trade relations with Russia following Russia's admission to the World Trade Organisation. However, the Act also provided the US president with the authority to blacklist Russian citizens who were suspected of international human rights violations. Blacklisted individuals face travel restrictions and asset freezes. In 2016, in response to criticism that the Act was limited to Russia, the US Congress passed the Global Magnitsky Act (GMA).[24] According to the GMA, the president can determine, given credible evidence, individuals to be added to a list of Specifically Designated Nationals, for gross violations of human rights including extrajudicial killings or torture, or having assisted or sponsored such activities. These individuals cannot buy, sell, or invest in the USA, and in keeping with the Magnitsky Act, all existing property in the US is frozen. Individuals who have been sanctioned to date include the former president of Gambia, Yahya Jammeh, allegedly responsible for armed violence against Gambian citizens; Francisco Javier Diaz Madriz, a Nicaraguan police official allegedly responsible for human rights abuses by the police; as well as four Burmese military commanders, Aung Kyaw Saw, Khin Maung Soe, Thura San Lwin, and Khin Hlain, for human rights abuses. Recently, other states have introduced their own unilateral sanctions mechanisms, including Canada.[25] Used wisely, such new coercive tools can fill protection gaps that arise when multilateral action is difficult given disagreement in the Security Council. However, unilateral authorisation of non-violent coercive measures is subject to some of the same risks associated with unilateral decision-making on the use of force, including questions related to right authority, due process, right intention, and balance of consequences. Here, as elsewhere, politicisation, in the absence of regulation, can have undesirable consequences.

Another recent development that will shape protection practices in profound ways going forward is cyber capacities and the way they relate to humanitarian protection practices.[26] The emergence of a cyber sphere carries both risks as well as opportunities. The emergence of new technology requires thinking by policymakers about how existing norms of protection may apply in the cyber domain. Generally, with regard to international law, the Tallinn Manual describes how existing laws may be mapped onto new circumstances and behaviour by states and non-state actors in the cyber domain. Similarly, policymakers and practitioners are needing to think about how protection responsibilities apply with regard to the cyber sphere. In 2018 Facebook took responsibility for a failure to prevent the incitement of violence against Rohingya in Myanmar on its platform. Members of Myanmar's military had launched a systematic campaign targeting the Rohingya. However, cyber capabilities can also be used in more direct ways, for example when an actor – state or non-state – targets the civilian infrastructure. Such attacks, which may be difficult to attribute, may have serious consequences for affected populations for example by crippling the cyber infrastructure required for banking or communications. Furthermore, the use of facial recognition and GPS tracking can help to facilitate the targeting of populations based on specific attributes. Furthermore, technology can be used to censor media, which in turn can make early warning more difficult. Finally, the manipulations of evidence can allow perpetrators to evade accountability. However, the misuse of social media can be prevented through early warning and effective response mechanisms. For this reason, private sector partnership is important. At the same time, coercive cyber capacities could also work as a tool for intervening in crisis situations to prevent harm to vulnerable populations. However, any cyber operations targeting a state would require authorisation by the Security Council. The same limitations may not apply with regard to non-state actors, which means coercive unilateral cyber operations targeting non-state actors involved in human rights abuses may not be in violation of international law; although criticism of a lack of due process can arise in the absence of multilateral authorisation, as is the case for unilateral targeted economic sanctions.

These trends, together, point to opportunities as well as challenges. While humanitarian and peacekeeping funding is declining, states now have new coercive tools at their disposal for responding robustly to crisis situations. Targeted sanctions and the use of new technologies can help to facilitate swift, decisive, and effective responses. These tools can also be used preventively, and to deter would-be norms violators. Given the increasingly transnational nexus between organised violence and armed violence against civilians, responses at the economic level can be helpful. At the same time, in the absence of UN or regional authorisation, the imposition of unilateral targeted sanctions or unilateral coercive cyber measures call for renewed debate on legitimacy criteria. In any case, these tools may provide a much more focused means of response that is more able to directly target individuals and groups implicated in systematic violation of human rights.

Current Crises, 'Black Holes', and the Future of Humanitarian Protection

The website of the Global Centre for the Responsibility to Protect lists 12 current crisis situations,[27] and the *New Humanitarian* suggests that ten crises, in particular, are likely to drive humanitarian needs in the future.[28] Among them is the conflict in Ethiopia, where war in the Tigray region and violent unrest in other parts of the state are resulting in a humanitarian crisis. In Venezuela, a shattered economy and the likely decrease in oil revenues are likely to cause even greater humanitarian crisis. In the Central African Republic, meanwhile, a new rebel offensive is threatening the peace agreement and to exacerbate the humanitarian crisis. In Yemen, the humanitarian situation is deteriorating even further, given reductions in aid funding, while violence has increased.

The question of how to respond to ongoing humanitarian protection crises where structural inhibitors are present and third parties that are contemplating a decisive response are faced with prohibitive costs for robust intervention is not new and ongoing systematic repression in numerous states attests to this. The concept of a 'black hole' suggested by Morten Pedersen describes a situation where a state is clearly failing to meet its protection responsibilities, but third-party assistance is unlikely to alleviate the problem or result in conflict intensification, spill-over, or prolongation. 'Black holes' also refer to situations where decisive coercive responses are deemed unfeasible by a prospective intervener given prohibitive geostrategic, economic, or human costs; and those coercive measures that may be considered or are already being implemented have insufficient coercive leverage to alter the cost-benefit calculations of a repressive regime.[29] For example, a protection intervention may endanger an intervening states' national security if the conflict threatens to escalate; a protective intervention may be costly in financial as well as in human terms; and it may negatively affect a state's trade relations. In these cases, states, which are bound constitutionally to act in the interest of their citizens, may struggle to meet their international protection responsibilities.[30]

The collective difficulty of confronting China over the domestic repression of minority groups serves as a current example. Arguing that R2P has been side-lined with regard to reports of mass atrocity crimes by the Chinese government, Rosemary Foot suggests it is unlikely that China will be held to account with regard to alleged occurrences of arbitrary detention, family separation, and forced labour.[31] Responding to China's repression of the Uighur in Xinjiang is difficult given that China is a permanent member of the UN Security Council. Still, states have responded in other ways. For example, the US government has imposed sanctions against Chinese officials and some Chinese companies. There have been calls for a UN fact-finding mission, as well as for a special session of the Human Rights Council. China has responded to these allegations by invoking anti-terrorism rhetoric. Similarly, in the case of Myanmar, China has blocked efforts for decisive action.[32]

In future, the humanitarian protection regime may have developed to a point where the consequences of a failure to protect were severe enough to compel all international actors to act decisively in the face of human suffering and grave rights violations. Such a protection regime would bring about the structural conditions necessary to raise the reputational and material costs of non-compliance at every level and encourage responsible action at every point of the response continuum: prevention, reaction, and rebuilding. A robust protection regime, were it to come about, would prevent the appearance of 'black holes', crises where the costs of direct confrontation are prohibitive, and the alternative, pragmatic engagement, blatantly disrespectful of human rights. Whether a structural environment that makes 'black holes' a thing of the past can be fully realised in the future remains to be seen. The chances of arriving there, and the speed of progress in this direction, depend on the actions of a range of actors including states, international organisations, and civil society. Not least, they depend on the actions of informed citizens, including the readers of this book.

Summary

- In 1986, at a speech in Oxford, former Secretary-General Perez de Cuellar suggested volatile political situations that are likely to escalate require a 'flexible and finely tuned response' by the international community.
- The three pillars framework of the Responsibility to Protect recognises states' primary Responsibility to Protect populations within their jurisdictions. It also recognises a collective responsibility by all states to assist states in meeting their primary protection responsibilities. Consequently, when responding to humanitarian protection crises, states and non-governmental actors must decide on the conditions for, and the extent of, engagement with authorities and de-facto authorities that are failing to meet their protection responsibilities and may be directly implicated in human rights violations.
- The Magnitsky Act is a legal framework in the US that permits the imposition of unilateral targeted sanctions against individuals and entities suspected of human rights violations and corruption. Other states around the world are adopting similar legal tools. Critics suggest the unilateral nature of such sanctions may interfere with their perceived legitimacy.
- The development of new technologies offers opportunities for more effective protection; however, it also poses new risks and dangers. Cyber capabilities may be employed to repress dissent, censor media, or target individuals based on group membership.

Questions for Reflection

- *Is it acceptable and wise to vary diplomatic strategies on a case-by-case basis? Should responses be tailored to each crisis individually, or should like cases be treated alike, proportionate in size to scale of the crisis?*
- *When ought third parties to engage with authorities that are failing their protection responsibilities; when ought they to cease or desist from doing so?*
- *Can unilateral sanctions regimes help progress international protection norms, and under what circumstances ought states make use of them?*
- *To what extent are social media platforms responsible for preventing human rights violations, and if so, how?*

Further reading

- Beaucillon, Charlotte, ed. (2021), *Unilateral and Extraterritorial Sanctions* (Cheltenham: Edward Elgar).
- Chouliaraki, Lilie and Anne Vestergaard, eds. (2021), *Routledge Handbook of Humanitarian Communication* (London and New York: Routledge).
- Doucet, Marc G. (2017), *Reforming 21st Century Peacekeeping Operations* (London and New York: Routledge).
- Fechter, Anne-Meike and Anke Schwittay, eds. (2021), *Citizen Aid and Everyday Humanitarianism: Development Futures?* (London and New York: Routledge).
- Glanville, Luke (2021), *Sharing Responsibility: The History and Future of Protection from Atrocities* (Princeton and Oxford: Princeton University Press).
- Kivimäki, Timo (2021), *Protecting the Global Civilian from Violence: UN Discourses and Practices in Fragile States* (London and New York: Routledge).

Notes

1 United Nations Secretary-General, 'Cyril Foster Lecture at Oxford University: "Human Protection and the 21st Century United Nations"', *United Nations*, 2 February 2011, https://www.un.org.

2 Steven C. Poe, C. Neal Tate, and Linda Camp Keith, 'Repression of the Human Right to Personal Integrity Revisited: A Global Cross-National Study Covering the Years 1976–1993', *International Studies Quarterly* 43, no. 2 (1 June 1999): 291–313, https://doi.org/10.1111/0020-8833.00121.

3 F. Stewart, ed., *Horizontal Inequalities and Conflict: Understanding Group Violence in Multiethnic Societies*, 2008th ed. (Basingstoke: Palgrave Macmillan, 2008).

4 Neve Gordon and Nicola Perugini, *Human Shields: A History of People in the Line of Fire*, Illustrated edition (Oakland, California: California University Press, 2020).

5 James Finkel, 'Global Approaches to Atrocity Prevention: Introduction to the Special Issue', *Genocide Studies and Prevention: An International Journal* 11, no. 3 (1 March 2018), http://doi.org/10.5038/1911-9933.11.3.1589; Cecilia Jacob, 'R2P as an Atrocity-Prevention Framework: Concepts and Institutionalization at the Global Level', in *Implementing the Responsibility to Protect: A Future Agenda* (Abingdon, Oxon: Routledge, 2020).

6 Outi Keranen, 'What Happened to the Responsibility to Rebuild?', *Global Governance* 22, no. 3 (2016): 331–48.

7 Jack Snyder and Leslie Vinjamuri, 'Principled Pragmatism and the Logic of Consequences', *International Theory: A Journal of International Politics, Law and Philosophy* 4, no. 3 (November 2012): 434–48.
8 See, for example, Chris Brown, 'Selective Humanitarianism: In Defence of Inconsistency', in *Ethics and Foreign Intervention*, ed. Deen Chatterjee and Don Scheid (Cambridge: Cambridge University Press, 2003), 31–50, http://eprints.lse.ac.uk/10253/.
9 Jason Ralph, 'What Should Be Done? Pragmatic Constructivist Ethics and the Responsibility to Protect', *International Organization*, 2018, https://doi.org/10.1017/S0020818317000455.
10 Outi Donovan, 'Norm Contestation and Pragmatic Ethics: Evaluating the Rebuilding Norm in Libya', *Journal of Global Security Studies* 6, no. 4 (25 June 2021).
11 Martha Finnemore and Kathryn Sikkink, 'International Norm Dynamics and Political Change', *International Organization* 52, no. 4 (1998): 887–917.
12 Luke Glanville, *Sovereignty and the Responsibility to Protect* (Chicago: University of Chicago Press, 2014).
13 United Nations, 'Guiding Principles on Internal Displacement' (OCHA, 1998).
14 United Nations, 'Implementing the Responsibility to Protect', 2009.
15 Adrian Gallagher, 'What Constitutes a "Manifest Failing"? Ambiguous and Inconsistent Terminology and the Responsibility to Protect', *International Relations* 28, no. 4 (1 December 2014): 428–44, https://doi.org/10.1177/0047117814552144.
16 Yasmine Nahlawi, 'Overcoming Russian and Chinese Vetoes on Syria through Uniting for Peace', *Journal of Conflict and Security Law* 24, no. 1 (1 April 2019): 111–43.
17 Nicholas Wheeler, *Saving Strangers: Humanitarian Intervention in International Society* (Oxford: Oxford University Press, 2003).
18 Matiangai Sirleaf, 'Regionalism, Regime Complexes, and the Crisis in International Criminal Justice', *Columbia Journal of Transnational Law* 54, no. 3 (n.d.): 699–778.
19 Justin Morris, 'Libya and Syria: R2P and the Spectre of the Swinging Pendulum', *International Affairs* 89, no. 5 (1 September 2013): 1265–83, https://doi.org/10.1111/1468-2346.12071.
20 United Nations Secretary-General, 'Responsibility to Protect: State Responsibility and Prevention', 2013, http://responsibilitytoprotect.org/SG%20report%202013%281%29.pdf.
21 Melissa T. Labonte, 'Whose Responsibility to Protect? The Implications of Double Manifest Failure for Civilian Protection', *The International Journal of Human Rights* 16, no. 7 (1 October 2012): 982–1002.
22 Kelly-Kate Pease, *Human Rights and Humanitarian Diplomacy: Negotiating for Human Rights Protection and Humanitarian Access* (Manchester: Manchester University Press, 2020).
23 The origins of the Magnitsky Act are described in Elizabeth Clark Hersey, 'No Universal Target: Distinguishing between Terrorism and Human Rights Violations in Targeted Sanctions Regimes', *Brooklyn Journal of International Law* 38, no. 3 (2013): 1231–67.
24 For a detailed discussion of the GMA, see Tom Firestone and Kerry Contini, 'The Global Magnitsky Act', *Criminal Law Forum* 29 (2018): 617–28.
25 Canada's introduction of a mechanism for unilateral human rights sanctions is discussed in Meredith Lilly and Delaram Arabi, 'Symbolic Act, Real Consequences: Passing Canada's Magnitsky Law to Combat Human Rights Violations and Corruption', *International Journal* 75, no. 2 (2020): 163–78.
26 A comprehensive discussion of cyber risks and opportunities can be found in Tina J. Park and Michael Switzer, 'R2P & Cyberspace: Sovereignty as a Responsibility' (International Conference on Cyber Conflict, NATO, 2020), https://www.ccdcoe.org/uploads/2020/05/CyCon_2020_7_Park_Switzer.pdf.
27 'Populations at Risk', Global Centre for the Responsibility to Protect, https://www.globalr2p.org/populations-at-risk/.
28 'Ten Humanitarian Crises and Trends to Watch in 2021', The New Humanitarian, 20 January 2021, https://www.thenewhumanitarian.org/feature/2021/01/20/ten-humanitarian-crises-trends-to-watch.
29 'Black holes' and the structural barriers preventing effective protection in the case of Myanmar are discussed in Morten B. Pedersen, 'The Rohingya Crisis, Myanmar, and R2P "Black Holes"', *Global Responsibility to Protect* 13, no. 2–3 (19 March 2021): 349–78, https://doi.org/10.1163/1875-984X-13020009.

30 Alex J. Bellamy, 'When Practice Doesn't Make Perfect: The Responsibility to Protect in Lived Reality', in *The Global Community Yearbook of International Law and Jurisprudence 2019* (Oxford: Oxford University Press, 2020).

31 International responses to the alleged crimes are discussed in Rosemary Foot, 'R2P Sidelined: The International Response to China's Repression of Muslim Minorities in Xinjiang', *Global Responsibility to Protect* 13 (2021): 29–32.

32 Pedersen, 'The Rohingya Crisis, Myanmar, and R2P "Black Holes"'.

Index

For Product Safety Concerns and Information please contact our EU
representative GPSR@taylorandfrancis.com
Taylor & Francis Verlag GmbH, Kaufingerstraße 24, 80331 München, Germany

www.ingramcontent.com/pod-product-compliance
Ingram Content Group UK Ltd.
Pitfield, Milton Keynes, MK11 3LW, UK
UKHW050232200926
475702UK00020B/2999
* 9 7 8 0 3 6 7 4 3 9 5 0 7 *